The Political Marketing Game

The Political Marketing Game

Jennifer Lees-Marshment
Department of Political Studies, University of Auckland, New Zealand

© Jennifer Lees-Marshment 2011

All rights reserved. No reproduction, copy or transmission of this publication may be made without written permission.

No portion of this publication may be reproduced, copied or transmitted save with written permission or in accordance with the provisions of the Copyright, Designs and Patents Act 1988, or under the terms of any licence permitting limited copying issued by the Copyright Licensing Agency, Saffron House, 6-10 Kirby Street, London EC1N 8TS.

Any person who does any unauthorized act in relation to this publication may be liable to criminal prosecution and civil claims for damages.

The author has asserted her right to be identified as the author of this work in accordance with the Copyright, Designs and Patents Act 1988.

First published 2011 by
PALGRAVE MACMILLAN

Palgrave Macmillan in the UK is an imprint of Macmillan Publishers Limited, registered in England, company number 785998, of Houndmills, Basingstoke, Hampshire RG21 6XS.

Palgrave Macmillan in the US is a division of St Martin's Press LLC, 175 Fifth Avenue, New York, NY 10010.

Palgrave Macmillan is the global academic imprint of the above companies and has companies and representatives throughout the world.

Palgrave® and Macmillan® are registered trademarks in the United States, the United Kingdom, Europe and other countries.

ISBN 978–0–230–53777–4 hardback

This book is printed on paper suitable for recycling and made from fully managed and sustained forest sources. Logging, pulping and manufacturing processes are expected to conform to the environmental regulations of the country of origin.

A catalogue record for this book is available from the British Library.

Library of Congress Cataloging-in-Publication Data
Lees-Marshment, Jennifer.
   The political marketing game / Jennifer Lees-Marshment.
     p. cm.
   Includes index.
   Summary: "The Political Marketing Game identifies what works in political marketing, drawing on 100 interviews with practitioners. It also shows that authenticity, values and vision are as much a part of a winning strategy as market-savvy pragmatism"— Provided by publisher.
   ISBN 978–0–230–53777–4 (hardback)
   1. Campaign management. 2. Political campaigns. 3. Marketing—Political aspects. I. Title.
   JF2112.C3L43 2011
   324.7—dc22
                                                         2010050921

10 9 8 7 6 5 4 3 2 1
20 19 18 17 16 15 14 13 12 11

Printed and bound in Great Britain by
CPI Antony Rowe, Chippenham and Eastbourne

This book is dedicated to my father, Peter Colin Crook, whom I have come to learn has passed on not only a sharp analytical ability, but the willingness to question the status quo in search of a more ideal reality.

Contents

List of Tables and Diagrams	x
Preface	xi

Introduction	**1**
Methodological approach	2
Structure of the book	9
1 Analysing the Market	**11**
The changing market and importance of market analysis	12
Market analysis methods	16
Individualising the market: segmentation, voter profiling, targeting and get out the vote	20
Candidate analysis	24
Predictive market analysis	26
Consultation	28
Consultants and clients	30
Using market analysis in politics	35
Summary	41
2 Strategic Development	**45**
Developing the product	45
Strategy	51
Positioning and the competition	60
Branding	66
Authenticity	73
Summary	75
3 Leading Responsively	**79**
Achieving change and new policies	79
True leadership: balancing leading and following the market	87
The advisor–leadership relationship	94
Summary	102
4 Marketing the Party	**104**
The value of marketing the party	105
Maintaining a long-term party organisation	105

Managing and developing volunteer activity   108
Marketing for money   115
Marketing vision and ideology   116
Internal unity   118
Summary   124

5 Communicating   127
Strategy and communication   128
Communicating complex policy   130
Selling policy   132
Communicating a leader   133
Communicating product change or re-positioning   136
Get out the vote   138
Election campaigning   139
Advertising   141
Targeted communication   142
Competition communication   143
Receiver-responsive communication   145
E-marketing   148
Authentic communication   153
Managing internal relationships   155
Managing the media relationship   158
Communication advisors and clients   161
Summary   163

6 Managing Delivery   167
The importance of delivery   167
Pre-election delivery   170
Delivery strategy   173
Making delivery happen   175
Managing failures in delivery   179
Communicating delivery   181
Public evaluation of delivery   185
Summary   188

7 Marketing Democratically   191
Overcoming potential problems   192
Realising the democratic benefits   200
Creating new ways to use political market democratically   204
Summary   210

Conclusion: Political Marketing, Democracy and Partnership **212**
   Winning the political marketing game 213
   Towards a partnership democracy 223
   Overall relationship: a partnership between politician and the public 227
   A partnership democracy in context 228
   Democracy in evolution 236

Academic References 238

Practitioner Interview References 252

Index 258

List of Tables and Diagrams

Tables

1.1	Rules of the game for market analysis	42
2.1	Rules of the game for strategic development	76
3.1	Rules of the game for political marketing and leadership	102
4.1	Rules of the game for marketing the party	125
5.1	Rules of the game for communicating	163
6.1	Rules of the game for managing delivery	189
7.1	Rules of the game for marketing democratically	211

Diagrams

1	Winning the political marketing game	214
2	Playing the political marketing game democratically	222
3	A partnership democracy	224

Preface

This has been a long and in-depth research project. It started with my first interview of Alastair Campbell in the UK in November 2005, and was only completed in 2010 after submission of the final post-review manuscript in July 2010. It is the longest project I have ever completed, but it has been worth it.

Thanks and appreciation are owed to a wide range of people.

Firstly, Auckland University for awarding competitive internal grants that funded travel for interviews and research assistant work in the form of transcription, literature searches and manuscript formatting. The research assistants themselves – Daria Gorbounova, Thomas Raudvaki, Jamie Turner, Laura Young, Edward Elder, Jess Peterson, Robin Campbell and Randall Potter – completed tasks including photocopying literature and transcribing interviews as well as using initiative and sensible judgement. They should know they made the life of an academic much more enjoyable and ideal with more room to just 'think', which for this book was particularly important.

The Centre for Democratic Citizenship at McGill and Laval Universities, led by Professor Elisabeth Gidengil, gave me a visiting professorship which part-paid for my trip to Canada in May–June 2009.

Dr Alex Marland of Memorial University and Dr Thierry Giasson of Laval who organised the political marketing workshop at the Canadian PSA in May 2009 invited me to be the keynote speaker, giving me the chance to present initial results from the study. Dr Jenny Lloyd discussed the idea with me at the beginning. Assistants to the practitioners helped arrange the time and location of interviews. Amy Lancaster-Owen at Palgrave took the time out to meet me on my second trip to London at the British Museum for a chat about the book and suggested not only linking it to democracy but, instead of identifying who caused the problems, looking for potential positive developments. Many academics and practitioners suggested people I might contact to interview, including Dr Kathy Smits at Auckland, Andrew Hughes at ANU and the aforementioned Alex and Thierry; the US Embassy in Wellington also helped me make connections. The two anonymous reviewers of the manuscript when it was first submitted in February 2010 for review offered constructive suggestions for how to cut the 150,000-word document down to a more manageable length.

And last but not, of course, least, the book would not exist without the practitioners who were interviewed. This book took me to five different countries, including four across the world from my New Zealand base. It was an experience to navigate around London/Washington/Toronto/Ottawa/Wellington/Sydney streets and public transport systems, and conduct interviews with a fantastic group of people from all areas of political practice and hear their experiences and perspectives. Particularly memorable were my interviews with Phillip Gould, whom I interviewed in his lounge while he stretched out on his couch, and Don Brash, where we did the interview in bare feet, as taking one's shoes off is the Kiwi custom when entering each other's homes. Also, the warm kitchen table and wonderful coffee of Judy Callingham and Brian Edward's home; the friendly coffee with Roger Mortimore near my accommodation in Kensington; the amazing Sydney skyline of Neil Lawrence's meeting room; the kindness of Su Inglish for getting me cups of water after I arrived late, hot and bothered at her BBC office, having got confused as to which White City building she was in and walked past hers to the other one to then have to walk back to hers again in a lovely English summery September; the patience of Nik Nanos for letting me catch my breath after rushing to try to avoid being late because of the previous interview being too interesting and running over time; and the many coffees or teas other people treated me to. Of course, the more formal places such as Scott Stanzel's office in the White House and Iain Duncan Smith's House of Commons office were also memorable, symbolic of the privileged opportunity I was gaining with all 100 interviews of a process that is often hidden from public view. The time and effort the practitioners put into making insightful comments were invaluable, and it is hoped that they gain something in return by being able to learn from the results.

Jennifer Lees-Marshment,
Manukau,
Auckland, New Zealand

Introduction

The electoral marketplace is unpredictable with its varying partisanship, emergent new segments, active media consumption, self-organising volunteers and global awareness of other countries' politics. This is not just confined to Western liberal democracies, even long-serving parties in Asia are finding the ground shifting around them. Politicians – whether they are a local councillor, regional or state parliament politician, minister in government, or prime minister or president – continually seek advice from and engage in marketing activities. Political marketing includes polling, focus groups, listening exercises, segmentation, voter profiling, get-out-the-vote (GOTV) activities, opposition research, strategic product development, internal marketing, volunteer management, voter-driven communication, e-marketing, delivery, voter expectation management and public relations. Political marketing offers strategies and tools that political elites can use to help them navigate the complex electoral game. Politicians play to win, but this is not just about winning elections – it includes trying to change the world.

This book explores the nature and implications of this quest by examining two questions: what works in political marketing, and what is the impact on our democracy? It sets out the rules of the political marketing game not just from academic literature but from those who play it: the strategic creative advisor who designs advertising; the pollster who presents data on voter preferences; the policy and media advisors who offer views on policy and the potential public reaction to it; press secretaries who manage the communication of product decisions; party staff who organise the membership and volunteers; strategic consultants who suggest future directions; public consultation managers; as well as, of course, the political leaders who make the final decisions. What really works – and not just to win votes, but to achieve change? Is political marketing forcing politicians to abandon their integrity in favour of creating inauthentic products? Or can political marketing be used to achieve change and progress? Is the party now redundant? Can communication develop from selling to two-way dialogue between elites and the public? What is the overall impact on representative democracy? How might democracy evolve in the twenty-first century?

Methodological approach

By integrating lessons from the experiences of those practising politics, the book challenges existing conceptions of politics and generates new possibilities for future development. Too often academia falls into the trap – for which we so often criticise the media – of focusing on what is wrong. Rather than elevating the difference between the ideals of politics and the pragmatism of political marketing, this book tries to reconcile them; instead of just identifying problems it explores potential solutions.

Ontology

The starting ontology for this research was firstly that we could better understand the empirical reality of political marketing by listening to practitioners, and therefore that their perspectives were valuable, and their activities potentially positive not just negative.

Secondly, that if the research included a wider range of academic literature on political marketing it would create a broader understanding. Thirdly, that it needed to be led by those two data sources to be open to new conclusions. Through this, we would reach a fresh 'image of social reality' with new 'claims about what exists, what it looks like, what units it makes up and how these units interact with each other' (Grix 2002, 177). It was therefore important to mitigate previous ontological positions and adopt a new openness to the material, thus engaging in a process called 'bracketing' where, as King (2004, 13) explains, 'the researcher must reflect on the presuppositions he or she holds, and remain alert to how they may colour every stage of the research process.'

Inductive approach

This research adopted a fresh epistemological position, whereby instead of taking marketing theory, adapting it to politics to create new theory and then seeking to find data to support it, an inductive approach was taken to data collection and data analysis. The research sought to cover all aspects of political marketing, choose a broad range of participants on different topics and integrated all political marketing literature and theories. This resulted in the collection of a large data set of academic literature and a substantial body of primary research. The very size and breadth of the practitioner and academic data set facilitated, if not necessitated, a departure from former epistemological and ontological perspectives, raising many new angles without a particular focus. Nevertheless, reflexivity was maintained throughout the project (see Desmond 2004, 268, King 2004, 20 and Slote-Morris 2009, 214) to mitigate any remaining potential bias. To maximise the inductive nature, multi-methodology was used with different methods employed at distinct stages of the research:

1. Data collection: inductive, reflexive, maximum variation sampling, qualitative in-depth elite interviews, practitioner perspectives and academic literature
2. Data analysis: analytic induction
3. Theory creation: contextual construction, relative generalisation, inference and grounded theory

Data collection

To ensure the academic literature was analysed comprehensively, a thorough literature search identified a range of political marketing literature, published to May 2009, in diverse publishing outlets. For the practitioner data, 100 interviews were completed with 97 practitioners (3 of whom were interviewed twice) in five Western liberal democracies: the US, the UK, Australia, Canada and New Zealand. Interviews started with Alastair Campbell in London in the UK in November 2005 and finished with Alexandra Evershed of Ipso Reid Canada in Ottawa in June 2009. When asking practitioners for an interview, the aim was to include as broad a range as possible so as to take a maximum-variation sampling approach (Kuper et al. 2008, 688). Some were already known; some were identifiable through being famous; others came from internet searches; and some were recommended from other interviewees. The response rate was approximately 50 per cent. There was no foreseeable pattern to who would say yes; their reputation, position, level, fame and my connections with them had no predictable influence.

While there have, of course, been studies of campaign consultants, particularly in the US, this research also included those working in government, parties and consultation, as well as politicians. These subjects were asked more varied questions about political marketing, rather than just about campaigning. Positions of those interviewed included Advertiser; Creative strategic advisor; Chief press secretary; Pollster; Public consultant; Head of the delivery unit; Political director; National campaigns officer; Journalist; Campaign manager; Fundraising manager; Party leader; Premier; Media advisor; Chief of staff; Deputy editor; Party president; General secretary; Head of political research; Shadow secretary; Minister; MP; Director of marketing; Political development manager; Head of political programmes; Civil servant; Head of strategic communications at Downing Street; E-campaign director; Communications director; National director; Member of the Office of the Public Liaison Presidential Transition Team; Director of Trainees; Policy advisor; Policy analyst; PR consultant; and Vice-President of public affairs.

Practitioners have always displayed understanding and appreciation of the potential nature and range of political marketing. Academia needs, of course, to occupy a distinct and independent position, but it also benefits from a close interaction with practice, which encourages a closer feel for reality and makes it easier to see change emerging. As Burnham, Gillard and Layton-Henry (2004, 245) said, 'elite interviewing brings the world of the practitioner and the academic together in a hopefully fruitful mutual dialogue.' It also helps to understand the complexity of practice. As one participant pointed out when asked about strategy: 'the first thing that you need to identify about the process of formulating strategy is that there is no one model and no one process. The process of identifying, devising a strategy comes out of a metamorphosis process' (McCully 2007). Political marketing is not just about a set of tools but a way of thinking, and, as Lilleker (2003, 208) noted, the benefits of elite interviews include 'insights into events about which we know little: the activities that take place out of the public or media gaze'. This is not to deny the weaknesses of elite interview data. Practitioners are only going to give their perspective, which is their opinion, their bias. This does not mean it is true. As Slote-Morris (2009, 210) observed, 'the majority of advice on interviewing elites assumes that the truth is "out there".'

The interviews involved mainly face-to-face interviews on trips to five countries: to Toronto and Ottawa in Canada, Sydney in Australia, London in the UK twice, Washington in the US twice, Wellington and Auckland in New Zealand, as well as a few phone interviews and comments sent by email. Interviews ranged from between 30 minutes to over an hour, with most being 45 minutes long. Qualitative methodology was employed in the form of unstructured elite soft interviews. Generic questions were: what worked in your role, what didn't work so well, what barriers did you face and what impact did the use of marketing have on democracy? However, the content depended on the experience and perspective of the practitioner, and, in most cases, the interviewees directed the conversation and topics. There was what Sarantakos (2005, 270) terms an 'absence of standardisation' whereby there was 'freedom to respondents to express their views without external limitations'. This approach was suitable for this type of project where the approach is inductive – we could not quantitatively test what we did not yet know. As Aberbach and Rockman (2002, 674) note, 'open-ended questions provide a greater opportunity for respondents to organise their answers within their own frameworks' and increase the validity of the data generated. Interviewees were often hospitable and engaged in generic conversation, thus building a relationship, as has been experienced by other researchers (see Herod 1999, 324, Berry 2002, 679 and Desmond 2004, 265).

The approach taken to the interviewees was positive, empathetic, respectful and accepting. The data were collected 'warts and all', accepting the perspective of people interviewed as it was offered because the research was seeking their views, biased or otherwise, and not seeking truth, to prove a theory, or to make an assessment of their performance or direct causality of electoral outcome. Rather, the research aimed to gather a collective understanding from multiple views. The variance of interviewees in terms of position, party, election experience and country and size of data prevented one interviewee's potential biases from dominating the results. The process was a chance to learn and be collaborative (see Slote-Morris 2009, 215). All participants were named but had the right to review the transcript of the interview and were given one month to change it and send it back before it could be used by the researcher. This precluded scrutiny of the interviewee but helped maintain the inductive approach. Participants were able to relax, be themselves and say what they thought, and in the end they displayed surprisingly self-reflectiveness, reflecting the experience of other qualitative researchers (see Leech 2002, 666 and Smith, K. 2006, 646–647). This method also followed principles of feminist interviewing (see Oakley 1981 and Kezar 2003, 399–403) with the emphasis on dialogue, openness and reciprocity, without pretending to offer unachievable neutrality.

Data analysis: comprehensive analytic induction

Data analysis was carried out in 2009 in two stages. The first was to produce two separate data sets, one of rules from the practitioner transcripts and the other from academic literature. Rules were produced by distilling a distinct clear point from the practitioner and academic views. Quotes from the interviews or literature that made this point were placed underneath the rule. Breaking down each transcript into a broad range of rules and putting them back together with other interviews maximised the potential to produce new results. This deconstructive approach, as Sarantakos (2005, 353) explains, involves going 'beyond the known': 'texts are converted to small units of meanings, free from previous meaningful connections, to other units and to contexts, and free from overarching, general assumptions.'

In the practitioner data set 675 rules were identified in total. No weighting was given to the number of interviewees saying the rule: this is a qualitative study with no attempt made to interview equal numbers of people in the same area. Therefore, just because only one respondent made one point does not mean it was any less valuable or 'true' than that made by ten interviewees. A final data set was completed on 31 August 2009. The total word count was 204,109. Academic data were organised in the same way as the practitioner data: into identifiable 'rules'. In total 366 such rules were produced. This analysis was, therefore, organic, allowing the themes, theories, rules and conclusions to evolve from the data.

The desire for as strong an inductive approach as possible prevented the use of coding by researcher-directed terms. Such rules were generated from the interviews themselves: that is, generated by the data, not theory or the author's opinion. The rule written to summarise the interviewee's points was the researcher's wording, and thus this process could be criticised for being open to the researcher's own bias. However, given the substantial list produced it would be hard to impose a bias on such substantial amount of data – and rules – even if this were the intention!

The main chapters were written by integrating academic and practitioner rules. Before analysis it was predicted that there would be many contradictions between the academic and practitioner literature. In fact there were few, and where there are these are highlighted. Rather, academics and practitioners either concurred or simply offered different but additional perspectives. During this writing process, the material was reorganised and reordered from the original data set to ensure a more logical flow and fit between the practitioner and academic data. Some rules were combined to provide ease of comprehension and avoid repetition. This resulted in a final list of 575 practitioner rules and 327 academic rules, and a first draft of the main chapters of the book was completed, which included all rules and quotes. Only then was the conclusion written and new theories created. The careful separation of different stages meant that the analysis took longer and the data set produced was larger, but this helped to maintain the inductive nature and mitigate potential researcher bias, not the least by there being a long period between data collection and analysis in most cases. After completing analysis and the first draft, cuts had to be made in the writing stages to make the book readable and the list of rules was, of course, cut down for presentation in the book at the end of each chapter to increase its usefulness and comprehensibility.

Theory creation

At the end of the project the methodology departed from the constrictions of the academic and practitioner data to enable a contextual construction of meaning – 'an analysis of the reconstructed materials' – and extensive interpretation of meanings to consider different possible meanings 'about the whole context of the phenomenon' (Sarantakos 2005, 353). Suggestions of how elites might win the political marketing game, but, moreover, play it democratically, were made to show how they could choose to use marketing positively. The theory of a partnership democracy was created with the aim of providing an understanding of how democracy itself may evolve in future. This was, therefore, a departure from being data led, but such interpretive analysis remained grounded (see Punch 1998, 162–169 for a discussion) because it was generated on the basis of the data. The one ontological and epistemological bias that has permeated the research from the initial conception to the final conclusion is to identify possible positives. This did not mean that problems in political marketing were ignored, or that negatives noted by practitioners and academics were deselected in the presentation of the data analysis. On the contrary, they were highlighted. But this bias did affect the final conclusions and without this it is unlikely that a partnership theory of democracy would have been created.

There remains the possibility that others could come to different conclusions from the same data. As Aspinwall (2006, 5) noted, 'facts are like holograms. Line them up one way and they look like one thing; line them up another way and they look like something completely different.' Similarly, Burnham, Gillard and Layton-Henry (2004, 50) said 'the interpretation of the data and the drawing of conclusions can be influenced by the values and disciplinary training of the analyst, thus we would not be surprised if a psychologist and a sociologist emphasises different findings and drew different findings and drew different conclusions from the same study.' The same could be said of the political marketing game data. The separation of this method from that used in the main body of the chapters was designed to enable readers to see where the author has led the discussion and be free to make their own alternative conclusions from the same data.

Finally, the new theory was related to the literature on democracy. The discussion used literature gained by a comprehensive search for democracy and related concepts such as e-government and participation, but most particularly in reference to consultation and deliberative democracy. Some 800 references were generated, providing a substantial resource to utilise, but, of course, one not without its omissions. Rather than conduct a literature review, the aim was to consider the potential for theories from the political marketing game and political marketing democracy to concur with democracy literature, and explore how that literature might offer greater insight and additional lessons political marketing needs to consider.

Overall reflection on methodology

The methodological design had significant advantages, sought to mitigate potential biases, and was reflected on throughout data collection and analysis. A range of methods were used: primary qualitative in-depth elite interviews using maximum variation sampling until saturation point was reached, collection of political marketing literature, integration of findings from both data sources and analytic induction to create detailed 'rules'; reconstruction of the materials to create new generalisations and therefore grounded theory; followed by more creative, emergent theory suggestion and discussion of the new theory in relation to a second set of literature; and the overall fitting of the triangulation approach, where there is more than one method or source drawn from the conclusions. Like all research, there remain potential weaknesses, and the conclusions are not presented as absolute truth. As Lilleker (2003, 213–214) said, 'following interviews it is often no longer possible to accept black and white analyses of events or people, instead you accept that there were at least different perspectives.' This is true of this research, with the methodology helping to provide new insights into what works in political marketing and the implications for democracy.

Structure of the book

The main body of the book is presented in eight chapters.

Chapter 1 'Analysing the Market' covers the changing market and importance of market analysis, market analysis methods, individualising the market through segmentation, voter profiling, targeting and get out the vote, candidate analysis, predictive market analysis, consultation, consultants and clients, and using market analysis in politics.

Chapter 2 'Strategic Development' discusses developing the product, strategy, positioning and the competition, branding and authenticity.

Chapter 3 'Leading Responsively' debates achieving change and new policies, balancing leading and following the market and the advisor–leadership relationship.

Chapter 4 'Marketing the Party' outlines the value of marketing the party, maintaining a long-term party organisation, managing and developing volunteer activity, marketing for money, marketing vision and ideology, and internal unity.

Chapter 5 'Communicating' goes over strategy and communication, communicating complex policy, selling policy, communicating a leader, communicating product change or re-positioning, get out the vote, election campaigning, advertising, targeted communication, competition communication, receiver-responsive communication, e-marketing, authentic communication, managing internal relationships, managing the media relationship, communication advisors and clients.

Chapter 6 'Managing Delivery' discusses the importance of delivery, pre-election delivery, delivery strategy, making delivery happen, managing failures in delivery, communicating delivery and public evaluation of delivery.

Chapter 7 'Marketing Democratically' explores overcoming potential problems in political marketing, realising the democratic benefits and creating new ways to use the political market democratically.

The final chapter, 'Political Marketing, Democracy and Partnership', is where discussion of the overall implications of the rules of the political marketing game in a democratic context takes place. It presents a condensed summary of the data findings to create a theory on how to win the political marketing game. Then it discusses what this means for democracy, using the principled points to suggest how political marketing might be used democratically.

The 'Conclusion' then considers how democracy itself may evolve, creating a new theory, a Partnership Democracy. It discusses this in the context of new trends in other subfields of political science, showing that there is support for a change in the institutions of democracy.

1
Analysing the Market

> The biggest danger for political parties is where they dismiss the feelings and the thoughts of the public.
> —Carter (2007)

> I can honestly say, hand on heart, I have never run qualitative research on anything with anybody where I haven't got a reasonable group of people together who can have a say on something, even if they don't really understand it.
> —Glover (2007)

> It's part science and part art...At some point you've gone through qualitative research, and focus-groups, and one-on-one interviews; based on your own experience as an individual interacting with other people, you just have to make a judgement call.
> —Muttart (2009)

How to understand the market is a fundamental issue in political marketing practice and study, not least because it informs decisions about all other marketing activities. At a base level, market analysis needs to be accurate and valuable if other marketing decisions are not to be taken on false grounds. But the real issue for politics lies in its influence on behaviour since it influences decision-making about policy, strategy and communication. This chapter will discuss the nature of the market itself, the importance of market analysis, methods of analysis (including polling, focus groups, quantitative and qualitative research, segmentation, voter profiling, targeting, get-out-the-vote (GOTV) activities, candidate or opposition research, predictive market analysis, global knowledge sharing and consultation), market analysis dissemination, consultants and clients, and the use of marketing analysis in political marketing.

The changing market and importance of market analysis

Political marketing is often criticised for encouraging politicians to pander to the median or floating voter. However, the political market is not just made up of voters but includes those who have a stakeholder in, or influence on, the party or politician. This can apply to anyone in society: voters, members or volunteers, internal party figures, voter segments, competitors and potential co-operators, donors, the media, the electoral commission, unions, party staff and professionals both internal and external, lobbyists, lobby groups, interest groups and think tanks, the public service or bureaucracy, professional organisations and groups (see Hughes and Dann 2006). As Hughes and Dann (2009, 252) note, 'the act of government is also one of meeting the broader stakeholder needs of society.' Nevertheless, academics and practitioners focus discussion on voters more than any other group. We already know from other subfields of political science that voters act more independently and are less predictable, given the decline of party identification and turnout as well as other factors (see Bartle 2001, 33, Mortimore 2003 and Bartle and Griffiths 2002, 24 for a discussion), but there are other more subtle characteristics elites need to consider when using political marketing. First, new cleavages are emerging that require politicians to segment the market according to ethnicity, race, lifestyle, stage in the life cycle and age (Bartle and Griffiths 2002 and Lees-Marshment 2008, 6), rather than relying on more traditional indications such as class and income.

The second aspect relates to communicating with voters. There are many products (not just political) competing for the political consumer's attention. Braun (2009) observed how what 'makes campaigns difficult is the shorter attention span that people have, and the flood of sensory input that they keep getting...you're really fighting for attention with so many aspects there'. Hyder (2009) explained that 'the average person is getting their news now in snippets. You know, it's like the tag line at the bottom of a newscast...the Middle East situation in a paragraph...if you've got two minutes to catch up on what's going on in the world – there you go! That's how people are getting the news.' When they do open up to communication, it is not just that sent by the party or candidate, or even particular media channels, because voters increasingly use a variety of sources of information to form their views. Muttart

(2009) noted how an analysis of media consumption habits in Canada found that 10–15 per cent of the electorate 'aren't reading newspapers, watching newscasts, listening to news bulletins on the radio' but still vote, so parties need to use alternative means to reach them. That the media are also more questioning of elites (Franklin 1994, Kavanagh 1995, Scammell 1995) makes market-researched communication important, as does the fact that voters question the information political elites distribute (Sherman et al. 2008). Changes in media technology means that citizens expect to control information themselves: 'online forums, blogs and networks demand active audience participation. Citizens are therefore empowered and given a voice in the public sphere' (D. Jackson 2008, 152).

Consumerism also affects voter demands and assessment of elites (Walsh 1994, 63, Butler and Collins 1998, 3, Needham 2003, 7, Scammell 2003, Lees-Marshment 2004, Lilleker and Scullion 2008). The overall attitude of the public towards government is negative and questioning, even though they have little understanding of the job politicians do. Langmaid (2008) commented that politics has become a negative brand: 'if you attack something over and over again it ends up tattered and battered, doesn't it?' (see also Mortimore 2003 and Sherman et al. 2008, 118). Gillan (2006) commented 'we once had a huge thing called the public understanding of science; we need that for politics. Most people don't know what an MP does and the long hours that we work.' This requires leaders to show they are listening and can provide a costed, tangible product with evident and instant delivery. Lilleker and Scullion (2008, 1–2) analysed speeches made by two British prime ministers on taking office – Attlee, in 1945, and Brown in 2007 – and concluded that 'a prime minister can no longer just argue that they know what is best for the country and deliver that, but that they must listen to the key concerns of the public and deliver specifically measurable outcomes.'

If a political product changes, it can take a long time for the public to perceive such a change. Duncan Smith (2006) said, when recalling his time as leader of the UK Conservatives and his attempts to change the image of his party, that 'it takes a long time to get those changes across. Word-of-mouth is usually important. Talking to people about who you are takes longer.' Mortimore (2006) noted how 'everything is very slow. People have very strong opinions of the politicians they know, very strong impressions of the parties...and it's pretty hard to shift those impressions.' As Collins (2006) argued, from the perspective of an advertiser, 'if you've got a big job – and the Conservative party has got a really big job to change perception or to win a general election – that's going to be a three or four-year project. You can't come in shortly before the election and expect to win for them.'

Overall the market is unpredictable; it questions communication; it is negative and consumerist, but is slow to respond to changes in elite behaviour, which makes market analysis particularly important. 'Research is crucial. It's vital in every case' noted Lavigne (2009), a party staffer; and Green (2006), an MP, noted 'you need the data. All the politicians think they've got a good gut instinct. But there is no substitute for actually asking people a set of sensible, nonpartisan questions to find their opinion, just finding out what they care about.' Pattillo (2009) also said 'better decision making, and better action comes from having a diversity of perspectives, and about seeing things in different ways, and I think it's about inviting more people into the tent.' Utting (2008) remarked that 'market research is such an integral part of any campaign...No campaign person can say "I'm not doing any market research"', while Braun (2009) claimed that 'you really need to ground everything you do in a campaign in research, because that's basically the only valid way to know...rather than spending a lot of money on something that you think might work, but actually doesn't.'

Reflecting the notion of the permanent campaign, there needs to be permanent polling, and politicians need to conduct market analysis all the time. Ulm (2007) recalled 'I can remember 20 years ago, when I was first starting to do this, that the odd numbered year was vacation year! There wasn't really work to be had. You couldn't work if you tried! Now, it never stops.' Government also needs market analysis to implement policies; as Ulm (2007) observed, 'they have to go into the same measures: have you thought about who's going to oppose it, why are they going to oppose it, what types of people is this going to reach out to to sort of expand our base, add to our base, everything!? It just never stops.' Gorbounova and Lees-Marshment (2009, 57), with their US Presidential Political Marketing Strategy Model, argued that analysis of presidents in power should include appraisals of stakeholders who may affect legislation and delivery as well as public perception of performance.

Market analysis uncovers unforeseen aspects and issues and helps elites understand the public more effectively. Middleton (2006) recalled 'one thing that came up which we thought was a bit surprising was 30–35 year old female real estate agents in Auckland really liked us, and we never would have never picked that. And probably property developers that we thought would have been more likely to like us, don't.' Carter (2007) recalls how UK public opinion seemed to be against the Iraq War and the Labour leader Tony Blair in 2004–2005, but more detailed market analysis found that 'people's frustration with Iraq was empowered by people who didn't necessarily disagree with removing Sadaam, but felt that Labour had stopped acting on issues that they were concerned about, like crime and law and order and issues back home.' It shows issues from different standpoints. As Carter (2007) said, 'you need to be able to see through the hysteria and to be able to solidly say what is the course of action, and research is actually very effective at doing that.' Research can check whether the daily critique common to 'planet politics' – the centre of political activity whether it be Parliament Hill in Ottawa, Canada, Wellington BeeHive and parliament in New Zealand, Westminster in London or Capitol Hill in Washington – is being felt by the general public. Brodie (2009) noted how 'a lot of the nonsense that got thrown around here, and got thrown around question period about what he [Stephen Harper] was or wasn't, turned out not be supported by the data.'

In the 2008 Czech gubernatorial elections PSB research was able to help a party that had no seats at the regional level gain every single one in the country. Braun (2009) explains how research found that incumbent governors were well known, popular and had delivered a lot of money from the EU, which was a poor situation for the opposition. However, what research also found 'was that the federal government, or the central government, [wa]s extremely unpopular, especially the health-care policies'. This gave PSB research a strategy: 'since all the governors were members of the parties that were in government we basically decided to position the entire campaign, which was a regional campaign, to be a referendum vote over national issues. ... and we completely succeeded in making people, sort of, voting to ... say no to the Prime Minister's government, and the result was going from 0 to 100.' Although of course other factors will have affected the result, this is an example of where research identified a strategy that was then implemented and followed by success. In this case the impact was enhanced because the party was the first to use research in the country. As Mills (2009) noted, 'it's a bit like the nuclear arms race. If you've got a full polling armoury and your opponents don't, they're in terrible trouble. There's a kind of matching; they know what you know.' Normally, research is 'never going to make 10% difference, but if an election's really close it's going to make 1–2% difference'. What also impacts its influence is how it is used, and the methods used to collect it.

Market analysis methods

Political marketing is characterised in terms of polling and focus groups being used to find out what people want, but the reality is much more varied. First, practitioners argue politicians should use different forms of market analysis in a variety of ways for a range of purposes and across different times. Utting (2008) said 'there's a whole spectrum of research techniques' that can all be used. At the end of a campaign 'it's really not going to have a big strategic influence on the campaign, it's really just more tuning things' or it is used for tracking support, whereas 'if it's right at the very start of a campaign, then it probably has a much bigger impact in terms of setting out what the agenda is, how people are going to be positioned.' Teinturier (2008, 148–151) explained how polls were used for a range of purposes in Nicholas Sarkozy's 2007 presidential campaign in France – including identifying swing voters and their motivations – to test reaction to the candidate's appearances in the campaign and to monitor opinion (see also Rademacher and Tuchfarber 1999).

Polling can be used more effectively if researchers ask for a range of opinions. They can discover nuances, rather than just for and against opinions, and use these to find unifying courses of action. Nanos (2009) said this was particularly important when discussing controversial issues: 'most of the polls you see focus on whether one is for or against the war in Afghanistan and the mission. When we do polling on the war in Afghanistan, however, we're asking Canadians: What do you think of the objectives of the war? Do you support or oppose the objectives? Do you think we're providing the necessary resources to achieve those objectives?...[then] the issue becomes determining how to improve a particular situation.' Similarly, qualitative research can provide understanding and background as to why and how, as well as what, the public thinks, using a range of techniques including visual stimulation and role play and analysis of body language. Rogers (2009) explained how it can put forward questions such as 'is this really what drives your votes or your opinion? Is it the top of your concerns?...Do you see it getting better or worse?...What other things does it look and sound like? How would you connect it with other things in your life?' Sparrow and Turner (2001, 992–995) argue that focus group research is now 'up-turning many assumptions made by elite politicians about the political world as experienced by ordinary people'.

Finding the underlying emotion or values is the key: Fenn (2007) noted how 'at the end of the day, it is really about what influences people's gut, what their hopes and dreams and aspirations are, and how a candidate taps into that.' Langmaid (2008) draws from 'gestalt techniques and bits and pieces borrowed from psychotherapy...you project the role of someone like your mum or your dad or your early carers onto the therapist and treat them as if they were reincarnations of those people. [In] the political frame, the leader is in a sense like a big therapist. He's going to solve the problems' (see also Langmaid 2006 and Langmaid et al. 2006). Muttart (2009) recalled how in Canada the Conservative Party's research found that right of centre voters responded to 'three key fanatic drivers', which were aspiration for 'something better for their families and their children' from their hard work; family, including those who get legally married; and 'a sense of localism' or cohesion. They then devised their strategy to tap into those broader themes emotionally as well as cognitively. Muttart observed the Australian 2007 election and found that 'Howard was campaigning solely on the cognitive ballot question – the narrow issue of the best place to run the economy – whereas Labour was tapping into the emotive ballot question which was an idea of new leadership, freshness, change, and they won-out over Howard's old structured, logical arguments.'

Less formal sources of market analysis are also used, one of which is the analysis of past elections. Noble (2009) recalls how staff 'interviewed people all across the country in the Conservative party. We talked to some folks in the UK and the US and really tried to get a sense of best-practices – what were the common things among failing enterprises, and what did winning campaigns have in common.' Chalupa (2007), who worked on John Kerry's 2004 presidential campaign, argued that US parties also need to do this: 'one of the things I was shocked about [was] that after the campaign...we're not even asked to do exit memos...it's just drop and do it again.' Governments can get feedback from people affected by policy – particularly at state level. Rogers (2009), who worked in both federal and state government, noted that the closer one gets to service delivery the more feedback one could get about the effect of policy on people's lives: 'when we were in power – there were some things that we dealt with on a policy level, the things that took up our time were the things that had pretty direct impacts. So, when you're closing a school, there is always a constituency of people that can stand up in front of you and say that they don't like or don't like what you're doing.' This rarely occurred at federal level where 'some statistical representative would come and testify before a committee. At the provincial government level you saw 1000 show up on your lawn' (Rogers 2009).

While most market analysis is carried out by central party headquarters in party-based systems, candidates can gather market analysis too, using informal methods and secondary data (Kotzaivazoglou 2009). Central organisations also use such on-the-ground feedback. Mehta (2007) trains US Democrat volunteers to gather feedback, telling them:

> I need you to come back to me and tell me what are you hearing? What are you seeing? When you knock on your neighbour's door and you have a conversation, are they frustrated?...What issues are they upset about?...Because we can sit here all day long and have all the polling and research...but nothing is more powerful than half a million neighbourhood leaders who talk to 50 of their neighbours 4 times over the next 14 months and who come back and tell me what they heard.

People send in their feedback to those in government; Clelland-Stokes (2009), chief of staff to Auckland Mayor John Banks, noted how 'people write to the mayor, we keep record...it's hardly scientific, but it is a measure of the temperature.' Borrowman (2006) talked of the value of gut intuition gathered by contact with the public: 'go to the pub, listen to what people are talking about, go on the village trip to France to see what they're complaining about. Walk down the street to see is there graffiti, is their rubbish falling out of bins, read the letters page in the local page.' Direct contact with the public can provide a reality check. Evershed (2009) recalled a time when, despite the 'noise' being made on planet politics, the issue was not resonating with the public:

> The government was faced with a situation where the opposition had banded together to defeat the government... This was a big constitutional crisis. But the Canadian people were just rolling their eyes.... during this crisis I was in the hospital and I was listening to the nurses talking to each other and they were saying things like 'Oh, can you believe this? I can't believe this is happening. We've just had an election! What are they trying to pull? Why aren't they focused on the serious issues that are facing the country?'

However, gut instinct needs to be verified by other sources. Middleton (2006) explained further: 'whose gut instinct should you use?...We probably put 40 hours a week into politics...our gut and the gut of the person who hates politics or politicians...[is] just not compatible.' Edwards (2006), advisor to former New Zealand First Party leader

Winston Peter, noted how the politician was 'one of the genuine gut instinct politicians, that generation that kind of knew just deep down what is right for a particular issue' but that, of course, 'sometimes you get that wrong'. Wilson (2006) noted 'we find sometimes with our research that the gut instinct is wrong, and that's something that counter intuitive is right, and once we put that into practice, we get results from it.' As Duffy (2009) observed:

> The great thing about polling is that it settles arguments among professionals. There's a wonderful line I quoted in a book I wrote from one of Canada's pre-eminent pollsters, a man named Allan Greg. He said 'Before polling, you could get into an argument about what was the most important thing to say, and old Fred, or old Bob would tell you "Oh, I know the people in the state of Alberta don't want to hear that." Well with a poll, you can say that Fred's full of shit actually. It turns out everybody down there is perfectly happy to talk about this.'

Regardless of method, the value of market analysis depends on the quality of its collection and its use. In particular, it needs to avoid moderator bias. Savigny (2008a, 53) notes that, in focus groups, 'question guidelines can mean too much focus upon what the researcher is interested in and not enough of what is of interest to the participants....each question tells the participant that this is relevant and important' (see also Sparrow and Turner 2001, 993, Savigny 2007, 130 and Wring 2007, 87). Practitioners acknowledged this. Edwards (2009), who advised New Zealand Prime Minister Helen Clark, was critical: 'you've got the subjectivity of the people speaking, and then on top of all that you've got the subjectivity of the interpretation of what that all meant...the amount of mediation that's going on there is extraordinary.' Similarly Mills noted that 'qualitative research places a massive premium on the skills and judgement of the qualitative researcher, especially in a campaign setting.' Mortimore (2006) also argued that 'obviously Gould is going a particular way with new Labour and I'd be surprised if any non-new Labour findings came out of his focus group...the time will come when they will start missing things that they can't see and it will block the redevelopment of the party product. They just won't be rethinking from the outside without thinking the product has to be a particular shape.'

However, practitioners also suggested solutions to overcome this problem. First, they queried the influence of one source of market analysis. Alastair Campbell (2005), Blair's chief press secretary, said 'focus groups are important, but you shouldn't overstate their importance.' Parties and politicians need to commission more than one source of market analysis to mitigate moderator bias on all forms of market analysis. Roozendaal (2008) said 'it's very dangerous to send your work all to one company, because natural prejudices can creep into researchers over time. That's why I think it's always good to run two different groups in competition of each other.' Parties can also use researchers with a range of backgrounds: 'so if you're researching with Maori, and that's a particularly important element, we would use at least one or maybe two Maori researchers who would talk to their community' (Glover 2007). Thus, although there are clearly problems with certain methods, if chosen and used carefully and if a range of sources and methods is used rather than just one, this helps reduce potential weaknesses and increase the overall value of the data collected.

Individualising the market: segmentation, voter profiling, targeting and get out the vote

Political marketing was often criticised for encouraging Downsian, centre-ground, catch-all-type behaviour among political parties, but practice in politics has recently become more sophisticated in how it breaks the market into new segments, which cut across old left–right ideological divisions to create new groupings, and can help to fill the gap where there is a lack of traditional political labels. As Beeson (2007) explains: 'Texas is a good example, where we don't have any party registration, so we don't know whether somebody is a Republican or a Democrat...so micro targeting is very helpful in saying OK...somebody lives in this type of house, drives this type of car, reads these kinds of magazines, goes to this kind of church, has this many kids, and they voted in these last 3 elections, therefore we can make some basic assumptions about them.'

The first step is that voters are profiled and the results put into a long-term database. Software such as Voter Vault and Mosaic offer tailor-made programmes to parties. Mehta (2009) explains how the US Democrats built a national voter file between 2004 and 2008: 'we invested about 10 million dollars in building an electronic voter database, where we now have information on voters from every single state in the country...now we have a voter file where if a voter moves from California to Nevada, all their information that we collected about them in California...instead of being lost forever, now moves with them to Nevada.' Such methods are not limited to major parties either: in New Zealand the minor party Act also built a CRM database. Wilson (2006) explained how they feed back any response from voters to their communication into a database, 'so we have got this voter profile of as many voters as possible. Some of that is going to so be people who detailed that they don't like us and don't talk to us ever again, but with others it is complicated information of members or previous members.'

Secondly, the market can be segmented according to various factors, including geography, behaviour, demography, lifestyle and political views (see Baines 1999, 405, Smith and Hirst 2001, Bannon 2004 and Johnson 2007), but, more recently, practitioners have been using deeper and more complex segmentation and micro-targeting. To reflect demographic change, the elderly or pensioner group now needs further division: as Davidson (2005, 1181) noted, 'someone in their 70s could be working full time and be fit and healthy, another person in their early 50s could be living with a long term chronic condition and [be] forced out of the labour market.' Therefore, in the 2005 election UK Labour identified different groups such as 'low income elderly', 'child-free serenity' and 'small town seniors'. In this way segmentation helps identify the varying needs elites need to meet. There are also more subtle changes, given that, as Penn (2007, xvi) argues, greater freedom of choice means that people 'segregate themselves into smaller and smaller niches in society'. As Carter (2007) explains, 'it's not enough to recognise that in any one constituency there are 15000 people that you need to talk to in order to win the election, but it's actually that those 15000 people may be able to be grouped into smaller groupings, each of whom has their own personal agendas and issues.' Mills (2009) notes how segmentation 'brings target voters alive e.g. females, 30–45, kids, in part-time work, under heavy costs of living pressures, concerned about their children's education, worried they're not spending enough time with their kids, not very interested in politics, don't read the newspaper, hate anti-smacking legislation, blind to nuances that it was a Green bill and National voted for it, etc, etc.'. Thus, in the 2005 UK election, some of the groups targeted were 'Symbols of success – Professionals who work in the big city, such as lawyers, surgeons and professors'; 'Burdened optimists – Modest qualifications; many have built up debts trying to emulate middle-class lifestyles. Made the Thatcher revolution. No belief in collective social responsibility. Place high value on personal freedom. Indulgence and immediate gratification sets the trend for everything' and 'Golden empty nesters – Wealthy older people living in provincial regions in 1930s houses. Lib Dems have strong challenge to Tories in this sort of neighbourhood. Support the National Trust. They are not concerned about the economy but rather with value for money' (Wintour 2005).

Mehta (2009) explained how, in the 2008 US presidential election, the Democrats used their national voter file 'to figure out what messages most resonated with them, so that when we sent them mail, when we made phone calls, and when we knocked on their doors, we were able to tailor the message to them'. The data can also be used to ensure volunteers contact those most receptive to the party message. Mehta (2009) explained how in the 2008 US presidential campaign:

> We created a brand new model of organising and it was called the Neighbour-to-neighbour programme. What that allowed us to do is any volunteer who wanted to help Barack Obama get elected could go on their computer, and go to his website to my.barackobama.com, and on that website they could type in their home address, and Google, using Google mapping technology, could find their home, and that would find 25 targeted voters.

It is used not just to influence what people vote, but whether they vote at all, through GOTV activities. There is no point having a lot of support if those voters don't actually turn out. As Mortimore (2006) noted, 'when you've got a situation whereby turnout has suddenly dropped by 20% over the last three elections there is still the potential for some of those people who used to vote being got back into a pattern of voting habit...it is logical to target your core vote, because if they vote, they'll vote for you rather than the opposition.' This is what the Bush RNC era did in the 2002–2004–2006–2008 elections. As Beeson (2007) said, 'we know very specific people we want to get to the polls...before I think we sort of looked at it like a baleen whale and we just came along and just scooped it up like krill and got it, you know, just tried to turn out a lot of people. In this case we're turning out a very defined universe.' They used mixed motivators to get people out, with not just the right message but also varied contacts including 'the most personal – a volunteer knocking on their door or a volunteer calling them and saying "hey, I live in your neighbourhood, I just want to make sure you're going to go vote"' (Beeson 2007). Parties can move voters between different GOTV universes to become more likely supporters. Beeson (2007) explains how the RNC broke voters down 'into a GOTV universe, which is people we know are going to vote for us or have a high propensity of voting for us. Then we have persuasion universe.

That's a group of people that we need to talk to.... We want...them to get a significant number of persuasion contacts...understanding that once they got a certain number of percentage contacts you could move them.'

Micro-targeting can be used to influence just a tiny number of votes. Beeson (2007) notes the importance of this in the 2004 US election: 'we weren't trying to move tens of thousands of people, we were literally trying to move hundreds of people.' Carter (2007) explained that micro-targeting 'helps organisations and politicians to understand...who are the people that you need to win, what are the messages that will most effectively move them'. The US Republicans sent a lot of mail and contacts to Hispanic females and single females with children in New Mexico because they 'responded to the President's no child left behind message.... and New Mexico was one of 2 states... [that] voted Democrat in 2000 and voted Republican in 2004. So those sorts of things make a difference' (Beeson 2007).

Segmentation, micro-target creation and voter profiling all lead to targeting – the targeting of policies, campaigning, voter contact and resources. Target selection depends on a range of factors: levels of support for the party or candidate is the starting point, but Bannon (2004) suggests more nuanced factors can be considered, such as how responsive the targets are to stimuli or how attractive or useful they will be to the party/candidate, as well as other factors, including long-term potential for growth; lack of, or weak, competition; whether the product can be differentiated to suit the segments' demands, such as local or single issues; a high-profile candidate; topical national issues; if attracting support from the segment will help achieve goals; and the ease, cost and effectiveness of access to the segment, for example, distribution of political literature is easier in urban rather than rural areas and it is also easier if there is an active local branch with good funds. In the 2005 UK election the UK Conservatives placed voters into distinctive voter vault cells and, as Seawright (2005) noted, they issued a training video to constituencies, advising them to contact those in cells where voters were strong party supporter or undecided, but were also likely to vote, because they could make more difference to the election outcome.

Although these methods are financially intensive, both academics and practitioners argue that targeting is more important for minor parties with limited resources. The UK Liberal Democrats increased their power in parliament by building up support in geographical clusters, with seats next to each other, which, as Russell and Fieldhouse (2005, 210) noted, enabled grassroots supporters to work across seats if needed and helped to build up 'shared credibility from having a historical and realistic chance of winning seats in the region'. As Ranger (2006) from the Lib Dems explained, 'if you're in Liverpool where there's only a handful of you, you could spend all the time trying to stand everywhere and not get anywhere. But if you spend all your time in one ward you can win the ward.' Staff from the minor Act Party in New Zealand also noted the importance of targeting resources. As Middleton (2006) pointed out, 'there are 3 million registered votes in the country, and if we have a campaign budget of 1 million dollars we can spend 30 cents on each of those, or we can say here are the people that are most likely support us, and we can spend a dollar on those or $1.50.'

Despite the growing use and complexity of tools to individualise the market, both practitioners and academics cautioned against relying on them. The method is limited by assumptions only made on data that may be inaccurate given that the data fed into the system are often collected by canvassing by party supporters or members on the ground, and thus elites may spend a lot of money communicating inappropriate messages to people. As Nelson (2007) explained:

> It's not like I have called you up on the phone and you have said 'I believe in X, Y and Z'. All we know about you is that you fall into a segment in a voter file that says there is a high likelihood that you want low taxes.... you can't say with great specificity that they support a reduction in capital gains taxes or the earned income tax credit... if you take the issue of abortion you might have a segment that is 75% or 85% pro-life, but you don't necessarily know how pro-life.... [so] a very hardcore message... [is] likely to alienate some people in that segment.

Micro-targeting can't tell you everything or solve every problem. Ulm (2007) argued 'we couldn't micro target our way out of this last election... you can't micro target our way out of, you know, a third of Americans strongly supporting the President. That's a brand issue.'

Candidate analysis

Opposition and candidate research is a technique that can derail campaigns. Candidates and parties research their own record and that of the opposition: as Fenn (2007) said, 'I'm a believer in doing very solid research on yourself and your opponent, in order to know what your strengths and weaknesses are.' Varoga and Rice (1999, 246) and Johnson (2007, 57–58) note how sources include elected official's records; campaign contribution records; records of the politician's voting; court files; personal and business records, including property records and property tax payment histories; media, including newspaper, magazine and journal articles and the internet; other behavioural records such as club membership and military service; comments from previous associates whether work colleagues, family, friends or former partners; and, more recently with the advent of YouTube, audio-visual footage. Candidates can expect their entire professional career to be scrutinised, even if it wasn't in politics. Private behaviour that contradicts public political positions rather than just the more obvious skeletons, such as affairs, can be an issue (Johnson 2007, 70–71). During the primaries Obama resigned from the Trinity United Church of Christ in Chicago he had been a member of for 20 years because of controversial comments made by the Rev. Jeremiah Wright and other ministers, which were at odds with the image he was trying to convey. Ulm (2007) explained that 'Americans actually care much less about their personal lives than most. What they do do though is, you know, if you're a businessman, have you run your business well? Have you ever been sued? Did you stick by your vendors?... there are firms that are year-round enterprises that work and do just this.'

Research is not always such a negative exercise and campaigns should use candidate research to defend the candidate's record and position and project positives. It is valuable to identify legislation assisted or blocked, grants obtained, votes cast, favourable ratings, number of visits to schools, support or criticism of government, and constituency work, and Johnson (2007, 63) notes how these can be considered in relation to key constituency groups, such as the elderly, by year in office, by media market, city and county, by issues and subject areas and by the names of individuals helped (see also Varoga and Rice 1999, 255). Another key aspect is identifying and justifying any changes in political position. Parties and candidates also employ policy researches to derive statistics and independent expert validation of their own policies as well as negative claims about their opponents. As Johnson (2007, 66) observes, while a change in position can indicate 'growth and maturity', in politics it is criticised as weakness or populism. If changes can be justified and explained, this can be defended. But otherwise they risk the candidate being accused of flip-flopping, lacking certainty and conviction, or only changing their position for electoral expediency.

Opposition research can help anticipate attacks and prepare a rebuttal. O'Shaughnessy and Henneberg (2007, 261) observed that in the 2004 US presidential election Kerry, despite his war record, which appeared positive in contrast with Bush, 'was vulnerable through the inherent contradiction in his Vietnam-era role and his post-service militant peace activism'. Kerry had no rebuttal ready when he was attacked by a Swift Boat Veterans advertisement, so the media were able to continue criticism. O'Shaughnessy and Henneberg (2007, 261) argue that 'such an attack should have been anticipated, there should have been capabilities existent in his campaign organisations that would allow him to instantaneously deal with the threat' (see also Varoga and Rice 1999, 255). Ulm (2007) explained that companies who specialise in this tend to be 'legislative experts' rather than those 'people who jump into dumpsters and hide and investigators', and that best practice is to 'do opposition research on our own candidates, so now there's no surprise... if we know something ahead of time, we can make plans to blunt it, counteract it, do whatever we need to do to explain it'.

Despite its potential power and visible impact in some cases, both practitioners and academics advise caution when attacking other candidates. Claims need to be verifiable and credible; false accusations backfire. A clear case of this was shown in the 2008 New Zealand election when a few weeks before the election Labour Party president Mike Williams travelled to Melbourne to conduct opposition research to uncover evidence linking National leader John Key to problematic financial management. When nothing came to light, this blew up into a negative media story about Labour's campaign methods (Lees-Marshment 2009c, 466). Fenn (2007) noted that in his experience 'the best example of the ridiculousness of our system was the whole impeachment craziness with Clinton. Finally, in 1998 the public got sick and tired of it and said, you know, enough already... and Gingtrich had to resign.' Politicians make the decision as to whether to use such research. Fenn (2007) observed how 'in one race I... found a complaint [that] one of the kids of the [opposing] candidate had filed one time, and there was a divorce in the family and stuff. The candidate... looked at that and said... I don't want anybody in the campaign ever talking about this.'

Predictive market analysis

Another aspect practitioners discussed was the need to conduct market analysis on future possibilities, not just where things are now. Gould

(2007) noted that 'whenever I do focus groups, you'd always move straight to strategy. I'm not interested in just doing some poll which says where the public are.' Callingham's (2009) experience advising New Zealand Prime Minister Helen Clark led her to say that 'one of the troubles with focus groups is that they're always backward looking... The focus-groups very seldom ask people "Well, what would you like to happen, how would you like to see the country move? What would you like to see her do? What would you like to hear him say?"'

Instead, market analysis can test the market and predict how voters might react to changes. Utting (2008) argued that research techniques had developed to allow more predictive analysis:

> [A] lot of the research we do, which is based on quite complex statistical theories, is sensitivity modelling... you can almost create a kind of black box situation where you can try different options within your model... it's only in the last decade or so that the statistical techniques have got to a stage where you can put together these models and... [test] if you change your position on something, or if the public changes their position on an issue, how that's likely to affect voting outcomes.

This enables analysis to explore the consequences of several courses of action the leader may take in advance of the decision. This is important, and may help politicians take a greater variety of decisions. However, too much testing can be problematic, as Ulm (2007) observed: 'in America... everything is tested. Everything is thought out beforehand. There's no "let's go with it and run with it and see how it works," just because of the price of failure.'

Nevertheless, work for Labour by the company Promise to help them, once in power, to reconnect (see Promise 2005 and Scammell 2008) showed that role play can be used to identify not just the problem but potential solutions. Promise's expressive techniques enabled people to reveal deeply held feelings, from which Promise could then reconstruct solutions for Labour. They asked participants to write letters to Blair, which identified what the public wanted him to do as well as what the problems were. Predictive analysis is as yet undeveloped and we need to understand limitations. Ansell (2007), an advertiser in New Zealand, said 'research is a great guide to the past, but not a terribly good predictor of what the public will do in the future. But they offer the campaign strategists some evidence and when they're accountable they're loath to ignore this.' Prediction is not easy.

Consultation

Consultation is another source of market analysis. It is carried out by local government, public bodies, parliaments, candidates and parties, and occurs in various forms, both formal and informal, with much potential but also many deficiencies in practice. Hillary Clinton engaged in consultation called *Let the Conversation Begin* in her bid to gain a seat in the US Senate and again in her bid to secure the presidential nomination, encouraging voters to submit their ideas and questions to her and responding to them, calling for a two-way dialogue (Lees-Marshment 2009a, 90). When the UK Blair government was beginning to seem out of touch, mainly because of the Iraq War, the *Big Conversation* was launched in November 2003. Such initiatives have, however, been criticised for failing to meet scientific market research principles; being more prone to bias, as they often attract a disproportionate number of party members or educated, middle-class participants; and only being a superficial exercise for public relations (see Wring 2005b, 60). The answer to this from practitioners is not to deny such weaknesses but to argue that the management and design of such consultations need to ensure that it does meet essential principles. As Levin (2008) said, 'consultations are almost always dominated by established interest groups. In general, the public doesn't come, the interest groups come. They're organised, they're resourced to write the briefs, so that's what you get in the consultation process, unless you're very careful with how you organise the consultations.'

Consultation needs to be carried out alongside a long-term decision-making process so stakeholder input can have impact. Pattillo (2009) cited the example of when she worked with the Department of Building and Housing on their review of the Building Code. Although the government had decided there was a need to change the code, it hadn't decided how, therefore the consultation had more potential to impact on the final legislation. 'That project started with engaging stakeholders and the public' so any revisions would 'work on the ground'. On the opposite side, less effective consultations are those where there is 'a little pool of their team beavering away for two years or something on a really complex piece of work, and then they'd pop out to the public, and give people two weeks notice and two hours to check about something, and then they're disappointed that their contribution wasn't in depth'. Humphrey (2007) said 'people pick up on whether you're serious or not.... if the government came out and went look, we're going to build eleven nuclear power stations... but there are public consultations going on and the public is invited to say whether they welcome it or not... that's the kind of thing I think means that people disengage, go why should I bother voting?' Consultation has genuine impact when several factors come together: genuine desire to consult before decisions are made, stakeholder interest in the issue and supportive leadership.

It is also important to report back to participants after a consultation. Karia (2006) conceded that 'when we did Labour listens, which is some time ago, people involved would accept that the infrastructure did not allow us to deal adequately with the results... in a Big Conversation we were a little bit better, we did go back to people, but, what we weren't able to do was to show them results in the discussion went into the policy document. It's quite resource intensive to do that.' Gill (2007) said 'I would never advise any party, ministry or minister or department to do a high profile public consultation if you're not prepared to then be as high profile in reporting back what you've heard, good and bad. And explaining that we can't do X, Y and Z, but we can do this, or we're looking into that.'

Consultation also needs to be co-ordinated to avoid consultation fatigue. Gill (2007) commented how 'you will always get the public saying they want to be listened to, they want to be consulted more... [but] this is then misinterpreted to mean that we have to go out and do lots of consultations and more polls and more of everything else because the public are demanding it.' Levin (2008) recalled how 'at one point years ago we were doing a lot of work on public dialogue and I asked one of the staff to do an inventory of how many public consultations the Manitoba government had going on at that particular point in time. There were 138 consultations going on through the government of Manitoba at that particular point, which is more than anyone could take part in.'

The methods used in the consultation obviously affects the quality and nature of the input received, so needs to be sound and suit the task and participants. As Pattillo (2009) explains, 'it depends on the question that you're asking [and] who you can say absolutely needs to be engaged in that conversation, and what would best work for them. For some groups, small community conversations work well. For others, doing stuff over the net offers quick surveys that [they] can do after the kids have gone to sleep works best. For others, being part of a community network of conversations that might be happening normally.'

Consultants and clients

A key factor in the quality and impact of market analysis is the nature of, and relationship between, market research consultants and political clients.

The clients

The client needs to want the research for it to be effective. Braun (2009) said 'at the end of the day, you're just a consultant to your client, so they can do whatever they want...the one in the Czech Republic, that party and especially the chairman, they became extremely fond of research.... [and] in that case it was totally worthwhile. There are other campaigns I worked on where they don't really trust research.' The client also needs to know what they want from the market analysis. Sparrow (2007) advised consultants 'don't even get involved if you're only being commissioned because the party thinks it ought to do it because the other party's doing it...agree with the party how you're actually going to use research...and how they're going to be integrated into policy decision-making'. Kavanagh (1996, 106) noted how 'difficulties persist, largely because party influentials differ among themselves about whether they want polling to help primarily with targeting communications, making policy decisions, or boosting morale (i.e. to report "good news" about voting intentions, and the popularity of existing policies).'

Practitioners said the best clients use market analysis for fine tuning only. Utting (2008) remarked that 'I really like to work with people who have got good instincts and you're much really there as a tuning, back up, safety check.' Nanos (2009) said 'if a politician or public policy-maker uses public opinion research as a first step, they run the risk of expecting the results to make decisions for them.' However, others argued that parties should only commission market analysis if they really want it, not if they already know the answer. Jones (2008) observed that 'the smart research for parties to do is research that is actionable, the stupid research for parties to do is research that just either A) tells you what you already know or should know if you pick up the papers or ask anyone or know intuitively; or B) seeks to persuade yourself of something that probably is isn't true.' Sparrow (2007) recalled how 'very often we were brought in to do research on subjects where the policy had already been announced. One example was something on The National Health Service, and the idea of a patient passport. The whole policy had been worked up, announced, this is what it's all going to be about and everything. And *then* they did some research!'

Politicians should let practitioners decide what/how to poll. As Braun (2009) explained, 'it's kind of like "give us enough room to do what we know how to do and then listen to us".' Stockley (2007) said it works 'when politicians are prepared to listen to the results and not try and either dictate results or screen it out when the results come back to them'. Kavanagh (1996, 105) noted how 'many politicians, not just on the left, have claimed that it is their job to know what voters were thinking and perceived polling as a threat to their status.' They believe they can judge public opinion more effectively, but the professional has a more objective outside perspective. Sparrow's (2007) experience with Hague 1997–2001 and the Keep the Pound campaign in 2001 reflects this:

> The important issues as far as people were concerned were health, education, law...[Europe was] at number nine...It was one area where the Tories had a lead over Labour, but it was right down at the bottom...And I remember presenting all this, and John Redwood said 'ah, this is all crap, I did my own research on Friday night over the dinner table...if we go on about Europe and explain to people what a threat Europe is, it will go up the list of priorities. And if it goes up the list of priorities, people will realise that we have much better policies on Europe than they [Labour] do, and that's how we win the election.' So you couldn't even say to this person that they should believe a list of issues people think are important, because [the politician felt] that's only unimportant because people don't realise how important it is!

Leadership support of market analysis is crucial for it to have any impact. Stockely (2007) talked about when he delivered a presentation which 'showed that the Labour electorate wasn't particularly Left-wing, it differed very little from the National-voting electorate....I remember one of the more Left-wing Labour MPs standing up in the middle of this thing [and saying] "what do these people believe in? Who are they?" And Moore [the party leader] saying "sit down and listen to this".'

To get the most out of the research, politicians should get training on how to understand and use market analysis. Braun (2009) observed how 'more and more, I would see candidates understanding the value of research.' Similarly, Glover (2007) said that politicians ask for more mature market analysis now:

> I've been doing this for 17 years or so and we used to get asked to do very simple questions like, "can you do a quick survey and find out if people want to build a second harbour bridge or whether they mind doing x because we are going to do x whether they think it should be done or not." And it used to be at that kind of level. Now most government departments, and certainly local government people have research and evaluation departments...and so we much more often get asked to explore what the issues might be...before we write policy.

The politician's ability to be open to results is important: Sparrow (2007) said 'very often you can come out of a focus group, politicians sitting behind the one way mirror and so on, and the politicians would've taken out of it the one person and the one phrase that just happened to support their particular view...they're coming to it from an angle...in the end, that's what you hear if you come to it in that frame of mind.' Problems can develop when research is used to justify a position internally (Kavanagh 1996, 102). Sparrow's position was very problematic:

> You've got people trying to mould the research questions before they ever get asked, and then I'm supposed to go along and see the leader and say this is the question we asked and this is the result we got, and efforts are being made to get him to implement whatever policy we're talking about on the basis of basically crooked research...it was Maurice Saatchi who knew the answer already and just wanted some research to back it up. Questions like do you think everyone should have the choices in health and education that today only money can buy?...about 43 percent said no...they actually realized what was behind it, which was greater use of the private sector and that kind of thing...Even with a crooked question producing a far less spectacularly positive result than an unbiased one would, it was still spun to say, you know, this glass is half full, at least, if not more! So it was just a thoroughly unrewarding experience.

The consultants

Market analysis consultants need to follow certain ethics. Humphrey (2007) said 'I think you've got to be honest with the client and...I don't think you should get into deceiving the public or helping the client to deceive the public', while Gill (2007) suggested avoiding just 'telling the client what he or she wants'. Gould (2007) also advised against hogging the data: make different forms and market intelligence results open:

> In the last 2005 election I introduced something that's basically called open source polling and there was lots of different polling companies doing the polling, lots of different techniques, there was marginal polling, there was message polling,... small internet samples, there were focus groups. I just made that available to everybody in the campaign. That worked very well because the idea that the pollster is the repository of wisdom when it comes to polling and then the others are seen as secondary somehow – you're the doctor and he's the patient – it's nonsense.

Consultants need to present recommendations, especially negative ones, carefully. Stockley (2007) recalled how

> UMR research did the research that showed that Geoffrey Palmer couldn't win or even have a half-respectable result.... it was shown very clearly that Mike Moore would have a better chance of winning in 1990, of saving more seats, saving more bums. This was, you know, delivered to the cabinet and duly appeared in the media and the effect, quite devastatingly, I think, it was the last nail in Geoffrey Palmer's coffin.

Humphrey (2007) said 'with politicians, the more it is about them as people the more difficult it is. So if you said to somebody you're ugly... or you have a very unfortunate manner... there are a lot of politicians who just won't have that conversation and there are an awful lot of advisors who won't attempt to have that conversation... [but] if you're a professional advisor you've got to at least try.' Carter (2007) noted how 'there's no way of getting around the data, and that's why research is so powerful at the end of the day... it's very easy to see in the period before 2005, the numbers show that Labour's numbers were going down, that there was an issue to do with trust, that people felt that the Prime Minister lost the public's respect.'

The best market analysis professionals suggest what to do with these results though: they present strategic options in product and communication. Ulm (2007) noted how 'we don't just do a survey and hand it off to the campaign. We're there from the beginning; we present the results in actionable terms. Here's what we need to do.' Humphrey (2007) noted that clients are now 'looking for something that would take you from research, to be properly rooted in research and evidence, through the analysis and the strategy element, through into engaging with people and supporting clients in their communications and their wider engagement with stakeholders or with the public or with their own staff'. Wright (2009) said 'you have to find the story, whether it's romance or adventure, in the data; there's a story there, find it. Everyone who does public affairs work has to be a good story teller. Otherwise you're just standing in front of clients with data and saying "well figure it out".' However, market analysis consultants should not make the final decision for the politician. Mortimore (2006) recalls how 'Bob Worcester used to say to me that the essence of his job was to say "this is what will happen if x, y and z happens." He said it is not his job to make the decision or even recommend that they *should* do XY or Z that is the politicians' job.'

The last point about collecting market analysis is a subtle but profound one: the value of market analysis lies in the interpretation – the ability to assess the results. It's not a golden bullet just by itself. Campbell (2005) discussed how they once received very negative feedback from focus groups, which was surprising given it took place after a period of positive events such as those that took place in Kosovo and Northern Ireland. However, what it told them was underneath it all was a concern voters had that the government was too interested in foreign affairs, and they wanted attention back on the domestic scene: 'so you have to interpret them very carefully.' Therefore, despite what the methods may suggest, as an activity in politics, market analysis is an art not just a science. Parties need to ensure they employ skilled and experienced pollsters who can interpret effectively. Mills (2009) recalled how 'during the time I was a political staffer I saw quite a few commercial pollsters in front of Ministers and most were completely unable to cope. They would certainly claim, as every research company does, that their findings were actionable but in terms of how politics works they weren't.' Ulm (2007) commented that 'when we hire people here, we found it easier to hire a political person and then turn them into a good researcher, rather than take a good researcher and make them into a political person.' Mills (2009) said 'there is art in both the analysis and in presentation and communication of those findings to the campaign team.' Therefore, although market analysis is often thought to be scientific, it involves judgement and interpretation and is less dictatorial to politicians than we might at first think.

Using market analysis in politics

The potential influence of market analysis on what politicians do and decide is strong. Academic research has identified many examples of politicians changing their product in response to the market. Newman (1999, 72–77) identified how, in 1988, presidential candidate Bush responded to the market desire for no tax rises. Similarly, Lees-Marshment (2001) and Wring (2005a) observed how UK Labour changed its communication under Neil Kinnock and then its policies under Tony Blair to suit voter demands. Global knowledge sharing has resulted in copied strategies from Bill Clinton in the US to UK Labour under Tony Blair in 1997, Helen Clark's Labour campaign in New Zealand in 1999, the SPD in Germany, the LDP in Japan, the Danish Venstre-Danmarks Liberale Parti and Kevin Rudd's Labor Party in Australia in 2007. 'Crosby Textorism', so-called after the Australian Liberal Party pollsters Lynton Crosby and Mark Textor, which creates strategies in response to core voters' fears of what they *don't* want to happen (as opposed to desires) on issues such as crime and immigration, succeeded for John Howard and the Australian Liberals in the 2001 Australian election, and was copied by the UK Conservative Party in 2005 and New Zealand's National Party in 2005 (see Lilleker and Lees-Marshment 2005, Turner 2009 and Lees-Marshment et al. 2010 for a range of comparative examples, also see Lees 2005, Rudd 2005, Lees-Marshment 2008 and Pettitt 2009).

Nevertheless, market analysis comes with a health warning, in that despite its essentialism and value (if carried out appropriately) to the political marketing process, there are generic rules about its limitations and how it should be used. Practitioners suggest there is a more nuanced, less direct relationship between analysis, the product and, in particular, electoral success. The overall process – and its consequences for electoral support – is more complex and less direct. As Edwards (2009) recalled of the 2008 New Zealand Labour Party's campaign:

> A lot of the stuff in these focus-groups is about the leaders and their personalities. So, they like this, they don't like that.... What it was that happened in this campaign was that the focus-groups seemed to be saying that John Key was nice, and that they were saying that what they liked about Helen Clark was strong, proven leadership. So, suddenly, based on these focus groups, everything was based around strong, proven leadership, and you were saying it again and again.

Thus, politicians need to be careful of being too slavish in following the analysis: there was 'a very powerful feeling that they had been locked into the focus-groups for so many years, it's a little bit like someone saying "Let go of the rail and swim." You're not going to let go of the rail, because the rail will hold you up.'

Other politicians talked about research being used to confirm that the chosen direction is working. Hide (2007), leader of the Act Party in New Zealand, noted how a poll found that 'what they [the public] liked was competition and choice, which I thought might have been quite hard. They like the fact that their MP was talking to the government on legislation trying to advance competition and choice, they liked that.' This was a surprise but confirmed his desired strategy. Alternatively, research can be used to make adjustments rather than whole-scale change. Rothmayr and Hardmeier (2002, 130–131) found the Swiss Federal government used polls to support arguments, existing decisions, criticise alternative proposals, inform social marketing and monitor public satisfaction with government services. Kiss (2009) showed how the Hungarian Socialist Party sought to win votes from youth using transactional marketing by changing certain aspects of the product: 'the government was very active in abolishing compulsory military service and the communication of the abolishment afterwards; a programme called Nest Building was prepared in order to help young people in their housing problem.'

Market analysis can have more direct impact in some cases. Hide (2007) recalls a clear example:

> I regularly do this 300 plus poll and put in questions of the day. And I put in a question in on the anti-smacking bill, and they were overwhelmingly opposed, I mean vitriolic. So that was pretty good because that's what we were, opposed to that bill. Then John Key did his about turn as he is want to do, and at that time we had some focus group work going on... and this focus group just said John Key, Helen Clark fixed it, it's gone. The issue was dead in a heartbeat... there's a couple of guys in the party... and they were fired up, 'were saying we are going to get 10 percent of the vote, all we need to do is say we are going to repeal the anti-smacking bill and we'll sail on to victory'. So they organised a meeting which they expected hundreds to turn up. We said no one would turn up but we went along with it and no one did. That was a powerful bit of research.

Market analysis thus identifies areas where politicians can't change opinion: Carr (2008) conceded that 'qualitative polling can help you, sometimes in identifying ideas that simply don't work.' It can also be used to find a way forward on controversial issues. Nanos (2008) gave the example of Barack Obama's speech at Notre Dame on abortion, when Obama said that all sides would agree to common goals, such as how to have the fewest number of abortions possible and maximise parents' access to adoption. Nanos believes 'his dialogue was the result of good political sense, but also of good public opinion research. The thought process was "What are the things that can unite us in regards to goals as opposed to dividing us and stopping a particular dialogue?"' Research can be used to give government more choices 'as opposed to saying "Abortion? Not going to deal with it because we're a minority view on it. We're not going to get what we want, so we're going to ignore this".'

Market analysis is therefore used for different purposes and strategies, and practitioners advise against over-relying on it. Callingham (2009) argued, regarding New Zealand Labour, that 'they went into the campaign wanting a fresh, new look – a fresh, forward-looking look, and unfortunately the focus-groups dragged them backwards.' Evans (2006) said:

> Research is essential in politics, but it can only tell you where you've been and where you are. It can't really tell you where you want to get to. It's like a rearview mirror, you wouldn't plan your journey without it. They can't tell you where you're going in front. It shouldn't affect where you ultimately want to get to but it can effect maybe how you get there. You have to believe in something in politics before you can go out and sell it.

Taylor (2008), who worked for President George W. Bush, said research was more useful in communication to tell them 'what groups did it resonate the most with... So women are more concerned about healthcare, teachers are more concerned about retirement planning.... President Bush [wa]s not somebody who was interested in sort of just, he just doesn't take a poll and decide what to talk about; he says here's what I'm saying, if you can help me articulate it in a way that resonates with people better, I'm all ears.' It helps highlight potential aspects to be exploited. Rennard (2006) commented that 'in the Lib Dems, people in the party have said if you're doing market research does that mean we have to change our principles and policies to suit market research? But I don't think that we've ever done that. Research helps us understand that some of our principles work better or worse than others.'

In 2003–2005, 'on foreign affairs, the Iraq War, our policy was very popular, particularly of course for minority communities and for traditional Labour voters.... [and] the degree to which we emphasised the Iraq War was strengthened by market research and guided us in Brent, and in Liverpool, and in Birmingham and by-elections like that. Having tested people's feeling on it, it was a good card to play.'

Research also helps ensure that MPs and candidates talk about issues that local people care about. Rennard (2006) explains how 'local politicians can be keen to talk about the issues they feel passionate about and it's quite right to see the passion in these people. But if they're very passionate about something which isn't actually the biggest concern of voters they are seeking to represent then we're not going to get the audience to listen to them properly.' He points out that, while a politician may be particularly concerned about housing, 'talking about slums in Glasgow is probably not the thing to talk about in Surrey [an affluent area] where you might be talking about tuition and top-up fees.' Policies remain consistent, avoiding conflicting messages, but the focus on which ones to communicate is changed according to the local area.

Market analysis can also be used to inform GOTV messaging. Lees-Marshment (2009c) noted that in the 2005 election in New Zealand the Labour Party, realising the election result was going to be close, sent direct mail shots to voters who lived in South Auckland in a state/council home. The mail was designed in the form of an eviction notice suggesting that if the opposition, the National Party, won it would result in state homes being sold and the tenants losing their home. Turnout went up among this segment – which naturally supported Labour anyway – helping secure an election victory.

Research also can be used to find the right words and way to present an argument and pinpoint which groups to communicate with. Brodie (2009) said [research] 'was helpful to us in terms of knowing what criticisms of the liberals would resonate, and then later on, what criticisms of the Bloc and the NDP would resonate'. It also told them that it was not clear what the Bloc, who dominated Quebec politics in Canada, could 'ever get done, because they're doing typical opposition stances and are quite small... So we ran the campaign against the Bloc in Quebec as "the Bloc is only in it for themselves, they're more interested in their parliamentary pensions and their parliamentary salaries and their travel allowances than they are in representing Quebecers. They can't get anything done for Quebec. The Conservatives are the ones that deliver the goods for Quebecers".' Roozendaal (2008) used research to test the words used in Australian NSW Labour campaign, giving focus groups key phrases to react to: 'it sounds very contrived, but there's just certain words and certain phrases that people will react better to, and there's ten ways to say the same thing, and if you can say it the way that most rings a bell with them, then it works.' Rogers (2009) described how research found that using the phrase 'cutting taxes' did not attract public support for policies of tax reduction; so they tested about 50 variations in language to describe reducing taxes until they found five words that would be received positively: ' "Lower taxes help working families".'

Just because a proposed communication does not receive a positive result it does not mean it should be dropped. Ansell (2007) recalled a time when a group's assessment of an advertisement was changed because of one participant:

> I remember one time everyone was bagging an ad – one where Don was talking passionately about his principles. The theme was, 'These are the things I stand for' (wise spending, say). 'And these are the things I won't stand for' (like waste). And it ended with the line, 'For me, politics is not about right and left. It's about right and wrong.' Well, I thought this was pretty stirring stuff. But one grumpy guy thought it was a bit over the top for his liking. He set the tone for the next few comments, all negative. Then just when I thought that was it for that particular ad, this woman pipes up, 'Actually, I think that's really strong of Brash to say that'. And, one by one, pretty much the whole room came round to her point of view. If it wasn't for that one woman, that ad would have rated a 3/10 rather than a 7/10.

Thus Ansell (2007) said, 'I'd abolish focus groups! (Really. Their responses bear little relation to the way people react when they're not being asked to analyse something)...a lot of the strongest ideas tend to get killed in research.' The leader of the National Party Ansell worked for, Don Brash (2007), confirmed Ansell's criticism of focus groups' predictive quality because in their experience the groups 'were not necessarily wildly enthusiastic about the [adverts], but it turned out they worked extremely well'.

Research can, nevertheless, be used to prevent miscommunication. Carr (2008) noted how they expected a negative attack campaign about land tax from the opposition in an Australian election, so they 'tested an advertisement that really explained how land tax used to work and how it works with our reforms. The polling showed that people liked it because it was informative.' Roozendaal (2008) recalled how they 'had a very interesting law and order ad which ended with handcuffs, and when the agency came to us with the concept I thought, "we're never going to get away with this thing"', but 'it tested its socks off as a great ad'. Carr (2008) explains how research also prevented mistakes in two campaigns. In one opposition campaign he thought of referring to the incumbent as 'a North Shore government' because a majority of its cabinet members came from Sydney's North Shore, but 'the party secretary came back to me and said look, we tested that, he said people don't care, people from Western Sydney don't care, it doesn't count, it makes you sound envious.' In another election he wanted to criticise the opposition leader for having very limited experience but 'qualitative polling showed that the remotest attack on her would be interpreted by softly-committed female voters as an attack on all of them' and could stop the party winning that whole demographic: 'we rigidly adhered to a policy of not criticising her...and we won big without criticising her. It was a classic example of the value of argument testing in qualitative research. That's where that works.'

Rottinghaus and Alberro (2005) explored how polls were used to inform the selling of the candidate Vicente Fox in the 2000 Mexican election at key chronological points, by revealing which candidate traits were the most important to voters (honesty, followed by reliability and good proposals). Fox connected all three in his speeches, talking of honest new faces to form a new government, declaring he was strong enough to do the job. Ingram and Lees-Marshment (2002) noted that in Bill Clinton's 1992 presidential bid for the US White House – as market research suggested voters were more open to changing their view of Clinton if they heard him speak at length – Clinton made frequent use of electronic town hall meetings, which allowed more direct and non-mediated access to voters, unavailable via traditional media. Rennard (2006) recalled that 'you know from the combination of formal research, and talking to people, whether leaders [have] got it or not. Paddy Ashdown and Charles Kennedy were good assets to us and that could be shown by scientific research and anecdotal evidence with people saying good things about Paddy and Charles. In our campaigns we always had Paddy and Charles very prominent in what we were doing. We would use them with our candidates to get attention.' However, market intelligence can't always predict how somebody is going to be perceived once they are a leader. Utting (2008) noted that 'from the day Kevin [Rudd, Labour leader and then prime minister in Australia] came on, the public just locked onto him, and it never changed. It was just like a hook went through continually. I think that with all the polling and all the published polling, in the year Kevin was there, there were probably 150 polls taken, and not one ever showed him winning. Once he got in the whole zeitgeist changed.'

Market analysis also helps identify competition weaknesses and devise an effective strategy to utilise them. Carr (2008) discusses how they used research in formulating a strategy against a strong incumbent, the Mayor of Brisbane – a woman by the name of Sally-Anne Atkinson – so that their unknown candidate Gibb Thorley managed to win against her:

> When the researchers said that she was even better paid than the Prime Minister, they didn't like that and they reacted to that quite negatively. And we were actually able to craft a campaign solely around that thing. To find that little chink and go right in on that issue in terms of the TV campaign that was then built around that. I think they called her 'Salary Anne'...the ad guys, they had a little jingle and they talked about 'Salary Anne.' And it really did the damage. It was sort of like a missile, it went in underneath the competence, the personality, the success factors, and it really hit the button...When I look back across my career, that's what I regard as the biggest difference, because it took a campaign that everybody thought had no chance, all the objective and analytical evidence showed that it had no chance, and it turned it around.

Summary

This chapter has shown that market analysis in politics is a multi-varied activity, and thus the criticism that political marketing means that politicians follow focus groups is a gross over-simplification. Instead, the value, purposes, uses, methods and attitudes to market analysis are wide-ranging. There are important practical lessons that need to be learned about how to make market analysis most effective and help politicians achieve a range of goals (see summary of rules in Table 1.1). Market analysis is part of the political process, but it does not dictate the outcome of decisions made, and thus practitioners have room to make considered choices, which will also vary the democratic implications. The next chapter discusses political product development, strategy and branding.

Table 1.1 Rules of the game for market analysis

The market and political consumer
1. Understand that voters are critical, negative and consumerist towards political elites without understanding their job
2. Be aware that there are lots of products (not just political) competing for political consumers' attention
3. Take into account that voters increasingly use a variety of sources of information to form their views and are questioning of them all
4. Realise that the political market isn't just voters but includes those who have a stakehold in, or influence on, the party, politician or government
5. Understand that the public wants politicians to deliver a costed product that suits their needs/demands
6. Look for new electoral segments replacing traditional cleavages, which need a distinct strategy
7. Accept that how the public vote is unpredictable; if they vote is uncertain; if they volunteer to help the party or politician, it has to be on their terms, not the candidate's/party's
8. Plan for public perception to take a long time to become more positive once changes have been made

Gathering market analysis
9. Don't just rely on gut instinct
10. Conduct market analysis continuously
11. Use different methods (polling, focus groups, in-depth interviews, talking to people on the street, analysis of past elections, counting issues raised in letters/emails, online, secondary data, internal committee discussions, intuition, policy/service users, role play)
12. Collect it from different sources – not just one organisation/person – to mitigate moderator bias
13. Use it for a range of purposes
14. Research multi-markets not just voters
15. Test the market to predict how voters might react to changes
16. Market analysis is an art not just a science
17. The value of market analysis lies in the interpretation – the ability to assess the results – it's not a golden bullet by itself

Segmentation
18. Don't try to get everyone: focus resources on key segments to maximise resource effectiveness and satisfaction
19. Don't treat everyone the same: we are individuals
20. Don't use old groupings: we belong to new segments now (consider geography, behaviour, demography, lifestyle, political views, likely support, family life, turn out)
21. Profile voters and build an effective long-term database incorporating deeper layers of analysis
22. Understand each segment (work out what they want, what motivates them, how they want to be communicated with; change communication and product to suit this so it is more likely to satisfy them)

23. Try to move people between different groups, e.g. from low to high support, from passive to active volunteer
24. Avoid sending conflicting messages; you'll get found out!
25. Include loyal traditional supporters
26. Micro-targeting can't tell you everything and is limited by data and assumptions made

Candidate analysis (opposition research)

27. Use research to identify strengths and weaknesses of both candidate and opposition
28. Use research to anticipate and prepare both attack and defence
29. Attack other candidates with caution: claims need to be verifiable or they will backfire
30. Research a wide range of sources and any aspect of the product: governing skills and record, voting record, policies championed, changed positions, positions against public opinion, non-political work, personal life where it contradicts public policies and positions
31. Be prepared to explain changes in position

Predictive market analysis

32. Avoid just analysing the past and the present
33. Understand 'now' (what do people think of you now?) but also the 'future' (what would people like to see happen? What could be changed?)
34. Explore possibility: test and predict how voters might react to possible changes
35. Look for a new path: for nuance, not just for and against
36. Ask for potential solutions, not just current problems

Consultation

37. Provide information in different ways to suit different needs
38. Consult particular groups to get more useful input: citizen experts, stakeholders. For each issue contact those living with the problem
39. Bring consultation within an organisation under one roof; avoid duplication and improve its quality
40. Conduct consultation alongside a long-term decision-making process so stakeholder input can have impact
41. Report back to participants after a consultation
42. Manage participants, otherwise consultations will attract biased participants such as interest groups
43. Avoid consultation fatigue: don't consult the public on everything
44. Don't do it just for show: it needs genuine desire to consult before decisions are made

Market analysis consultants and clients

The client needs to:
45. Know what they want from the market analysis
46. Support objective market analysis and caution other people's protest against the results
47. Let consultants do their job

Table 1.1 (Continued)

48. Get training to understand results
49. Understand research does not dictate the decision; it just informs it
50. Only commission market analysis if they really want it, not if they already know the answer
51. Let researchers do scientifically sound research

Consultants need to:
52. Commission market analysis in time for it to be useful
53. Present recommendations carefully, especially negative ones
54. Suggest options for what to do in response
55. Let the politician make the actual decision

Using market analysis
56. Use market analysis in decision-making to find new groups to represent, find who to talk to and how, put resources in best place, confirm existing decisions, make adjustments, change parts of the product, change for particular segments and identify where you can't change opinion
57. Use market analysis in communication to ensure candidates talk about issues people care about, communicate issues politicians care about, check assumptions, test controversial ads, avoid unpopular attacks, sell policy/candidate, decide candidate/policy prominence, identify unknown insights, identify blocks that have to be dealt with and, identify and manage weaknesses
58. Make sure you don't rely on market analysis for product ideas, or necessarily drop ideas because of a single piece of analysis
59. Research does not tell you everything

2
Strategic Development

> Strategy is the most important thing for winning and losing elections by any measure.
>
> —Gould (2007)
>
> It is always political ideas that are the currency of politics, if it becomes reduced to a tactical game, then you lose sight of the whole reason to be there... Because it's a marketplace to do with political values and political ideas; one can play lots of games with that.
>
> —Evans (2006)

A second key area of political marketing is how politicians decide what to offer to the public in relation to public demands. Developing the product and brand involves consideration of a range of factors. Strategy interlinks with several other marketing areas, influencing the product, communication, internal marketing and leadership. Positioning involves more tactical thinking in relation to the competition. This chapter will discuss a range of factors involved in developing the product, strategy, positioning and branding, finishing with a discussion about the need for authenticity.

Developing the product

The first point to understand about the political product is that it is more than just policies: it includes everything a party does, including its organisation, conferences/conventions and events, and also the behaviour of many different people, including the key party figures and leaders, elected politicians and candidates, membership/supporters, staff and advisors (Lees-Marshment 2001). It also includes less tangible aspects. Baines et al. (2003, 229) add in parliamentary representation (belongingness and social identity) and a voice in government (social participation and identity), while the Lloyd (2005, 41–43) concept of the political product argues that it also includes delivery management and skills, accommodation in terms of how parties understand and respond appropriately to the needs of the electorate, accessibility to the public and the return given to stakeholders on their money, time, effort and emotional investment. For example, the campaign of Hillary Clinton in the 2008 Iowa and New Hampshire primaries focused on a range of personal characteristics such as her experience, gender, bipartisanship, compassion and her hardworking nature, as well as her overall responsiveness to the electorate (Gorbounova and Lees-Marshment 2009). The political product is continually evolving (Newman 1999, 46–47). Stockley (2007) commented that 'no one actually comes erupting into a room and says to the policy committee or to the party leaders...we have to change this, we have to change that because the polling says so. It's part of a cumulative process.' This partly reflects how many different factors contribute to political product development. Academics have debated whether the main driver is voters or political elites, but practitioners' perspectives suggest that such a dichotomy is too simplistic and, therefore, this chapter will discuss a range of influences.

First, parties can use policy research to add rigour and data to support their proposals. Somerville (2007) said 'you could safely say that policy, at least a third, should be informed by the attitude or society, and a third by some of the values held centrally, and then maybe a third on evidence.' In opposition, Jones (2008) noted the Conservative research department tried 'to provide the rigour, the data and the thinking behind what the party did'. This is true of government also: Glover (2007) noted that 'that's most often where we get involved because the strategists...are not quite sure how it all should work, so we end up presenting the community's view, but also trying to pull together the community of interest groups'.

In government, the public service and communication staff are involved in this process. Macken (2008) said that, as a policy advisor, he worked on pre-decided policies and on developing new ones: 'you'd try and develop policies that would win *and* respond to...who was saying the government should really do something about men's health or planning reform.' Staff need to be included in the process: as Rogers (2009) noted, 'the worst thing that you can do is to...insert a decision that hasn't gone through the rigours of the process, because it will ultimately fail, either because it was poorly thought out and inappropriate, or because public servants will sabotage it because it isn't rational.' Communication staff also need to be involved from the beginning: Reid (2009) noted that a 'model where the communications director or the press secretary is the person that comes into the room after the decisions have been made, and then they say "OK, go sell this"...[is] a bit of an antiquated model.' Communications staff can offer predictions as to the potential reaction from the public, whereas policy staff are too close: Evershed (2009) said 'it is a hazard of their work – I call it living inside...the stamen of the flower, because they're so knowledgeable about their particular area, and so interested in it, that they have a hard time understanding that not everybody is immediately interested and taken with their ideas.'

The product is also determined by events. Robertson (2006) noted 'you can't completely control the agenda because stuff gets chucked onto it, like we would've never said anything about foreshore and seabed in 2002...yet that was the dominating sort of issue for that term in government.' Macken (2008) recalled 'you've got to respond to the political environment you're in...suddenly there's a dead person in a hospital and you've got to say why is there a dead person in the foyer of a hospital, why didn't they get them into bed? And you have to amend types of access protocols and that sort of thing.'

Product development must take into account the history and beliefs of the product/candidates. Medvic (2006, 20–23) argued that the candidate is the foundation of the strategy. Ulm (2007) said 'I have never had a candidate ask me "What should I believe on this?" Never had. Never had it once. Usually the candidate has a core history, a core set of beliefs, and you're trying to figure out of all those, what's the best way to win?' Mellman (2007) explained that 'if your message is we need someone who's tough and you have a wimpy sort of candidate...that can't really be your message.' Stanzel (2007) said of President George W. Bush, his character impacts what they advise him, given that voters 'see him as somebody who's pretty direct and if he says something he means it. Sometimes that's, more often than not in my view, a good thing, sometimes that can be seen as a bad thing – that the President's too direct or too blunt.' His manner also 'impact[s] the way reporters act around him, he's someone who's very, very easy to get along with and very engaging with people, so when we have opportunities, it's my view that he is the person that we would most want to have talk to reporters, because he is better at making the case, he's impassioned about the issues that he cares about'. This is also true of the party as a whole, while smaller, minor parties may be even more constrained by principle. Billot (2006), president of the Alliance in New Zealand, said 'we're a changing society party... we have to actually cause debate and discussion... by being controversial and possibly even unpopular with a larger section of the population.'

Nevertheless, the product is often changed in response to public opinion and market analysis, but in different ways and to varying degrees. Parties can appeal not to all, but to the next tier of potential voters. Lavigne (2009) noted that 'you can't embrace policies that will alienate your next tier of voters... What we want to do is we want to break through to that next grouping of individuals... it's a prudent kind of market share strategy.' Smaller parties can modify their policies to suit public opinion without whole-scale abandonment of principle; staff from the Act Party said 'we are never going to cave in and have the same policies as the Greens on climate change because it just doesn't work for us' (Middleton 2006), 'but on the other hand... some of these people might love our education and tax policies but because we are seen as so anti-green, they couldn't afford to vote for us, whereas if we were just OK on the environment then we can actually get [them]' (Wilson 2006). A less ideological approach can attract support in unusual states/segments. Mehta (2009) noted of Obama that:

> By campaigning in 50 states he had to have a message that worked in 50 states, and that meant abandoning traditional democratic or republican talking points and really talking about the core issues that the voters cared about... because Barack Obama was A – a democrat, B – somebody who had been giving that message about change, and C – an outside Washington person, so he wasn't tied to the policies that are cast by either party... that greatly helped us in some of the historically republican states.

Of course there are limits that public opinion place on political product development. The success of a product depends on the market reaction, not just the worthiness of position, or public policy value or the skills of the candidate. One example is environmentalism, which despite environmental protests and lobbying for decades only became part of the mainstream major party agenda more recently, aided by former Vice-President Al Gore's work around his documentary *An Inconvenient Truth*. However, it is too simplistic to conclude that this means every policy is made to fit voter demands. As Macken (2008) said, 'sometimes you've got to fess up and say this is, this is, we need to do this, this is hard, but we're going to close this hospital or whatever, but then sort of for good clinical reasons and it's really unpopular and of course there's a huge kafuffle, but sometimes you've got to articulate that. At other times you've got to tailor your policies so the spinners can get it out there as potentially a good thing.'

Internal demands also need to be considered in product development. Lilleker (2005c, 573) notes that 'if the party moves away from the core principles that motivate members to join and be active supporters, some will withdraw their support and membership.' Adjusting the product to suit internal demand is crucial in the Canadian context, according to Paré and Berger (2008, 57). The Canadian Conservatives managed to appeal to both markets in 2006 'by designing and marketing a product offering that struck a balance between the interests of specific segments of the voting public (i.e. the desire for efficiency, accountability, and direct benefits without a radical ideological shift) and the interests of internal party supporters'. However, meeting internal and external demands is not easy in practice. Lavigne (2009), from the Canadian minor party, the NDP, said that his party risk 'upsetting and alienating the base, who will either stay at home or flee, in an effort to go get that next tier'. Leadership candidates for parties obviously need to respond to the internal market (see Ormrod et al. 2007 and Gorbounova and Lees-Marshment 2009), but they have to be careful about not putting on record a position or comment that, while helping them become selected as nominee or leader, will deter voters at election time. In the 2000 presidential campaign of George W. Bush, he stressed traditional conservative Republican themes during the primaries, but after securing the nomination moved back towards the centre and focused on issues that opinion polls had shown to be of paramount concern for most Americans in the 2000 election: education, social security and health care. However, he retained traditional Republican themes such as tax cuts, smaller government and a stronger military (Knuckey and Lees-Marshment 2005). Getting that balance is important. Rennard (2006) noted that 'you need volunteers to feel motivated and feel passionate about core party beliefs', but 'with the Liberal Democrats, you may well find in the gathering of members that they are extremely interested in the detail of the House of Lords reform for example. If you then went out to the country and said, we need to look at the election of House of Lords, you are not going to command the attention of the voters.' Pettitt (2009) argues that the product should not be adjusted too much 'because the compromises necessary to avoid dissent would dilute the new product too much'.

Parties also need to present a capable and representative team. Parties try to broaden their candidates in terms of gender and ethnicity, but with mixed results. As Gillan (2006) said, 'you can't market yourself unless you look like the population you are trying to represent.' Bray (2008) made a pertinent observation of the 2007 federal election in Australia:

> One of my most searing memories was standing in the main street in Eastwood...the centre of what was John Howard's electorate. And they had this street party parade...about a month before the election...the seat had the greatest number of languages spoken in it, and you had these people in dragon suits, and the corrections marching band, and a bunch of Scottish highland dancers, and Japanese, and Chinese, and Korean...and right in front of us was this raised stage with 15 old white men...and it just struck me, this is why this guy is probably going to lose, because you've got this very rich huge multicultural country, [but] at the top, it's the same people that have been running it for 20 years. [The] elite haven't recognised that they need to change.

The likelihood of getting into government affects product development. Mills (2009) noted how 'you can be a bit more free and easy with following the polling in Opposition, especially if you are a minor party, but a major party still faces the constraints of having to govern in future'. Griggs (2008) talked about how the promises made in Australian NSW premier candidate Bob Carr's campaign in the 1995 campaign made government difficult, as they said they would 'halve the waiting list within eighteen months or Bob would make Andrew resign. We essentially did it, but it blew the budget out to buggery, lasted about three months before the waiting lists went skewed again.'

Gould (2007) explains that 'in the early years of the opposition... you're just wanting to kind of develop political positions, develop issues, exploit weaknesses and polling is absolutely key to that. In government...ultimately you're making decisions on the merits of the case and so polling has to be less important.' Lobbying provides expertise to change policy into legislation: as Harris (2001, 1151) noted, 'politicians become increasingly isolated and short of quality information, effective lobbying fills up that vacuum and allows good decision making.' Somerville (2007) cited an example in the UK of 'baby bonds...an idea that was rooted further in academia and was adapted by IPPR, and promoted by Tony Blair himself, and then became policy'.

Strategy

Strategy is about setting goals and sticking to them to keep focused. Political elites have multiple goals other than just winning elections, such as to pursue a particular ideology, cause, policy or piece of legislation, change the agenda/general political debate, change behaviour in society, increase their support from the last election, gain support from new segments in the market, become a coalition partner in government with another party, increase membership or involvement in their organisation, ensure long-term electoral success, not just for one election, win control of government and wanting to 'change the world' (Lees-Marshment 2009a). Practitioners then need to form a strategy and plan to work towards these goals (Barber 2005, 212). Hide (2007) said 'that means actually setting targets...So getting my book out is a big tick, having a good launch, good tick. We set a media plan, tick, tick, tick. Now I've got a sales target, tick, tick, tick. Then I've got a membership drive, tick.'

Practitioners argued that strategy must be created first, before any other decisions are taken. Gould (2007) claimed that 'unless you've got a strategy that is robust, long-term, linked to serious political projects, you're not going to win elections.' Hide (2007) said 'the first principle is to establish what the objective is...it's not just a matter about winning an x percentage, I want to be there having articulated fair policy.' Lindholm and Prehn (2007, 20) quote Claus Hjort Frederiksen, a minister in the Danish Fogh government, who said that 'without a clear strategy, you have to jump from stump to stump. A strategy helps you to prioritise between the important and the insignificant.' Without a strategy problems occur. Nelson (2007) recalled of the McCain presidential nomination bid initial stages 'what was the strategy? I don't know...! It changed.' Duncan Smith (2006) recalled how the idea to focus on the vulnerable and highlight party concern with the less-well off was hindered by not completing the strategising in advance: 'I don't for a minute pretend that the strategy I was trying to implement was completely and fully thought through....maybe part of the problem was that we were still finishing it off it as a work in progress while we were doing it.' Even in the campaign 'everything should be dictated by the strategy' (Carson 2006). Lawrence (2008), who advised on the Rudd/Labor 2007 Australian election campaign, observed:

> It's axiomatic that you can't have good creative without great strategy. Stuff that looks good, but if it's not firmly rooted in...a really sound political strategy that then translates into a very sound

communications strategy and the expression of that is kind of irrelevant, maybe dangerously irrelevant. So that's where you start. The first year was nearly all strategy...once Kevin Rudd took the leadership that was kind of a long marathon run. But before that there was a year of putting in place the framework for everything that we did.

Leaders need to think strategically and support the strategy. Fischer et al. (2007, 185) conclude from their comparative study of strategy that leadership is crucial: the advantage with Tony Blair was a prime minister 'who thinks and acts in strategic terms...encourages others to do the same' whereas the former German Chancellor, Schroeder, was noted to have 'a situational and not entirely consistent leadership style that focused on immediate needs rather than the big picture' and thus was 'detrimental to the development of a coherent strategy'. Harris (2006) said 'you can report to the party chairman but really it's the relationship with the leader that counts. But all those things were out of my control. We didn't really have a fighting chance to create an appropriate strategy.' Strategy needs to become 'a core process' involving the central players, including leader's staff, senior MPs, deputy leadership and party officials, with the job of the last group being 'to try and impose a strategic pattern' over the behaviour of the party (McCully 2007). Another aid is to form a strategy unit. Fischer et al. (2007) argued that such units help encourage new thinking and change the nature of the civil service to reward strategic thinking. The UK Labour government created a Prime Minister's Strategy Unit in 2003, its second term in office, which looked at spending reviews and five-year strategies for different departments.

Strategy is like a ship, and it needs to continually evolve and respond to change (see Glaab 2007, 67). Gould (2007) explains how:

> Strategy in itself has got to be both fluid and...there's got to be a constancy about it, but there's also got to be a fluidity about it....everything changes all the time. So you have to have a way of acting through your strategy, but at the same time you have to know where you're going. A good metaphor is sailing a ship across, sailing a sailing boat across choppy waters. You know where you want to go, but you're constantly adjusting how you get to it.

Robertson (2008) recalled of his local campaign to be elected MP for Wellington Central that, although he had an issue focus before the campaign, he 'altered them a little as the campaign went on...as different things became clear at meetings and so on... things people were asking about I made sure I included them as well'.

Strategy is organic; it evolves out of different processes and from different groups of people. As Stockley (2007) explained, 'I've never been involved with one where there's a strategy and it's written down on a bit of paper and it's all gift wrapped and everyone knows what it is and everyone's bought into it, and it's like the invasion of D-day, where it's all written on one piece of paper.' McCully (2007) recalled how leaders have to bring together the staff, the caucus and the party people, and get them to work with 'the process of focus group work, polling and other intelligence... [then] you see a process unfold that changes its character as you go', which involves 'sitting down and spending some time unravelling the complex strands that are there and trying to configure things in a way that makes logical sense. This is not a science.' Thus strategy is hard to measure, although more recently scholars have tried to develop more quantitative measurements (see O'Cass 2006, Ormrod and Henneberg 2006 and Strömbäck 2010). Academic models show that strategy formulation involves a range of factors, including the nature of the market, history, culture and governance, economic and political principles, the media, the product, the grassroots, polling and image (see Baines and Lynch 2005, 2, Newman 1994 and Medvic 2006, 20–23). Thus strategy is particular to the unique situation: 'strategy depends for its success and its power on circumstances in which it's formed and created. And I think that all political campaigns are essentially unique... it is developing the strategy that meets the uniqueness of that moment that works now' (Gould 2007). As Carter (2007) commented on the UK Labour 2005 campaign strategy, 'it wasn't enough to repeat those techniques of the past; they had to be built on and changed', especially as in 2005 there was 'an elephant in the room, which was to do with the conflict in Iraq and the consequences of that conflict and what it came to symbolise.... the fact that they perceived there to be too much of a focus abroad and not enough of a focus at home.'

There is, therefore, no comprehensive blueprint to follow but there are some guidelines. Strategy should respond to market analysis. Stockley (2007) observed how 'the polling side comes in to it almost by osmosis, it's one thing they're thinking about all the time. There are other things they have to think about, like what if they win what can they deliver.' Academics suggest that adopting a market-oriented strategy, where politicians listen to and respond to their markets to provide voter satisfaction, can help achieve goals (Newman 1999, 35, Lees-Marshment 2001). In Canada, Paré (2009, 50) notes how the Conservative Party's product designed for the 2006 election was built around specific policies in five areas that appealed to individual interest and personal concerns – political accountability, heath care, crime/security, tax relief and child care.

Strategy also has to be localised. Parties often get ideas from global knowledge sharing, which can be effective given the similarity of market demands across countries. As Carter (2007) said, 'when you listen to voters in focus groups in different countries, they will tell you very similar things. Even though their experiences are different, even though their circumstances are different, there are some common trends and themes.' It is not just about Americanisation: ideas are shared in all directions. Ranger (2006) noted how, in the 2004 democratic primaries, 'Howard Dean's campaign had a version of hand-written envelopes at the end of the campaign that [the Liberal Democrats] use. One of the guys we worked with took that back over from us.' In the 1980s the UK Labour Party ran a Labour Listens exercise, which was copied in New Zealand and Australia. Griggs (2008) recalled how the NSW Labour Party ran the programme 'to overcome twelve years of, you know, some of the perceived arrogance of [previous leaders]' and how they 'pinched it from what the Brits did in the '80s'. The UK Labour Party's idea of a pledge card used in 1997, 2001 and 2005 to communicate potential delivery was also copied by the New Zealand Labour Party. Collins (2006) observed: 'with the pledge card that's a tool. Now if you used exactly the same card with the same issues that would be a problem, but the concept of it is I think a transferable communication tool.'

However, both academics and practitioners argue that because each country is different, consultants can't just go from one country to another (Plasser et al. 1999, 90–91). Practitioners acknowledged this. Collins (2006) conceded that 'Karl Rove has an instinctive feel for Middle America, as does Bush. They've got a really good gut instinct based on experience and research but also, if something happens, they've got a kind of feel for America. But could Karl Rove come to the UK? Well what he could do is analyse the research, see some trends, suggest clear messaging; he's not going to have quite the same gut feel as somebody in the UK will.' Humphrey (2007) said 'in at least 2 or 3 countries we've come across... American consultants who'd come in and said, you know, we did for Dole like this, or we did it for Clinton like this, you've got to do it the same. And it just doesn't work and the client gets really fed up with it.'

The answer is to ensure they get hold of that local knowledge. Muttart (2009) said that 'you just have to make sure you've got your local-reality lenses on when you look at [other countries].' As a Canadian he could learn 'tactical and a technological' lessons, 'but it's really hard to learn big-picture branding and position lessons from the United States because the system is just so fundamentally different from Canada'. Market analysis helps advisors learn quickly; as Braun (2009) observed, 'you sort of transform yourself into somebody who doesn't know anything, or almost anything to, to knowing more about the local voters than all the politicians who have lived there the whole time.' They also look out for differences: 'in Asia, especially in South-East Asia, it's very difficult to do negative campaigns. They don't like conflict...so if you do an aggressive negative campaign, like American-style, it would be extremely weird and strange and people wouldn't accept it.' Consulting in developing countries is obviously very different. Braun (2009) recalled 'in the developing world you deal with stuff like: people are hungry, or they need services of water. It's quite a different game.'

Thus practitioners look across a range of countries for tools to suit their particular election. Muttart (2009) explained that, although Britain has some commonalities with Canada, such as the same voting system, the country is smaller and 'British campaigns don't have to plan forty-day campaigns that extend over five or six time zones, and they don't have to plan TV campaigns', whereas in Australia, which has a different electoral system, 'they do have to plan leaders' tours which go across a large geography, and television advertising is part of Australian election campaigning'. Therefore, consultants working internationally can suggest 'the best examples to offer to the client' from multiple sources (Humphrey 2007). Ideas can be borrowed, but they must be adapted to suit the context. Ranger (2006) noted how parties in other countries had adopted the UK Lib Dem idea of sending out Focus's – a newsletter – but then in South Africa 'they said well how can you adapt that for the townships where people can't read, so we came up with the idea of cartoon Focus's – the same kind of message but in cartoon form'. Ridder (2007) argued: 'there's a rule no matter where you are that you can't make Adolf Hitler into Ghandi.... you bridge the gap by (1) rely on local expertise so you don't impose US values; (2) rely on local linguists – so you don't create problems in polling; (3) you understand the political history enough.'

More recent academic research (Lees-Marshment et al. (eds) 2010, 279) found that systemic differences do not determine the way political marketing is used; rather it depends on the circumstances facing each election. Practitioners need to develop a unique campaign each time. Carter (2007) argued 'I don't believe that you can write a blueprint for a campaign and then just stick to it. I think you have to keep applying it to the circumstances.' Gould (2007) therefore concluded:

> I don't believe in absolute campaigning truths that travel. I think what worked in one campaign will not work in the next. I think more that each campaign has to move on from the last campaign...all the great political campaigns and great governments were very much based upon home-grown projects, not transplanted projects and not artificial. You don't win an important election on the basis of a campaigning technique, you win it on the basis of a project and a vision and a kind of set of values that are the basis of that which you seek to govern the nation.... distinctive to that country in so many ways.

The pattern of knowledge transfer is, therefore, much more globalised and works within the local context.

Strategy also has to suit political ideology. As Mortimore and Gill (2010, 258) noted, 'a successful market orientation does not entail a party being led by the nose by its pollsters. The optimal strategy will involve taking into account ideology and party traditions, the historical context of the political party and party system and broader considerations of party and leader image – unless the voters themselves reject these as irrelevancies' (see also Lees-Marshment 2001 and Kotzaivazoglou 2009). Thus, Lindholm and Prehn (2007, 28) argued that strategy formation should involve and consult the grassroots to help test new initiatives and ensure that members feel that they have some ownership of the new strategy. Mills (2009) said 'politicians have to consider what are the views of their core party supporters. There are costs if you go with a more popular position that demotivates your base.' McCully (2007) explains that:

> One of the challenges is to get an alignment between the party and the parliamentary side of things because during the bulk of the parliamentary term the public face and the substance of what is on offer by the political party is delivered by the leadership in the parliamentary wing, and yet you move into a brief phase around election time where the party organisation outside of parliament has control of a very substantial advertising budget an election program...if you have a misalignment between those two...you end up with confused messages and fundamental flaws in your communication strategy and delivery. So each leader from time to time has to shoulder tap people in the staff and within the caucus to work alongside the party people.

Some leaders are successful in appealing to both their internal and external market. Hughes and Dann (2010, 88) noted how 'Kevin Rudd's leadership of the ALP suggests that the party is willing to become more market-focused to achieve electorate success without feeling the need to sever ties as 70 per cent of the front bench candidates have strong union or party official backgrounds.' Lees-Marshment and Pettitt (2010, 122–123) also observed how David Cameron sought to appeal to internal as well as external demands when he took over as leader of the UK Conservative Party; maintaining positions on grammar schools while aiming to appeal to former Labour voters by pledging to protect the NHS. Strategy also considers ideology. Political marketing strategy does not therefore result in a unidimensional response to public opinion. Lilleker, Jackson and Scullion's (2006, 252–254) edited study of the UK 2005 election concluded that the parties did not really engage directly with voters in designing the product. Parties exhibited both leading and following traits, with Labour showing more following than any other party.

There is a strong temporal dimension to strategy. It needs time to develop. Nicolle (2007) said 'one of the things I've learnt over the years is you have to allow time for that thinking. Sometimes there is a time to fish, and there is a time to cut bait.' This is not easy to ensure, however, as 'often parliamentarians, by nature of their occupation get very focused on the day to day tactics and forget about the medium term strategy' (McCully 2007). It also needs time to work – braver strategies need more time and need to be started sooner. As Levin (2008) explained, 'maybe it takes a period of years, sometimes it is being bold, sometimes it's a matter of saying we're just going to have to go really slow on this while we do the groundwork.' A strategy may work in the long term if not immediately. Brash (2007), a former National Party leader, said, 'we were interested in wining electorates not because of the effect it would have on this year's election but the effect on the next election. If you are the incumbent MP you have a number of advantages; you have the local media approaching you for comment, you go to schools celebrations etc, whereas if you are a list MP you don't. So having a constituency MP had some advantages for the longer term.' Lindholm and Prehn's (2007, 59–69) advice for strategists was to be very patient. In the 2008 New Zealand election Labour adopted a theme of trust, which, although not successful in winning, perhaps mitigated losses, which will help the party rebuild and respond in the long term: 'we were soundly beaten but...we weren't wiped off the floor...so we aren't starting from a really bad base. We're starting from an extremely energised solid base' (Robertson 2008). Strategy also needs to be implemented at the right time – a strategy that has failed at one election can be successful for the next leader. As Duncan Smith (2006) commented, 'you can be right, but in the wrong era. It could be said of the time I was there, it just wasn't the right time, but we did the right things. We set the ground enough for David Cameron to start making some of those changes.'

The ability of a government to implement its strategy depends on its political power, and thus the proximity of elections, and public and parliamentary support (Barber 2005, Fischer et al. 2007). In or out of power, strategy implementation requires management of the party. Barber (2005) argues that often strategies fail due to internal party conditions. When Tony Blair took over as leader of the Labour Party in 1995, he faced a very different set of circumstances and found it much easier to impose a particular strategy than previous Labour leaders, because the party was power-seeking after losing so many successive elections from 1979 to 1992. Reforming Clause IV of the party's constitution was part of the overall strategy as it helped to re-position the party in the public mind (Barber 2005, 73). Strategy is more successful if politicians can anticipate the consequences of actions before implementing them. Carson (2006) notes:

> So often what you do in politics... is that you might think ok, well I need to pull that string down because that's an obvious string to pull down, but another one goes up. So for example the National party might say cuddle up to the [Maori] party, it's going to take some of Labour constituency away, because there's an element in the Maori party that's actually a bit right wing, there's a bit... they both hate Labour most of the time, because many of those Maori people are ex-Labour people, there's nothing worse that a reformed smoker, is there? But the consequence of that might well be that there's a chunk of the Maori party which actually says we're not having a truck of this and break away... there's always a consequences and sometimes they're really unexpected ones as well.

Indeed, the practical reality is that all the strategising in the world can't predict everything: Edwards (2006) said 'sometimes it is just beyond your control... if you allow it to frustrate you too much, then basically you give up and stop playing the game.' Macken (2008) recalled an example where they tried in NSW in Australia to improve health provision by moving hospitals from inner city suburbs where there were lots of hospitals out to the western suburbs where there was a higher population but fewer hospitals. They knew in advance it would be difficult politically and 'sat around for two weeks looking at how we were going to do it'. They tried to get support from the nuns who ran one of the institutions they were going to close 'by saying we're going to give you St. George hospital...you'd be able to continue the St. Vincent's mission for another one hundred and fifty years but in a hospital that's perfectly built and growing and much newer...and the nuns said yes!' However, unexpectedly, the doctors at St George protested and marched through the streets 'because they didn't want to be told what to do by the nuns and that. Even though they were going to get all this money, all these theatres, one hundred and fifty extra beds....my boss then was nearly sacked. The government backed down, reversed everything, St. Vincent's hospital is still there today; St. George is still an underfunded hospital.'

In another case what they thought was going to be a big issue turned out not to be. They were putting rents up to improve the funding and provision of public housing overall. This was a problem because, as Macken (2008) explains, 'these are Labour voters, because we're putting the rent up for three hundred thousand of our poorest people in our society, we thought this was going to look terrible. And we did it, we did it, we did a big announcement in parliament house, question time, full thing, put press releases out everywhere, and the shop, DOCS (Department of Community Service) and everything. And it didn't get a run. Didn't get printed in a single newspaper....We spent weeks thinking about that and, you know, convincing the backbenchers this was going to be OK...we felt we were putting on the helmets and getting ready in our trenches for the bombs to start coming over. And nothing was there.' The reason was that the public thought people in state housing were unfairly getting something for free, but the strategists had not known this in advance.

If problems do occur, practitioners advise not to abandon the strategy quickly. Fenn (2007) argued that the US Republicans succeeded in 2000 and 2004 by sticking to their strategy: 'the Bush folks...had a plan of how they were going to carry out that campaign and they weren't going to deviate from it very much. The Kerry people kind of lurched from one thing to another.' The director of marketing for the UK Conservatives 2003–2004 faced a change in strategy:

> *I remember when we talked when you were still working there you said that there was this plan to create something positive.* 'Yeah, I had a great strategy.' *So what happened?* What stopped that going through? 'Well

basically Michael baulked; he didn't want to do anything that...He thought the prime duty of opposition was to oppose. He thought that if you keep knocking away they'll just give in. The thing is that the economy is a key factor in voting. How do you get out an incumbent government that isn't mis-managing the economy is another question.'

(Harris 2006)

Positioning and the competition

Positioning links to strategy uses market analysis to assess where politicians and parties are in relation to each other, and informs how to respond to competitors (Baines et al. 2002). Wilson (2006) argues 'it's important both at a very basic level, kind of setting the scene, just so that you know where is National heading where is Act heading, where are we positioned.' In response to the competition this can include making sure there is a distinct difference between you and them, considering relative strengths and weaknesses, sometimes co-operating with them and sometimes changing position. Positions need to be clear, consistent, credible, have a competitive advantage and be easily communicated: Bannon (2004) argues a voter needs to know where they are, so the organisation needs to offer a consistent and sustained approach, and the position needs to be credible (see also Baines 1999). Baines and Worcester (2004) noted how Dick Morris's advice for Bill Clinton was to create a third position between and above the traditional stances of the two parties, Republican and Democrat, to attract the support of supporters from both parties and appeal to the maximum amount of voters. One example of this is how Clinton implemented previously promised tax cuts for the middle classes, but instead of generic change focused these on people who took personal responsibility, such as college students and those saving for their pension.

Butler and Collins (1996) suggest that parties occupy different positions in the market – market leader, challenger, follower and nicher – and they must follow a strategy that suits each position:

- Leader: has to appeal to a broad range of voters and is subject to continuous attack so needs to use defensive strategies and try to expand or increase market share.
- Challenger: takes on new issues at first out of line with public opinion, and has to show differentiation or superiority. They can try to characterise the leader negatively and use a back door strategy of

identifying and branding a new issue, which in the long term will gain support once the issue becomes more salient.
- Follower: subject to attack from other competitors, especially challengers, and must avoid alienating large segments of the market to protect existing support. They can copy the leader, but in interest of existing customers they should imitate but with some differentiation; adapt the leaders' product, perhaps to suit different market or segment; and protect their stable market share.
- Nicher: specialises in serving the needs of a niche better than other competitors, so has to protect this niche. They can use highly focused product positioning but need to employ effective communication before changing direction.

Gorbounova and Lees-Marshment (2009) note that, when Hillary Clinton bid for the Democratic presidential nomination in 2007–2008, she started out as the market leader because she was seen as the inevitable nominee and Obama was the challenger, the underdog. Obama made her original position as leader a vulnerable one, criticising Clinton by 'painting her as a stale Washington insider'. Clinton 'defended existing market share, such as the women's vote, and attempted to expand it to incorporate younger voters in New Hampshire, but made few gains...[while] Obama took most of the female vote in Iowa'. The outcome was that Obama emerged as the new market leader.

Differentiation is important but not easy. Lees-Marshment (2009c, 467) notes that in New Zealand in 2008 the National Party had their major strength eroded when Labour also adopted a tax-cut policy, however, their cautionary approach led them to accept many popular Labour policies to avoid alienating and losing any voters: 'John Campbell, a current affairs presenter, hit the nail on the head when he interviewed Key in June 2007 and said "so you're just Labour with tax cuts".' Byrne (2006), Head of News and Current Affairs at Channel 4, recalled how, in the 2005 UK election, 'we went out on the street, and we asked people to guess which party had produced the [Labour] pledge. They virtually all got it wrong, but the reason there was no distinction between them was because they were meaningless. One of the things Labour was promising was a better life for our children. How could you possibly be against a better life for children?'

It is harder for incumbents to re-position than those in opposition, as they are bound by their previous behaviour and record (see Baines and Worcester 2004 and Smith 2005). Smith (2005) noted that, in the UK 2005 election, Labour was in a negative position due to the gap between perceptions of its promises in 1997 and its delivery by the end of two terms in office. Labour had little room for re-positioning because if it moved to the left it would open up the market for the Conservatives, if it moved to the right it would open up other sections of the market to the Liberal Democrats. Nevertheless, Labour enjoyed positive points of difference (POD) over both its competitors, being perceived to hold better policies on the two most important issues, health services and taxation/public services. As the market leader, Labour defended its position in health by attacking Conservative proposals and making the Conservatives appear to be a threat to a national health service. Although the Conservatives attacked the government in terms of trust in its leader, re-branding by Labour had helped to mitigate that weakness.

When it comes to attacking the competition, therefore, politicians should take advantage of incumbent's longevity or other weaknesses. As Lawrence (2008) noted of the 2007 campaign against the Howard Liberal government in Australia, 'our research indicated the public increasingly saw it as becoming stale, a government that had lost touch, that was clinging on to past glory and past paradigm. And all of this was able to be ascribed to the leader, to Howard.' Therefore, they focused their own campaign on the future partly in response to that. Alternatively, another successful strategy is not to just highlight weaknesses but to attack competitors on their usual strengths, to undermine voter loyalty and get their traditional supporters to consider switching. Fenn (2007) noted how in the US 'the flip-flop campaign raised the questions about [Kerry's] military service...you go after their strengths and do what some of us call a bit of jitsu move on them, you use their strength and then flip them.' Borrowman (2006) explained how attacking local Conservatives 'on financial incompetence and crime...makes conservative supporters sit back and think well maybe I should at least stay at home and not go out to vote'. Negative attack needs to be believable, however. Hyder (2009) argued that the reason Bush's attack on John Kerry, which claimed Kerry was indecisive, worked in the 2004 US election, despite all the weaknesses of Bush, was 'because, the shoe fits. The shoe fit on John Kerry.'

Guerrilla attacks aim to weaken and demoralise an opponent through a series of small, unpredictable efforts to secure permanent elector support, such as the use of testimonials, case studies and special events to suggest grassroots frustration with an incumbent (see Marland 2003). The guerrilla approach fits with comments from practitioners about taking the opponent by surprise: Boscawen (2009) recalled how 'Rodney only won by 3,000 votes; had to pick up a lot of ground from the position at the beginning of the campaign. One of the reasons was we totally caught the National Party unaware', and Brodie (2009) remembered how the Canadian Conservatives achieved success because 'in 2006 the block didn't consider us to be a threat. So we took them by surprise. They never responded. By the time that they responded they responded on the wrong grounds.'

Another form of attack is copying successful policies. Robertson (2008) explained how in New Zealand in 2008 'National adopted a pretty convincing 18 month campaign of policy inoculation...They knocked off every single thing, so when I knocked on people's doors and they'd say that it's time for a change, it'd say "Do you like Working For Families?" Yes. "Do you like interest free loans?" Yes. Well they're Labour policies..."Oh yes, but National is doing them too...".' However, Labour had also copied National's tax-cutting proposals, so such inoculation worked both ways. The difficulty for minor parties is when major parties co-opt their issue and re-position. Although this means the minor parties have succeeded in putting their policies on the agenda, it erodes their point of difference and rationale. One notable story is from the Act Party, who lost support suddenly in the 2005 election:

> Things were going fairly well, we stayed at 9 Mps in 2002. In late 2003 Don Brash became leader of the National Party; in 2004 about March, he gave his Orewa speech. Don Brash is a very Act like person in his personal philosophy, and he appealed very much to our supporters...and all our supporters looked at us and looked at National and said well if National is going to be like Act, why would we want the small party when we can have the big party?...The first poll after the Orewa speech had National on 49% and us on 1%, and we had been on 5% and so basically we saw ourselves vanish in the polls, and we all thought oh well, you know, my, that's interesting but it will go away, because we had been at 1% before!
>
> (Middleton 2006)

> A lot in the party were all very excited because, hey look at Don Brash, here is one of our guy's, he's succeeding, and Don's going to lead everyone into a National government, and Act is going to along there as well.
>
> (Wilson 2006)

[but then] We didn't have an electorate seat, and we were polling well below 5%. Coming into the election campaign we had the worst of both worlds: if I vote for those guys, will they be back? and that basically ended up being our election campaign. We had done all this research, and all this targeting, and you know, we had all these ideas. [but then voters thought] why vote for a small party when you can vote for a big Act, the National Party? And then the second problem was you know, just that whole yeah you know, why would I vote for Act when I can vote for Don Brash and get the big show you know, or I could vote for Act...National basically stole the ground out of their small coalition partner.

(Middleton 2006)

Attacks need to be anticipated. Lawrence (2008) noted how the Australian Labor Party had been criticised by the Liberals in previous elections because interest rates had been so high under previous Labor governments, so for 2007 they 'knew that overcoming the scare campaign on seventeen percent interest rates, and at least not letting them own the economic competence-management area all to themselves, were critical'. To build a strong enough defence against this potential attack took a long time: 'that was two years of work, it's not the sort of thing you turn around with an argument or an ad'. And what they did was attack the Liberals on the same issue to undermine *their* credibility, as there had been nine increases in rates recently. Utting (2008) said 'all the time you've got these doubts...when's the counter attack going to come? How is the counter attack going to be established?'

Whichever tactic is used, being proactive is important. If you lose your original position, find another one. Hide (2007) noted how with Act he found a new position as an outsider: 'I'm outside the hurly burly of politics and I can put myself above it and I couldn't get involved in that. Actually I couldn't get involved if I wanted to because with two MPs no one cares. So you write a book and say you need better politics, which is true, and allows me to come at it from another angle.' Parties can also stake their position and force other parties to react to them. Carter (2007) noted how the UK Labour Blair government refused to move from its position:

A judgment [was] made by the Prime Minister on the government and the party that we had to remain firmly located on the centre ground of British politics...so there were key strategic decisions taken throughout the parliament, many of which were tough and controversial, but which actually located in the public's mind the Labour party and the Prime Minister Tony Blair as being fighting for the centre ground. What that actually meant in election time was that both the Conservatives and the Liberal Democrats fought the election from the margins of politics on the key issues that people saw as fundamental to their lives. So the Conservatives ran a very aggressive, high-profile campaign on asylum and on immigration which was a point of connection with the public and controversial, but an issue. The Liberal Democrats almost exclusively talked about the war in Iraq. And both of those issues are important, but in many ways they were not the defining issues on which most people make up their minds when they go to vote...It was not chance that the election was fought by the Conservatives and the Liberal Democrats on the extremes of politics. It was only because the Labour government had made a firm decision to occupy the centre ground.

Parties all consider each other when marketing. Edwards (2006) noted how with New Zealand First 'it's not simply just marketing you, it's marketing you in relation to Labour, you in relation to National'. Similarly, Robertson (2006) said, with regard to the Labour Party in New Zealand, 'you're not working in a vacuum, you have to be aware of what the policy you opponents are going to put up and how that might affect what you're proposing. I was very satisfied when Don Brash launched National's student loan policy (a tax write off for part of the interest) because we already knew that we were going to have 0% interest so we were quite happy that that went out before we knew what they were doing.' But that has to be done without losing your own position. As Fenn (2007) said, getting the message right was also about keeping a sense of your own vision: 'do you get caught arguing on their turf and getting all balled up in he said-she said-he said-she said kinds of arguments, which take you off of your basic message?'

A final point is that attack is not always the only way to respond to the competition, and co-operation can be more appropriate especially given existing or potential coalition arrangements. Middleton (2006) recalled how 'we couldn't be seen to be attacking National, because even though that had absorbed all our former voters and stolen all our funders, and taken all our policy ground, our people, even the people we had left really really liked them, and especially liked Don Brash, and if we went and attacked them we risked losing what we still had!' Edwards (2006) explained that, once Winston Peters, leader of New Zealand

First, became a minister in the Labour government 2005–2008 through coalition, 'that does impact on the tactics you use...he has got to be more careful, he is a Minister, that restricts the amount of attack that he might [use]'. Gorbounova and Lees-Marshment (2009) also noted how in the US primaries 'criticism of fellow candidates is problematic: it can alienate potential primary party voters who might otherwise be persuaded to switch support; intra-party animosity could undermine the prospects of the eventual nominee by weakening them and the candidate may want to keep the option to become a presidential running mate open should they not win.' Thus politicians need to be open to all competitors. Whichever tactic is chosen in the end, they need to operate alongside longer-term strategy. McCully (2007) concluded that 'the strategic and the tactical levels need to operate in tandem.'

Branding

The political brand is a more psychological entity, made up of impressions, associations and the overall perception of a party or politician. Brands are long term, created by past behaviour and harder to change. As Smith (2009, 224) noted, for example, UK parties have been held back by previous negative brand personalities, with Labour being perceived as incompetent in the 1980s–1990s, and the Conservatives as too rough and nasty (see also Lloyd 2006). Brands can evoke emotions and images, and thus Cosgrove (2009) argues that one weakness of the 2007–2008 Clinton primary campaign was that it did not do this. How voters perceive a brand can affect how they judge the product. Smith (2009, 210) reported a study in the UK where two groups of voters were asked what they thought of a policy, with only one group being told it was the Conservative policy. The group that had no party attribution attached to the policy perceived it more highly than that which was told it was the Conservatives' policy. Similarly, Schneider's (2004, 54) research in Germany found that CDU supporters rejected the proposal to abolish national service with 62.5 per cent against the policy, but when it was presented as a CDU proposal, the number against fell to 46 per cent. Thus, political branding has important potential impact on the success of political marketing.

The leader should be viewed as a brand. As Ansell (2007) said, 'a political party leader is...a brand. He should be aware of his brand's strengths and weaknesses, and play to the strengths and work to improve the weaknesses.' New Zealand Prime Minister 'John Key is very self-aware in this department.' Langmaid (2008) argued that although 'there has been quite a strong resistance to the idea that political leaders are iconic in the same way that nationally or internationally known brands are. And that people project a lot of fantasies onto them' yet:

> Of no politicians in the UK has that been more true (truer) than of the Blairs. You only have to replay the footage of their arrival at Number 10 in 1997 to see that nothing really short of adulation was going on. So they cease to be people. And they become, you know, the best of us in a way that a brand is the best of its class. And they then, they carry all of our hopes with them.

The physicality of the leader influences perceptions of the brand. Smith (2009, 214) notes how 'the physical appearance of politicians allows for personality inferences to be made', so a younger new leader is easier to portray as offering a fresh product than an older, well-known one. As Ietcu-Fairclough (2008, 374) observed of Basescu in Romania, he succeeded partly by making sure his way of talking and behaviour embodied or enacted the values of his party's brand, which included justice, honesty, anti-elitism and radicalism. However, Lloyd (2006) argued that appearances by the UK Lib Dem leader, Charles Kennedy, on a television comedy show in 2005 encouraged participants to dismiss his party brand as not being serious enough.

Unpopular leaders can be re-branded. Scammell (2008) notes how, in UK Labour's second term, they enlisted the company Promise to work with strategists and develop ways to reconnect Blair to the electorate. Roy Langmaid (2006), from Promise, described how their 'work encompassed brand analysis and qualitative research on behalf of the Government, and looked at the incumbent New Labour brand, the reputation of prime minister Tony Blair'. They noted how people's needs had changed from the original 1997 Labour brand and 'hypothesised that the New Labour brand, personified by Tony Blair, had lost its attraction for the British public. Some of the disillusionment stemmed from developments in respondents' relationships with Blair on a personal level...we needed to look at Blair's brand as a leader and how he could reconnect with the electorate.' When interviewed, Langmaid (2008) noted that:

> Iconic brands in politics follow similar patterns to iconic brands in the marketplace...what had been a good Tony, became a bad Tony. The idealisation is always followed by denigration...in the marketplace we do brand tracking...when a product or a service loses

its way, if it has any sense, it instantly starts to reengage with its customers and find out what's gone on in their psychological process that's made them leave. In Blair's case... it was that he hadn't, that he wasn't there for the British people, seen to be hanging about with George Bush more than he was hanging out with us.

Promise suggested solutions. Langmaid (2006) explains that they found that 'attributes such as competence, integrity and teamwork came through as three of the most important elements for any brand. These three issues had been undermined for voters by the perceived inability of the Prime Minister to listen (principally over Iraq), the divisiveness of the media and the infighting within the party.' They suggested a strategy for the party to reconnect with the public, which Scammell (2008, 105–106) notes was implemented at the party spring conference in February 2005, when Blair's speech followed Promise's advice by using phrases such as 'I understand why some people are angry, not just over Iraq but many of the difficult decisions we have made.' The prime minister was put on television with aggressive interviewers and hostile audiences to visibly demonstrate that Blair had heard the public's discontent. Scammell (2008, 127) concluded that the evidence suggests the strategy had some success, not so much because of a relatively inevitable win over the less popular Conservatives, but because the party's and Blair's rating improved during the campaign, which had not happened in 1997 and 2001.

Smith and French (2009, 218) note 'there is a shelf-life with most brands' which has to be managed and changed over time. Cosgrove (2007) remarked how the previously successful US Republican brand lost seats in the 2006 mid-terms by forgetting to maintain the brand and allowing candidates to act more as individuals, thus enabling the Democrats to brand them negatively. This, in addition to President Bush having tarnished the brand, meant that they reduced their chances of success. When the brand had worked, they had been united behind it. Neglecting it lost them their unity and distinctiveness. Furthermore, the Republicans 'added nothing to their brand since 2002 that was relevant to the voters' concerns. In such a circumstance, consumers will always start to look for something different.' UK Labour's brand succeeded through three elections by changing each time. Scammell (2008, 108–109) noted how it varied from one election to the next. In 1997 it was about 're-assurance' that New Labour really was *new*; in 2001 Labour re-freshed the brand to show bold leadership; and in 2005 '*new* New Labour needed to change tack again and re-establish "Tough Tony" as the listening, caring, in-touch leader that target voters thought he was when they first elected him.'

Negativity in a party brand has to be removed before re-branding can begin, otherwise just a single image can reactivate the negativity in the public mind. Smith (2009, 212) notes how 'brand knowledge is made from individual pieces of information (called nodes) that link together in memory to form more complex associative networks... thus, the stimulus of seeing Tony Blair on television can activate from memory other associations such as the Labour Party, Cherie Blair, weapons of mass destruction and the case for going to war in Iraq.' The UK Conservative leader David Cameron 'began his leadership acceptance speech by acknowledging the party's image problem' (Smith 2009, 210 and Lees-Marshment and Pettitt, 2010, 122) and then sought to decontaminate the UK Conservative brand with visible clear change such as focusing on new areas of environmentalism and social responsibility. Similarly, Stephen Harper, leader of the Canadian Conservatives who lost in 2004, underwent a re-branding exercise for the 2006 election, appealing to Quebec voters in particular (Paré and Berger 2008, 51).

Successive leaders need to re-brand to offer a distinctive position from the previous leader. Lloyd (2009) noted that the ability of Blair's successor, Gordon Brown, to re-brand the party or present his own brand was challenged by him having held a central position in the Blair government. Brown needed to convey his own 'brand' of Labour politics and convey a positive and distinctive position in the political market, not only from the competition but also from his predecessor. He could have focused on his more positive personal attributes 'such as sincerity and integrity' but would still have had to face the constraint of expected delivery from the party brand overall, since it had been in power for three terms. Needham (2006) observed how Bush senior and John Major also failed to win a second election because they failed to offer an alternative brand to their predecessors. In a similar way, Al Gore failed to win the presidency the first time as he tried to distance himself from the problems of Bill Clinton but in doing so could not then take credit for the achievements of the government.

The party brand is also important, even in candidate systems, as it influences the electoral fortunes of individual candidates. Rosenberg (2007) said that in the US 'parties frankly have been ignorant perhaps in understanding the importance of the party brand, which arguably in many ways is perhaps the single most powerful political brand in America today'. Ulm (2007) noted how individual candidates had to try to manage the negativity of the Republican presidential brand in the US in 2004–2008. When 'the brand is flawed you need to overcome it with, you know, some way in the big picture, we demonstrate independence'. Equally, it can help candidates. Rosenberg (2007) recalled how the US Democrats 'ran party building ads which, based on our research had a positive impact on a part of the debate that was outside the control of the candidate which was then an indirect way of helping the candidate'. Such methods helped build long-term support: 'we continued the innovative Spanish ads in 2006 connecting Democratic and progressive values to soccer during the World Cup... recognising that for at least this population soccer is, like most of the world, a religious thing, something that is more a religious experience rather than a sporting one.'

The lack of a coherent brand hinders political marketing strategy. Sparrow (2007) remarked that this was the case with UK Conservative leader William Hague's attempts to market the party between 1997 and 2001:

> 'You had to have a firm idea of the core values around your brand and everything has to support those core values' but the party 'had somebody responsible for policy on Europe, health and education and so on... and they went off and... said what they liked, and you hope that all of it added up to something that was kind of Conservative. And in some cases it did and in some cases it didn't. In some cases it added up to something that one might call a modern interpretation of conservativism, and in some cases it added up to something that looked like very old conservativism.'

As Smith and French (2009, 213) noted, 'when a party becomes disunited and/or sends conflicting messages to voters, the perceived cohesion of the party brand breaks down, its credibility is lost.'

A new logo and use of colours can help communicate re-branding. Cosgrove (2009) remarked that the Obama 2008 campaign 'sold itself more like the Conservatives have sold themselves than it did in the Democratic tradition. The campaign has a specific logo [and] uses the red, white and blue color scheme.' UK Labour was hindered by its old cloth and cap and red flag image, tying it to socialism and working class voters, and the party lost support in the 1970s and 1980s. It thus changed its logo to a more generically appealing red rose in 1986, but this was introduced somewhat surreptitiously internally. Peter Mandelson (quoted in Gould 1998, 66) explained that it was at a report during a Press and Publicity sub-committee NEC meeting they played it down, 'didn't say it was a change in corporate identity for the entire party, merely referred to it as a logo to use in our campaigns. They didn't know what a logo was or anything... It was all sort of "yes, very good" and that was it and all agreed without anyone noticing.' When the new logo was revealed at the party conference it came as a shock to the NEC: Gould (1998, 66) notes that 'they hadn't really understood what we were up to.'

However, this upset internal supporters who had an emotional attachment to the old brand (Lees-Marshment 2001); the brand needs its users (party supporters) to accept and portray the change. Smith (2009, 215–216) notes how party members 'provide strong clues to the wider public as to the personality of their party'. The UK Conservatives were held back between 1997 and 2005 because their older, white, middle-class membership was unreflective of society. Rudd and Miller (2009) remark how the minor New Zealand party Act tried to re-brand in 2001, as the new party president, Catherine Judd, a public relations consultant, began *The Liberal Project* to convey a more positive image and appeal particularly to young, urban liberals. However, the branding exercise was incomplete: 'the use of the liberal branding was still limited, with the word not used in the party manifesto or on Act's election billboards and advertising.' Judd consulted the internal members about making the re-branding more formal, but 'conference delegates at the "Scenic South" conference in 2002 were reluctant to change Act's branding'. The existing brand had too much familiarity and the attachment of liberal was never completely achieved.

Successful brands simplify the product, are differentiated, reassuring, aspirational, symbolic of superior internal values and credible (Needham 2005, 347–348). They make voting for the party seem less risky, evoke a positive vision of a better way of life and deliver on their promises. Cosgrove (2009) noted how obviously the 2008 Obama brand met the aspirational criteria, given that 'the main selling point to the Obama campaign is the notion of providing "hope" for America.' Scammell (2008, 108) observed how UK Labour's 1997 brand was about reassurance, because market analysis showed voters were concerned the party might go back to the old policies of tax-raising and control by the unions. Regarding differentiation, Needham (2005, 349–355) argued that Tony Blair 1997–January 2005 and Bill Clinton 1992–2000 called their parties New Democrats and New Labour, following the Third Way. Langmaid (2008) argued that 'the interesting thing [is] the same sorts of ideas that are at the centre of the political debate, at least in this country and [in] most of Europe, where most people try to aim [for] the centre, or the pole position in the market. And so the issue – which is a classic one for branding – of differentiation becomes key. So how do you tell Persil from Ariel?' Lloyd (2008, 305–310) observed in the 2005 UK election that parties were using negative brands, which were not based upon what they stood for but what they didn't. Voters were then distinguishing between brands on the basis of those they disliked least. However, Lloyd noted that this 'has left respondents unclear as to what the respective political brands have to offer'. When interviewed in *Time* Magazine (Von Drehle 2008), Obama conceded the lack of distinction of his brand:

> I know that people have said what does this change word mean? You know that it's sort of ill defined. Actually we defined it pretty precisely during the campaign, and I'm trying to define it further for people during this transition. It means a government that is not ideologically driven. It means a government that is competent. It means a government, most importantly, that is focused day in, day out on the needs and struggles, the hopes and dreams of ordinary people.

Credibility is about delivering the brand promises, in relation to what Smith (2009, 219) argues are important characteristics for political brands – sincerity, competence and thus trustworthiness. Cosgrove (2009) explained that the decline of the Bush/Republican brand 2006–2008 shows that 'the brand promises must be kept or else disaster can ensue.' In 2008 weaknesses in the delivery of the brand were exploited by the opposition: 'the Obama campaign built on the sense that Bush and the Republicans had not kept their promises.' However, the difficulty for Obama is that given it was clearly an aspirational brand there were questions over its definition, and it could be more difficult for it to satisfy voters in government. Failure to define the brand, as with the product, can raise expectations beyond what can be delivered.

Brands also need to have positive brand personalities, which Smith (2009) argued in politics are honesty, spirit, image, leadership, toughness and uniqueness (see also Smith and French 2009, 215). Smith (2009, 220) suggests that honesty conjures up ideas such as reliability, wholesomeness, sincerity, realness, being down-to-earth and friendliness. Spirit includes being spirited, daring, imaginative, up to date and cheerful. Image includes being smooth, good-looking, trendy, young, cool, exciting, contemporary. Leadership consists of being a leader, being confident, intelligent, successful, hardworking and self-assured. Toughness equals masculinity, ruggedness and being outdoorsy, while uniqueness traits include being unique, independent and original. However, creating such characteristics in practice may not be so easy.

Political branding can also be used to develop a long-term relationship between voter and government. One advantage is that brands help political consumers make a choice and feel a connection with politicians – as Schneider (2004, 52) explains, brands create sentimental utility 'from a feeling of solidarity with a group of like-minded voters in the sense of a community of values or a feeling of identification with the party or its candidates' (see also Smith 2001, 991, Reeves et al. 2006, 423 and Smith and French 2009, 211). Cosgrove (2009) notes how brands are 'constructed to build durable relationships between the consumer and producer'. Carson (2006) commented that they try to build 'brand communities – long-term, ongoing relationships with people. So you not only recruit, but you retain them ... so they won't just vote for you once but they'll vote for you next time and so on.'

Authenticity

There is one final, but very important aspect to discuss, which is important for practical and normative reasons: strategy, product development, branding and positioning needs to be authentic. Newman (1999, 42) argues 'there is nothing wrong with the use of marketing research so long as a candidate or leader does not use the information to build an image-based campaign that makes promises that he or she knows never can be fulfilled. Unfortunately, candidates are building campaigns by crafting images or themselves that, in many cases, have no resemblance to either them or their ideas.' As Evans (2006) said:

> If you are not authentic you will fail, maybe not initially, but ultimately. I think you have to find your way through the political smoke of conflict that obscures the vision. We can see individual politicians that are successful are always the ones that are most authentic and true to themselves and are comfortable and know themselves. Politicians that aren't tend to be found out in an instant.

Sparrow (2007) noted how Al Gore 'was stopped from talking on the environment, because he was told that people don't care about the environment, talk about this. So he tried to talk about something else, but he didn't feel passionate about it...if you feel passionate about it, that's the thing you've really got to talk about it, because in the end that's the only way you make any communication with people.' Reid (2009) observed that Harper, the Conservative prime minister of Canada came into power as a hard-core Conservative – 'smaller government, shrink-government, less change, more status quo' but as a consequence of global economic crisis has ended up allowing the greatest expansion of the public state in over 70 years. Although his government would get credit for doing what people needed and having the right motivation the problem is that the way he argued for the massive expansion of the state showed that it was not something he believed in: 'you've got to be authentic....these are the three fundamental tests of public communication.' Even though pollsters obviously believe in the importance of their work they do not argue politicians should always follow the results. As Nanos (2009) explains:

> Politicians commonly use public opinion research as a substitute for making decisions, and they even lose themselves in the process because they think that's what people want. What they don't realise is that people have an innate sense of whether someone is genuine or not. Sometimes politicians can cover it up in the short-term, but in the long-term, when you're the leader of a democratic country and you're in the news, things either ring true or they don't. Many politicians weren't successful because they're not true to themselves and voters will say "There's something I can't put my finger on that's not right there".

The New Zealand National Party leader Brash doubled his party's share of the crucial party vote in the 2005 election by making the overall brand seem responsive to public concerns, but Johansson (2009) contends he failed to actually win due to a loss of support in the final week of his campaign after Labour opponents asked voters to consider if Brash was likely to pursue a different set of policies to those promised in the campaign once elected. This attack worked because voters did not completely trust 'the authenticity of National's primary brand agent', as Brash had demonstrated more right-wing views throughout his previous career. The National Party's placement of him at the head of the party brand made it lack authenticity. Smith and French (2009, 219) note how 'for consumers to see a political brand as authentic it requires it to be seen as "disinterested." That is, driven, not by a self-serving motive to achieve power and govern.'

Practitioners therefore advise politicians not to change position to suit the polls all of the time. Mills (2009) explains it succinctly: 'polling may show that right now 75% of voters favour "Policy A" but if you had declared passionately against "Policy A" a few months back you can't now advocate "Policy A" without a cost to your personal credibility.' Munro (2006) noted:

> You can overreact to polls. The Labour party has a permanent pollster and that company is providing data all the time to the party through polling and through focus group testing, focus group activity. That information is very important, it's obviously taken on board when you're considering how to run an issue or respond to an issue. But I think that the risk is that you end up like a reef fish and suddenly changing direction depending on what the polls are saying.

Utting (2008) said that 'it's much better to have a consistent position and I'd say be slightly out of centre than make that desperate dash to the centre and weaken any kind of credibility that you've got.' This doesn't mean, however, that politicians can never change, as leaders will lose if they stay rigid forever. As Lawrence (2008) noted of the Australian Liberals led by Howard in 2007: 'they held to rigid old positions. His younger and more progressive people in the cabinet were saying let's get on and sign Kyoto.' Change just needs to be logical and justifiable, for example, due to new information or knowledge about the issue.

Summary

Developing the product, strategy, position and brand is a complex activity influenced by a range of factors. There are a number of guidelines about what works, including that despite the need to consider the market internal party views and traditions, the candidate's character and record are also important considerations, not least because the product and brand needs to be achievable, accepted internally and authentic to gain public support, as evident from the rules of the game summarised in Table 2.1. To explore this aspect further, the next chapter will examine political marketing and leadership.

Table 2.1 Rules of the game for strategic development

The product
1. The product is continually evolving
2. The politics product is more than just policies, and more than tangible identifiable parts, such as overall perceptions of representativeness and capacity
3. Consider a range of markets, not just voters; attractive and also unpopular but necessary policies; and existing and desired supporters/markets
4. Involve a range of people – policy advisors to add rigour and data; communication staff to check public appeal; the public service in developing policy in government; think tanks who can offer policy knowledge, novelty, more creative ideas; and the internal market within the party

Achievability
5. Balance internal demands and practical realities
6. Avoid overpromising because, if elected, events, crisis and change will hinder delivery

Considering internal demands in product and strategy development
7. Consider a range of stakeholders: voters, members/volunteers, donors, internal staff, external staff, politicians and candidates, lobbyists and think tanks, public/civil service, professional groups, the media, regulatory bodies, competitors, co-operators, citizen experts
8. Consider the candidate – their history and beliefs
9. Consider the party – appeal to both the internal market and new target markets but avoid adjusting the product to suit the internal market too much – members' demands are different to those of the wider electorate

Strategy
10. Strategy is about setting goals and focusing on sticking to them
11. Devise your strategy first – set achievable goals (not just winning votes) then figure out how to achieve them
12. Allow time for strategy development: make it a core process with leadership support
13. Strategy is never written down
14. Strategy evolves out of different processes and from different groups of people
15. Strategy is particular to the unique situation
16. It should respond to market analysis but also involves other factors, including belief, constraints, resources
17. Strategy is like a ship: needs to continually evolve and respond to change
18. Make the strategy localised: adapt ideas from global knowledge sharing to create a unique campaign each time
19. Strategies don't always work immediately; timing has to be right
20. Braver strategies need more time and to be started sooner
21. A range of factors help strategy succeed, including party culture, resources, leadership, skills and links between strategic thinking and decision-making

22. Strategy units may help
23. Keep on the right strategy regardless of criticism and media commentary and avoid abandoning strategy too quickly
24. Anticipate consequences of actions before implementing strategies
25. All the strategising in the world can't predict everything: be prepared for the unexpected

Positioning
26. More immediate tactics need to operate alongside longer-term strategy
27. Positions need to be clear, consistent, credible, differentiated, have competitive advantage and be easily communicated
28. Explore counter-intuitive targets which work across left–right divisions
29. Stake your position early to force other parties to react to you
30. Minor parties need to respond if major parties adopt their key position, as this could lose them core support
31. It's harder for incumbents to re-position
32. Use counter-intuitive events and images to convey a changed position

The competition
33. Anticipate attacks and be proactive in response to them
34. Do the ju-jitsu move: attack them on their usual strengths to undermine voter loyalty and get their traditional supporters to consider switching
35. Go negative early and make opponents follow, then go positive so that's what voters remember about you
36. Don't just attack the competition without thinking about those with similar visions or who have taken your policies or whom you (may) co-operate with
37. Co-operate with the competition if it brings benefits

Branding
38. Understand that the political brand is broader than the product
39. A political brand is more psychological than a functional product, and has an emotional aspect
40. It is also long standing, built on past behaviour, influenced by many difference factors, and thus hard to control and change
41. How voters perceive a brand can affect how they judge that brand's product; the party brand can affect candidates
42. Understand that all political figures/organisations (politician/party/government/department) can be seen as a brand
43. Make the brand: Clear and coherent; Differentiated; Reassuring; Aspirational; Symbolic of superior internal values; Credible & competent; Sincere; Trustworthy
44. Make sure it delivers
45. Manage the brand's product life cycle – expect it to decline and plan to reconnect as part of a long-term brand relationship
46. Re-brand unpopular leaders when needed
47. Decontaminate a negative brand before re-branding – just a single image can reactivate the negativity in the public mind

Table 2.1 (Continued)

48. Even the best marketing research and advisors cannot ensure that the re-branding of a party will be successful
49. Branding is not the new magic bullet

Authenticity
50. Make sure the branding, product and positioning is authentic
51. Any changes in position to suit polls need thinking out and justifying
52. Negative attack needs to be believable
53. Integrate ideology and vision to win and achieve goals

3
Leading Responsively

> I think the idea of a poll-driven government is well overdone. It's really not like that.
> —Robertson (2006)
>
> Politicians should neither blindly follow nor blindly ignore polls.
> —Mills (2009)
>
> Sometimes politicians come to us and say well this is what I've decided to do, what I need you to do is tell me... how do I get people to support that?
> —Mellman (2007)

Political marketing presents dilemmas for politicians. Market analysis, strategy, product, branding and positioning all contribute to the complex reality of the context in which politicians make their decisions. On one hand, political leaders need to be seen to be responsive and in touch with the public; on the other hand, they need to consider other stakeholders, be genuine and take the 'right' decision so to achieve change. Politicians also receive advice from a range of advisors on how to manage conflicting demands and problematic situations. This chapter explores three main themes in this area: achieving change and new policies, true leadership by achieving a balancing between leading and following and the advisor–leader relationship.

Achieving change and new policies

The first important rule is that, contrary to what might be expected, market analysis can be used to help politicians achieve change, not change themselves. As Utting (2008) explains:

Often a lot of research is to nuance people through difficult situations... If you've got a client and they say 'Look, we're locked into this position...' what the research really becomes about is understanding what are the advantages of this position, what are the weaknesses of this position.

Research can be used to overcome opposition: Duffy (2009) argued that 'the best use of market-research, in my experience, is... it can show you a pathway through what appears to be an insurmountable barrier.' He cited an example of publicly owned utilities, and how polling that directly asked 'We want to privatise this, we as a government are thinking of privatising this. What do you think?' received a negative response from the public. This had 'inhibited successive governments for about 20 years from doing this privatisation', despite potential benefits. Yet, hypothetically, research could find a way to link the agenda and policy to conservation in aid of environmental best practices, which would be more positively received. Research can help leaders take positions which are ahead of time by generating a greater understanding of opposition and finding alternative arguments and policy adjustments. Nanos (2009) remarked how 'as a researcher... one can usually tell how savvy [politicians] are within five minutes because if the first thing they say is "I need this to make a decision" then you know that they're probably not thinking about public opinion research in the right frame. However, if they're going in saying "I have an objective," then they are on the right track.' Analysis can also assess the risk of moving against public opinion. As Evershed (2009) said, 'it's about understanding where the minefields are, so that you can negotiate the minefield, and you can bring your important policy to fruition, if indeed it is an important policy.'

Goot (1999) details how the Australian Liberals were able to use polling to win support to implement a previously unpopular policy – selling off the publicly owned phone company Telstra – once they were in power. Pre-decision-making polling suggested the party would lose votes with the privatisation policy; that the policy's associated price rises could facilitate attacks from the opposition. However, market intelligence also identified strong public concern with public debt and the environment. Therefore it was announced that funds from such a sale would go towards reducing the public debt and environmental projects. The proposal thus appealed to voters concerned about the environment as well as those who were opposed to privatisation. This research reflects what Gill (2007) said: 'my experience at Mori has very much taught me that public opinion can be lead and changed very substantially on a lot of issues, because most of the time most people aren't thinking about these issues that politicians and government are thinking about very much.' As suggested in Chapter 1, politicians choose how to use the market analysis. As Goot (1999, 215) concludes, a 'party's purpose in commissioning a poll need not be confined to locating majority opinion or tracing the median voter; it may be just as effective as a means of working out how to galvanise support, neutralise opposition or convert those who might otherwise be reluctant to see things the party's way.'

This does not mean leaders can ignore public opinion, of course. As Durdin (2009) commented, 'they can shape public opinion to a certain degree but essentially they're working on their behalf...In politics it's much more of a two-way street, about being responsive to what people think they understand and what they need.' Politicians can only achieve change within some constraints. Rottinghaus (2008, 151) studied three cases of presidential decision-making and public opinion in the US and concluded that US presidents were constrained on foreign policy issues: 'crafted talk can work, but possibly only in conditions where the president already has support, public opinion is malleable, where the public is more likely to agree anyway, where the frame is acceptable to the public.' However, the leadership–public relationship is variable and nuanced and marketing analysis can be used to help negotiate with the public and make changes over time, with compromises on both sides. Both Duffy and Nanos talk of the need to help the public see what needs to be done sooner than would otherwise be the case, while respecting their views:

> What you're doing is you are trying to prepare the public and lead them into addressing a set of challenges that they probably haven't thought of yet, or that have sprung very quickly upon them and you need to react quickly... to get the public to think in a way that maybe they haven't thought of before.
>
> (Duffy 2009)

> Think of it as a learning process. Compare to the dating process. You don't meet someone and say 'I love you. I want to marry you. We're going to have four kids. We're going to live here.' Instead, you're going to shake hands and learn about each other. It's going to be a gradual learning process. If someone started a relationship and said 'If I can't get everything I want, then I'm not doing anything,' the relationship is not going to be successful. Politics is no

different. The politicians that understand that concept and have more of an incremental and gradual approach are more successful. They are hedging on their personal abilities to communicate, educate, and to slowly nurture and get the country moving in a particular direction, even if the majority is not there at that particular point of time.

(Nanos 2009)

Practitioners offered other suggestions in how to achieve change. Politicians can disseminate market analysis to build internal support for potential change. Mortimore (2006) explained how 'there is a role for dissemination, if done properly... it can help gain support for the changes necessary to make the party win.' Ranger (2006) also noted how valuable it can be to help activists, who have different views to the mainstream electorate, to understand the electoral reality: 'voters are much more concerned about the bread-and-butter issues, so market research is quite important to be able to say to activists, look, actually these are the things that people are concerned about and they are the things we need to address. If we expect them to vote for us we have to give them a reason.'

Leaders need to know when they can sell something and not be too cautious. On reflection, Bob Carr (2008) said of his time as NSW premier, 'I was a bit hesitant on some issues seeing that I had support; I think there were a few issues where I could have leapt in more strongly and said "No we oppose this – here's our alternative."' Somerville (2007) criticised UK New Labour for 'cautious leadership', and Byrne (2006) said 'we need politicians who are willing to step off this hideous roller coaster that we're on together and say I'm now going to tell you something very difficult... The big issue is can our politicians do it? Can they be brave?' From his work as a minister, Roozendaal (2008) agreed:

> You've got to be brave. All the decisions we took on young driver reforms were brave. A lot of people didn't want us to do them, and we had the motorist organisation opposing us, and I took a decision, because I was going to do that, I was going to save some lives with these new rules. First year drivers using their mobiles in the car... we banned... and one speed ticket you loose your licence. Tough – not popular. We did it. I think that was good. I think introducing speed cameras into school zones, and using the money generated from those to build more school zones where they have these big flashing lights; that was very controversial, especially in government. Took

that decision, it was the right decision, and it's delivering, I think, good outcomes. You've got to have a bit of balls.

Leaders do not always need to follow public opinion on important issues if they can change it. Carr (2008) said 'a strong leader can shape public opinion. You might look at a bit of polling information that shows 55–45 division, but by simply staking your case... you can see that flip over. Secondly, the issue might not be in the media for that long. So even if you're behind, it may not hurt you.' He cited the example of when he tried to get support for embryonic stem cell research:

> I knew churches were opposed to it and there were some opinion leaders who wouldn't understand it.... I thought that it would be possible to shift opinion once you've pointed out some basic facts... [but] the party secretary had reservations about me leading on it. I invited Christopher Reeve to come to Australia, made public statements and was something of a leader for the other state premiers, state and territory leaders, took a position before John Howard had. I made public comments... at press conferences, at spinal injury centres, helped shape public opinion I think to the extent where he had to not block it. I'd say I moulded it. Now, another politician might have been told by his or her instincts to avoid the issue, but I rather enjoyed taking on people who opposed it. But doing polling was not part of this. I thought it was important to win it, I was confident enough in being able to shape it.

It is also important to be cautious of responding to media criticism, because it is not the same as public criticism. Paxman (2007) said 'it requires sufficient self-confidence or worldly wisdom to be able to recognise that the fact that the *Daily Mail*, or the *Daily Mirror* or *The Guardian* or whoever chooses to make a song and dance about a proposal doesn't mean that that proposal isn't worth considering.' Hide (2007) noted that once a newspaper criticised him in an editorial for talking to people in Epsom as Epsom is very conservative, but 'we were just getting the results of a poll we did in Epsom and the Epsom people loved it. And it's interesting how you find that time and time again that the voters think differently to the commentators.' He said 'the great thing I've worked out about the media is that they write about politics and no one reads it... the only people who read it are the people who are interested in politics and have already made their mind up... so I don't actually worry about them.' Similarly, Campbell (2005) observed that the 'media go with what they're interested in, not the public.' Journalists themselves acknowledged this. Paxman (2007) commented that 'the media attributes far too much importance to their own role. In the end, you know, all that it's going to do is exercise at most a little influence', while Armstrong (2006) said, 'I don't think we have a huge influence, It is really hard to say.'

There are examples of success against public and media critique. Firstly, Rogers (2009) tells an important story about a necessary decision a new Canadian Premier John Ham took in 1999, which received substantial opposition and media discussion:

> The three major promises that the government had been elected on were to repair the healthcare system, to balance the budget for the first time in 42 years, and to dramatically reduce government spending, namely in the form of shutting down a coal plant in a place called Cape Breton in an island off of Nova Scotia... which had declined dramatically. In 1968 a British company had announced the closure of the steel plant... [and] the premier of the day stepped in and said that the province would take temporary custodianship... In 1999, the province still had custodianship of the company, and it had added about 35% of our net debt.... It was a sap on the taxpayers in the whole province... [but] it still had about 2500–2700 employees, still critically important to the economy of the island... It was probably the most difficult thing we did, because every time we tried to have a legitimate public policy discussion, of course the communities were very affected, and you want to make sure they're being heard, but who have an interest at stake.... our premier made the commitment that he would always tell the workers any policy development first, but we couldn't fly in because they would picket the airport if we tried to fly up because the wanted to embarrass us on the news. There were threats of physical violence. We were under constant police protection at one point.... At the same time you're trying to move the public policy file forward... The premier stuck by his decision, even though that would hurt him electorally and our party electorally in the area for some time. He began liquidation, and he said that as part of liquidation that we were going to blow it up, just to make sure that it's never opened again. We look back now, less than ten years later, if we hadn't blown it up it would have been reopened.

Secondly, Fitzpatrick (2008) gives an example of where a leader succeeded in focusing on the non-media-friendly issues of public housing and mental health. Morris Iemma, former NSW premier, was 'determined to get his agenda up in these areas', but it gained very negative coverage in his first 6 months as premier: 'the criticism that was put to me by a lot of the people in the media was basically you know...his stories are boring.' However, because he had been a health minister 'he had no problem in being able to explain what the issue was and pursue it publicly', and his government even succeeded in getting it onto the national agenda in the end. Fitzpatrick said 'that's one of the rare moments where I've seen them blindsided a bit'. The advantage, in addition to making progress on policy, was that it was 'a great way of showing people what he was about and really characterised him as a guy who genuinely cared'.

Politicians should not give up trying to change the way politics works. Duncan Smith (2006) notes how he tried to change the infamous UK Question Time at Westminster, in response to public concerns, but faced barriers from parliamentary politicians in his own party:

> It is by and large largely irrelevant. It's just weak theatre. Most of the public don't want to watch it...but....it's become about who can make the place laugh more, what the jokes of the day are, and that's fine if all you want to do is go away feeling good about yourself, but if you want this thing to be worth something, then it ought to be about issues. So I was often criticised for being pretty boring at because I was trying to make it issues-based, but in the end I gave up and went to jokes because you just couldn't win. All I did was get clobbered by the sketch writers, because they said he was dull and wooden...they wanted to be amused, so eventually I gave that up, and in the last six or seven months I said well I'm just going to play this for red meat and treat it as street theatre and go out and do some real politics after it's over.

However, sometimes you just can't make it work and have to give up. Durdin (2009) explained how John Tory, the Conservative leader in Ontario, committed the government to funding all religious schools in one election, and although this won support in the Muslim and the Jewish communities the reaction from elsewhere was negative: 'his caucus was telling him to back off, the polls were telling him to back off, his advisors were telling him to back off, everybody was saying "back off back off this issue is not working for you, you should pay attention to what people want." He wouldn't back off. Finally three-quarters the way through the campaign he tried to soften it a little bit but it was too late. So he really single-handedly managed to lose the election because he adopted quite strenuously a very very unpopular position in Ontario and stuck with it.' Making the judgement as to when to go ahead and when to back down is not easy. Tyson (2008) said 'let something fly for a day or two, then the press back down; you've really got to stick it out...your one bad story does not make two bad stories...If a week down the track things are still not going well and it seems to be escalating then you perhaps need to rethink things.'

Thus, as Macken (2008) noted, at 'times you just can't do the right thing because it's too politically unpalatable...in the offices that I worked there was always a battle between the media unit and the policy team. The policy people [are] the ones who actually want to do something, whereas the media guys...say...you're going to make our boss look like an idiot...I've seen people fighting and punch-ups in offices over [this].' Mike Munro (2006), the chief press secretary for Helen Clark when she was prime minister for New Zealand, remarked that 'there's been a couple of issues where the government's just found itself in a situation where we just weren't getting any cut through at all with the public and the polls were telling us that and media commentary was telling us that. And even though the decision that was taken was sound from a policy viewpoint, the Prime Minister just made the call that look, let's just cut and run on this one; make a break before it gets any worse.' He cites the example of a levy they considered putting on farmers of agricultural cattle in New Zealand who produce emissions – which are one of the biggest sources of greenhouse gas – with the levy funding resource into the problem, but:

> That levy became known as the fart tax. And it just dragged us down...even though it was a sort of principled and sound policy, it had to be pulled at the end and Helen did that pretty much by seeing what the polls were telling us, which is that people thought it was pretty much an attack on farmers and ridiculous – 'for goodness sake, what are we going to tax next in this country?'

Duffy (2009) quoted Bob Ray, who was the premier of Ontario for the Social-Democrat Party and then became a liberal: 'Democracy's important, inclusion is important. So too is understanding when the conversation is over, and you have had your say, and sometimes you carry the argument, and sometimes you don't. You've got to accept it when you don't carry the argument and move on.'

True leadership: balancing leading and following the market

Given this, while political marketing makes politicians more aware of market opinion, how leaders respond to this needs to vary. Firstly, leaders should seek and listen to a range of market analysis from multiple sources. Blumenthal (2007) noted how 'in the case of Bill Clinton, he was interested in as wide a network of people informing him as he could. He wanted as many facts and opinions from informed people as he could get.' Carr (2008) said 'political leaders have got several constituencies and one is the parliamentary party, the people and the men and women who keep them in the job, more specifically the cabinet [and]...you've got your party outside the parliament, party conference; you're widening circles as you got the electorate of the capital city and then the regions, remote areas. And so you've got to be calibrating all the time the effect.' Leaders also draw on their staff. Therefore, Mills (2009) argues, 'polling...is only ever going to form part of the mix from which decisions are made', while Mellman (2007) agrees that public opinion is 'only one factor in their decision-making process'. As Utting (2008) noted, politicians have to balance multiple demands, and 'a real test of a politician is to be able to take all these factors on board, and to position yourself in a public space in a way to enjoy support'.

Leaders can also be proactive in response to market analysis. Gould (2007) said that Tony Blair 'listens to the polling, but he's doesn't say I'm going to do that, he just uses it as a sort of jumping off point for his own strategy...he's proactive in his response to polling, not reactive'. Hide (2007) remarked that 'I'm not a politician that operates without belief. But in terms of the actions that I take, and the things that I do I very much reference to a group of people and we do do a wee bit of polling.' Mills (2009) said that 'most [politicians] are totally responsible in their understanding of both the value of and limits of the use of polling findings.' Strategically, leaders need some kind of position and should not just follow. Utting (2008) claimed 'you have to know where public opinion is. At the same time, you have to have positions.' Leaders also spoke about the need to be positive and focus on certain goals and try to achieve the impossible. Hide (2007) recalled going on the show *Dancing with the stars* and that 'what I do now is that I go about politics with joy and happiness, with a view that I can achieve things'.

Market-*led* campaigns may not work but neither do leadership-led campaigns. Mellman (2007) noted that John 'Kerry...wasn't all that interested in the polling, so it was probably less useful to him because it just wasn't his thing... on the message side, I mean, you know, there are certainly various points where, you know, he was not, you know, particularly enamoured of what it is we were suggesting for various reasons, had his own things he wanted to do, what he's talking about'. However, Kerry lost against a problematic incumbent. Duffy (2009) noted how former Canadian Prime Minister Paul Martin 'cared a lot of things that the Canadian public didn't really care about. He cared passionately about reconciling European descendant and aboriginal descendant Canada... all of us back-room geniuses said to the Prime Minister "Look, there are no votes in this stuff. Will you stop carrying the torch for it?" It was one of the only times that he ever simply pulled rank to end a discussion that I was involved in, and he said "No, I don't care. This is the right thing to do... if you scratch any social problem in Canada and look at the statistics, you'll usually find that it's really concentrated enormously in one of the aboriginal populations... so, don't tell me that it's non-viable. I really don't care. We're going to have to do this."' The problem was that he not only got no political yield from the position, but once the new government came in, they undid it all. Brash (2007) conceded that 'the reality is that politicians are terribly loath, and I am included in that, to say something which the public is strongly in disagreement with', and explained how their policy was affected by opinion:

> A lot of the policies we had were quite popular. Even in the tax area the focus we made was on reducing tax rates for middle New Zealand. Now if you are interested primarily in driving economic growth, you wouldn't do that, you would reduce the top tax rate, because those are the people who actually have the potential to save, invest, to take economic risk etc. But in a situation where I was the leader and John Key was the finance spokesman, there was no way we could propose to reduce the top tax rate, which would be seen as Don Brash and John Key looking after themselves and their mates.

If leaders override the market they lose popularity. Blair's popularity declined after decisions such as going to war in Iraq. Another case of losing touch and public support is that of Arnold Schwarzenegger, governor of California in the US. In 2005 he called a special election costing hundreds of millions of dollars to allow voters to decide on eight propositions, all of which California voters rejected, losing him considerable support. The main reason, according to Mehlman (2006, 12) was that Schwarzenegger first attracted support by being bi-partisan but then moved to the right, working against his allies instead of with them and abandoning his key supporter market.

Leaders do, therefore, need to avoid becoming too remote and marooned on planet politics, even if this doesn't mean following every focus group. Virtually all practitioners who have worked with prime ministers, premiers or presidents conceded this potential issue. Campbell (2005) noted that, given that Westminster is 'in a political bubble', you 'need to step outside the bubble and get back with the public'; 'it's very hard' to stay in touch. Callingham (2009) explained that 'they may meet thousands of people, but they're still meeting them as a Prime Minister.' Reid (2009) noted how the government apparatus is isolating so that 'incumbency starts to equal complacency, and complacency starts to equal self-interest, and you can start taking it [being in government] for granted'. Rogers (2009) explained how the resources cabinet ministers get access to can make them feel more permanent than they are: 'Cabinet ministers come to work either driven in a car, or in a car given to them by the government, they have a coterie of personal staff, they have a whole department of people who will only refer to them as Minister, who never disagree with them, aside from very rarely.' Robertson (2006) said 'I think it's a trait of government that the longer they go on, the less they remember to think about that. The more ministers become ministers, they think as ministers rather than thinking as politicians.' To overcome this, Rogers (2009) said he would try to get his staff to reconnect with ordinary people:

> Every year I issued a little strip of paper that I asked them to tape to the side of their monitor, and they were questions from polls that I had asked. For example, is it a treat for our voter or the average citizen to take their family to McDonalds once a week? Now, no one that works in my office thinks that's a treat, because everyone that works in my office makes a decent income, they have a university education, they're probably childless, they probably live downtown; so they are not our voter.... it's very hard to be empathetic towards people you don't see every day, you don't talk to every day. You've never walked a mile in their shoes, and you don't understand their experience or their journey, when they in fact are the people who have hired us to be here.

Success and power discourages the market analysis that could help prevent the decline. Mills (2009) noted that, in his experience as a pollster, 'a Government when it is way in front in the polls is not as interested in what the polling says as it is when it is behind and especially when it is well behind.' Braun (2009) said 'it's more based on where they stand in terms of poll numbers' and that those not doing so well are more likely to hire consultants. Government is a very different environment as it brings into play a whole new set of resources, information and advice, including the civil service or bureaucracy, and also think tanks who want to influence the detailed construction of legislation, but also reduces the time to think strategically (see Lees-Marshment 2008). The comparative study by Lees-Marshment et al. (2010, 282–283) found a range of example whereby governing parties who have been in power for more than one term have moved towards selling rather than listening; such parties include the Labour parties in the UK and New Zealand, Liberals in Australia, PASOK in Greece, the MKT in Taiwan, the LDP in Japan and the APRA in Peru (see also Lees-Marshment 2009b, 209).

Mills (2009), however, argued that the problem is due to an inevitable change in public perception of politicians in power: 'I don't think they go out of touch, it's just that all the imagery has been power imagery for sort of six, nine, 12 years, seeing overseas leaders in limousines surrounded by people...I've been close to people in that situation and I don't think they're out of touch...The solution though is that leaders must not forget the need to campaign for re-election and be even more responsive when in power.' Griffin (2006) who worked for New Zealand Prime Minister Jim Bolger noted how:

> He would often be avuncular rather than engaging, there was a level of arrogance that we found difficult to supplant during the election campaign...what you have to do when going into an election campaign as an incumbent Prime Minister is swallow your pride, forget you are the Prime Minister, and go back and petition people – you are asking people to vote for you, that's not a mandate for you to tell them how clever you are, and how well your Government has done.

Indeed, Edwards (2009) said 'a politician needs to be more conciliatory towards the electorate as time goes on, than that they needed to be at the beginning.' Lees-Marshment (2009b, 211) argues that governments need to 'maintain a responsive relationship with the public, continuing to consult a range of markets, to reflect and review delivery progress, offer appropriate leadership and engage in strategic product development in the context of government realities'. Leaders therefore need to be flexible and willing to change position if a new idea is not accepted.

Tyson (2008) said politicians need to have 'the courage to acknowledge that maybe it wasn't the right issue, if the weight of the community reaction or other stakeholder reaction is such that you know that they're suggesting that this isn't doable at this time, you're simply saying; look we have under stepped the mark, it was ill considered, we apologise'.

While this might seem like abandoning principle, Carr (2008) noted that 'societies stick together through compromise. Compromise is a part of life. Interest groups can't get what they want. That means compromise. The property industry wants all taxes on property removed. They can't get it. If Government revenues are high; they might get a measure of tax relief. But that's a compromise. That's how societies have avoided dictatorship; there's no way around that. The US constitution is designed to enforce compromise. No branch of government is strong enough to get its way.' Taylor (2008) said of President Bush's failure to get through measures on welfare that 'the president has the bully pulpit and there's nothing more powerful, but at the end of the day the Congress has to support it. So if they chose not to, you know, it's not going to happen. It's our system of checks and balances sort of at work right there.'

Not all policies may be amenable to public views and Gould (2007) observed how 'the leadership-listening conundrum comes really acutely when it comes to issues of war and peace and life and death issues... there are real limits to it.' But on controversial issues leaders can use the party/government committees as a check. Carr (2008) said 'Cabinet's a good filtering process... The subcommittee to cabinet are good filtering process... when you get into trouble is where you ignore that process or short circuit that process and try to crash trough or dash forward.' If leaders ignore this and continue to go against the market, then they need to at least show awareness of public criticism. Blair regained some popularity after following solutions decided by Promise from their role-playing market research. This enabled people to express deeply held feelings from which to then reconstruct solutions for Labour. They used Two Chair Work, where one of the people in a chair was a voter and the other one played Mr Blair. In the first role play, the participations played Blair as voters currently saw him, suggesting he would simply argue that he was in charge and did the right thing. In the second, however, participants played Blair as they would like him to be, where 'he' acknowledged their discontent and was more humble:

> I understand your feelings and I realize that there are many who do not agree with me over Iraq. I realized this as I listened to more and

more people over the past months. I still believe on balance that we did the right thing, though I have been shocked to appreciate the depth of frustration among those who disagree with me. I solemnly promise to spend more time at home in contact with our own people and to debate these issues more seriously before we launch on such an endeavour again.

(Langmaid et al. 2006)

There is no difference in policy position in either case. But the difference to role-playing voters was significant. Leaders need to acknowledge differences with the public. Overall, it is clear that leadership requires a balance between leading and following. Gould (2007) discussed this in relation to the UK Labour government 1997–2007:

It may be a fair criticism to say in the early days that it was poll-driven or too much, I don't know, public opinion-driven, certainly. In the later stages, it's a ridiculous claim; almost nothing Tony Blair did was popular. Everything was based on conviction.... It's absolutely crucial to listen in modern politics, but equally important to lead.... you have to balance flexibility and resolution. What I call soft–hard politics. You have to be soft, you have to be flexible, you have to be listening... you have to be participatory. But you also have to have the courage and your convictions. Now that's very hard. The art of politics, modern politics, is kind of being able to perfectly blend these two together and to make them work. I mean, if you become too much of a listening party you just get nowhere. If you become too much of a leadership government, then you start to disconnecting your voters, which is bad also. If you're too flexible it's bad, if you're too inflexible it's bad, so you need to balance these.

Henneberg (2006, 17) argued that there are two main dimensions political elites can choose from: 'they can try to lead, knowing their political product is essentially right, so marketing if used is only to help fulfill a certain mission, and involves convincing others of the benefits of a proposal or policy', and 'they can try to follow, so marketing is used to guess, anticipate or analyse the demands of the market or a particular segment, and create a political product that integrates market demands, so marketing is used to develop the actual political offering.' However, they can also do both. In practice, it is also not either follow or lead: it is follow in some respects blended with leading in others, with compromise from both politicians and the public.

The difficult bit, and where the debate among practitioners will lie, is in getting the mix right. Furthermore, public opinion itself is not always clear. Munro (2006) recalled how, when working for Helen Clark in New Zealand:

> These refugees were sitting on a ship off the Australian coast. Their rickety boat was about to sink and they got picked up by a big Dutch freight ship or cargo ship and transferred to the ship. John Howard in Australia more or less refused to take them, he said, we're sick of refugees swamping our shores. And there was a standoff for several days, and eventually New Zealand intervened and decided to take these refugees. They became known as the Tampa refugees. Public opinion was very divided on that... So it was quite a controversial decision but it was a humanitarian decision and it was incredibly popular sort of outside New Zealand. The liberal community in Australia thought it was brilliant and they used it to say how much of a more humanitarian and liberal Prime Minister Helen Clark was compared with John Howard. So it won us sort of kudos in trans-Tasman politics. But beyond New Zealand too it was greeted with acclaim by others or social democratic countries who said it was a fantastic humanitarian gesture. But at the outset, people here weren't too sure about it, you know, we didn't sort of want these dirty, unwashed refugees on our shores either all of a sudden. But in the end it worked out well.

At the end of the day, leaders still have to make the decision – marketing cannot do that for them. As Carter (2007) said, researchers are 'are able to bring to the table very effective tools to be able to show people what would be most effective, what would work best. At the end of the day, the responsibility of the leader at the top – that's the CEO or the Prime Minister – needs to be able to make judgment calls based on the knowledge that they have.' Marketing does not remove the problem of leaders having to take decisions on key and controversial issues to which market demand may be opposed, or even unclear. As Mortimore and Gill (2010, 259) noted, 'the leadership function is crucial, and that leader must exercise judgement when to follow the dictates of the market and when to defy it.' Political marketing does not replace leadership even if it informs it. Furthermore, how the leader manages input from marketing and advisors depends on them and the advisor–leadership relationship, which the next section will focus on.

The advisor–leadership relationship

The advisors

Advisors need to have a good relationship with the leader to be effective. Harris (2006) was director of marketing for the UK Tories for only a year and went back into business marketing afterwards, and he made insightful comments about this:

> The things that matter in politics are first and foremost, shoring up your position with the leader, which means face-time, wining and dining, and being out on the road with them. It's basically a whimsical dictatorship. You've got to be there the whole time. If you spend all your time in the office crafting your message you're never going to get the chance to apply it because the leader isn't going to believe in it... if you look at people have been successful such as Alastair Campbell, like or loathe him he was basically indivisible from Blair for the first two years of his premiership. That was his greatest strength – that Blair completely trusted him. And so from there he could give good advice but if you haven't got that then you really struggle. It's not a matter of how good you are and how hard you work. It's about being liked.

Lavigne (2009), who advised the Canadian NDP leader Jack Layton, noted how 'one of the most important things that we were able to do was develop the relationship – all relationships take time, and we gave our relationship the so much time that we are very close.' Fitzpatrick (2008) explained that 'that relationship is very important, and what you'll find is that because of the closeness of that relationship, the media advisor often becomes a very significant part of the rest of the process – because they're there with the minister at meetings with departments or meetings with third parties or community groups.'

Advisors still need to be able to be frank and offer long-term strategic advice, however. This is not always easy, as Muttart (2009) explained:

> I have known Stephen Harper since I was 17 years old when I was a youth activist in party politics, and although I did not know him as well then, as I do now, it was still easier to talk to Stephen Harper when he was Chief Policy Officer of the Reform Party than when he was Prime Minister of Canada, right? You're talking to the head of government of a rich, prosperous, G8 nation. When you walk

into his office, you're walking into an office of state. Even for people who know their leaders well, and have worked with them for a long time, I still think that to a certain degree, they still find that intimidating.

Macken (2008) said, 'most of time you've just got to be frank and fearless.' As Scard (2008) remarked, 'there's no point in taking the Emperor's-New-Clothes approach to political advice, because it doesn't get you anything, it doesn't get you anywhere – nor the person you are advising'. This doesn't mean opposing everything, of course. As Nicolle (2007) outlined, 'what you have to do is help dispose of some ideas, develop some of the other ones.' Munro (2006) said of Helen Clark, 'I'm paid to be the advisor and she knows that and I won't always give her advice she wants to hear... most of the time we did agree... but sometimes, yeah, she disagreed with me and she'd let me know. And if I disagreed with her I'd let her know.' Similarly, Campbell (2005) had an 'open and frank relationship' with Blair and 'never had any qualms' criticising Blair; he had the ability 'to be brutally honest, and also to have a laugh'.

Part of the job of advisors is to be a filter of market analysis, both informal and official. As Carr (2008) explained:

> Paul Griggs, an advisor, came into my office once and said you've got to make a decision about forests on the South coast, this is after the '99 election. I was reasonably familiar with the issue, but I said what's the range here, and he said there can be strong pro-Green, which means they need 100 new national parks between Nowra and the Bega valley. He outlined the other options. I said how's the local member line up on the issue? We picked the set of South coast and he said he's comfortable, he's a marginal seat, in fact we want to hold it beyond that term. He said he's comfortable with it. I said well, that's really all I need to know here, and there's a bit of a compromise from the last term in the North coast forest decision, because we accommodated some logging interests, and the context is generally pro-conservation there. I said let's go for the bold, the boldest of the options. That's all I needed to know in a case like that.

Advisors have to reach a balance in being honest but also remembering the leader is still a human being. Callingham (2009) observed how:

They are surrounded, once they get to the top, by the yes-men, and the yes-women, and sometimes you have to go towards them, and it's quite scary, and say 'I'm sorry, I think that's wrong. I'm sorry; I don't think that's the way to do it.' If you do that, if you have the courage to do that, eventually you become part of a very small group that's trusted to give an honest if sugar-coated opinion.... everybody hates to have criticism, but put correctly and put well, it actually ends up that you're not one of the mass of people that gets eliminated from opinion because they can trust it. Brian, over the years has actually sent some quite firm emails when he hasn't agreed with Helen or one of her Ministers.

Not surprisingly, advisors need to present advice on their leader's image carefully. Edwards (2009), who advised Helen Clark on her media image, found that she 'was very reluctant' to receive advice at first; 'she wasn't interested in all that stuff about changing your hair, and changing your voice, and changing your teeth – all that sort of thing' but then they advised her for a single session and gave feedback after her media appearances and this began to build a trusting relationship and boost her confidence. Callingham (2009) explained that their 'contribution to the improvement in Helen's performance and therefore in her ratings was as much or even more to do with the positive reinforcement we gave her (constant praise) than with any technical changes to that performance. That is often the case with media training and advice. Think Supernanny. Media training is perhaps a form of parenting – yes, it involves critiquing performance but the most important thing is praise – when it is deserved of course.'

The other skill to advising is to have good political antennae and gut instinct. Campbell (2005) said the first thing to do to stay in touch is to 'be conscious of the need to keep in touch'; 'you've got to fight to stay outside the bubble'. Borrowman (2006) observed that 'you've got to have someone who can tell you what's going on. All the victories go to people who have that gut instinct. Not everyone has it.' But they should also back up advice with more than gut instinct. Brodie (2009) noted how Canadian Prime Minister Harper 'is an extremely rigorously analytical guy, and so on strategic issues, on marketing issues, on branding issues, on policy issues, on organisational issues, on parliamentary issues, on rhetorical issues; you really have to have your case well thought through to get through the door of the office. He would engage, read everything you sent to him.' Permanent internal advisors need to support outside consultant advice. Langmaid (2008) noted how advisors' success in getting Blair to listen to their advice on re-branding was in part because he 'had some pretty astute people around him. One or two of whom thought similarly to us...you need a sponsor if you're going to do something different. And we went through three presentations before we got to the share time with the prime minister.' He recalled: 'they found our way of talking about the reaction that we'd met out in the population really fresh and new. At the time when they were looking to re-describe things to Tony, so that he might take on the re-engagement strategy, rather than the presidential strategy.'

Advisors also say that it is important not to just tell the leader what to do. Just as advisors should challenge leaders, leaders should 'challenge your advice...you'd prefer at least to say no I don't agree with that, and that you can have a debate about it or then move on if they're not going to take your advice' (Tyson 2008). Munro (2006) explained how, with Prime Minister Helen Clark, 'my advice might have been to say I don't think you should do this interview for these reasons and she might say no, no I don't agree and I can go out there and handle him and she'd overrule my advice. That's fine, it's her call, she's the one that has to front up there and do it.' Nicolle (2007) said of his experience in the Act Party, 'I always had an opinion and it wasn't always accepted. I wasn't hurt over things like that, I've been around politics for a long time. And when I worked in the real world I worked for senior management and used to give advice and things, this is just the way life is.'

What advisors should do is help keep the leader focused on the strategy. Carr (2008) said 'they've got to be thinking of the next election and not allowing you to blow your election prospects apart.' Lavigne (2009) explained that 'one of the key things for the advisors to do is to constantly monitor where the leader is at, and make sure that the ideas that are being presented, or the directions that are being implemented, fulfil that mandate...the leader has many inputs. In any given day, the leader will talk to dozens and dozens of people.... Layton...[will] come and say "So and so advises this." And, we'll say "That's good, but this is outside of that – that goal." You just go back – how does this idea or initiative fulfil that?'

Advisors also have to work around the leaders' capabilities and style. Di Lollo (2008) noted that in politics people have 'very varying abilities in very senior management roles', and advisors need to understand 'their communication style, their way of learning things...on a individual basis'. He said that most politicians are used to face-to-face communicators and want orally accepted information, although 'Rudd is very different; he's famous for not only reading every single word of a brief, but probably understanding it better than the person that had written it by the time that he had finished.' In contrast, the former Australian Labor Prime Minister, Keating, 'was known to never turn more than one page of a brief, so we could get the brief for him onto two pages and that was fine, but he just wasn't going to read past the end of the second page'. Robertson (2006) recalled how he learnt to adapt to suit the minister he worked for:

> In my first few months I was sort of doing politics 101 on [the minister] and trying to get her to behave in a certain way and do certain things. And quickly I realised that it was a stupid thing to do, she was very intelligent and capable person, she just had a different way of going about stuff. And I needed to work with that and help her be 'the best "x" she could be', not be some other politician. I think that's a really important part of it, knowing your minister and knowing how to work with them and what they need to do.

Brodie (2009) concluded that 'not everybody leads an organisation in the same way, which is fine. So, organisations either adapt to the leadership style of the person who's running them, or else they collapse. We adapted before we collapsed.' Advisors also need to accept situations when leaders ignore their advice and, by doing so, create a problem. Tyson (2008) said 'it always happens, you provide advice, then it gets ignored, then you go and fix up the mess', while Nicolle (2007) commented, 'you just deal with it and fix it because we all stuff it up.'

The influence of advisor varies depending on the leader: 'the role varies depending on the personality that you're dealing with' (Tyson 2008). Macken (2008) said 'there are some ministers you just can't tell what to do. They just won't follow advice. They have it in their own mind what they're going to do and the best you can do is try and clear the bush around them as they go burrowing through the jungle...Keating never followed advice. He would often do things the staff would yell at him for.' Mellman (2007) recalled 'I've had clients say just stop telling me that, I don't want to hear, you know. Don't tell me that anymore, just tell me more what I have to do, I don't want to know what people are thinking. Other people get angry. Some people want to, you know, I want to meet these people, I want to talk to them and tell them why they're wrong, you know.' The difficulty is that feedback is all about the person: if 'someone doesn't like Crispy-Os, the CEO doesn't really feel that bad, he says OK, we better change Crispy-Os. But when someone says well, I don't really like you as a person, you can't just say be a better person.'

Nelson (2007) said that while John McCain was 'happy to have the discussion, he is happy to talk about most anything... he is a very principled person and part of his belief in his principled positions is that there needs to be some consistency over time... it was very hard for him to look at an issue and think about it, and think about changing the position that he held.' This does not mean nothing can ever be done. Nelson (2007) recalled the one time McCain succeeded in changing his perception of his own views of himself was on the issue of ethanol in Iowa. McCain started out thinking he would be against ethanol as most people would perceive him to be. Instead, Nelson argued a more subtler point: 'my point was you are against *subsidies* for ethanol. Whether somebody puts ethanol in their vehicles is, you don't care about that, if ethanol is competitive in the marketplace, who cares. What you don't want is subsidies, and he did come around to that, it was a process for him, but he did come around to the idea that he could be against subsidies without being against ethanol. And he started to talk about ethanol as being one way to deal with our dependence on foreign oil.' Nicolle (2007) said 'I might suggest something and then get no response, but then a week later they were actually following your advice.'

The leaders

Leaders need to get a loyal team ready from the start. Duncan Smith (2006) was asked *is there anything that with hindsight, you would do differently?*:

> Yeah I think you need to only become leader with a fully fledged, fantastic team, all singing all dancing and unfortunately I didn't do that! I was putting that together for the first nine months, and that's where some of my biggest problems came from. So my advice to any would-be leader, is your personal office is the most critical thing. It has to be good, it has to be functioning well. It needs to be completely dedicated to you and you need to have the absolute sense of loyalty around you, so that you can work knowing that your discussions will be kept confidential.

In contrast, Lavigne (2009) noted how he 'worked on Jack Layton's leadership campaign in Toronto for the 2003, and what I think is vital – I also believe this to be true for other leaders in other parties – is the leader needs to encircle him or herself with his or her people who are part of the leadership race if possible'. Callingham (2009) observed that Helen Clark had 'a small group of people that she talked to regularly, the same people as well all the way through. We were there to be turned to. If Helen wanted another opinion on something, or wanted to say "What's your feeling as to how people are reacting out there?" or "What would happen if we did X?" It was on a purely ad hoc basis mainly.'

Leaders need to avoid being too sensitive to take honest advice. Langmaid (2008) commented 'I really like Gordon, but...he does wear his heart on his sleeve and he is very passionate and easily hurt by things that are said about him.' As Munro (2006) said, 'it's just a matter of finding professionals and people who she's [Clark's] going to be comfortable with. Because if you get the wrong person and there's no chemistry between the two it could be disastrous. It really has to be somebody the Prime Minister is familiar with or has met before.'

Leaders need to ensure advisors/consultants can still get access to the leader in power. Mills (2009) cautioned that 'the relationship between a pollster and a Government is generally harder to maintain than with an Opposition.' Consultants also feel that they should be paid, and it should be understood that they can't always drop everything and work on planet politics' time. In the conversation with Langmaid (2008), he said:

> *Is there anything in hindsight from the UK case that you'd do differently in the future, or with other clients?* 'I'll be absolutely candid. It's very difficult to do this work unpaid. Which we did for the Labour party. So it's very difficult, because the political storm is so fast-moving and furious that you get calls from Number 10 "can you come in that afternoon?" And I don't think any government is going to behave that much differently. Because they feel like they're in the eye of the storm. And so this kind of work is tremendously demanding.'

To get the most out of consultants, leaders need to give the advisor space and time to make real change. Harris (2006) was asked *so what would you do differently?* and he replied 'the first thing I do is try and buy myself more time. So I'd say to Michael, look I'm not going to fix this problem in three days. This is a three-week exercise to work out what we stand for. Instead we had one dinner at his house. We had a weekend in Southsea, where I had to present what I thought we should do.'

Through all the advice, and input, leaders need to remain strategic and keep the mission in mind. Hide (2007) remarked that 'to be honest when I took over the leadership I didn't have that [a clear strategy and goals], and so I got run down.' Leaders need to 'stick with the principles and the strategy. That's the hardest thing in life. The easiest thing in life is to be busy. It's better to stop and think, [but] it's the hardest thing to do.' The leader has to take responsibility for this: Lawrence (2008) claimed that 'the key to this, absolutely was Rudd. And many of the things that we tried and the strategies that worked I don't think would have without him and his discipline, you know.' Once in power, however, this is not easy but it is just as important. Carr (2008) explained that 'you can't see what issues are going to be weak, they're going to be brought in, you know, next year, you can't foresee it. You've just got to be flexible; you've got to bear in mind what your strengths as a government are, so that they're not diminished.'

Leaders also need to have a good gut instinct and the ability to judge advisors and advice. Ulm (2007) noted how some 'truly gifted politician[s], which both Blair and Clinton are...don't need pollsters' help...they know how to connect policies with politics and voters and communicating. And it comes to them as if it was instinctual.' Hide (2007) remarked that experience helps politicians choose their advisors carefully: 'you become adept at evaluating what people are telling you and you also discover advisors over time who have a good instinct.' But politicians also have to manage conflicting advice. As Carson (2006) said, 'they're getting a lot of advice from a lot of different directions and what they want to be able to do is to quickly distil the advice...it's only 24 hours in a day. A lot of them don't sleep that much. They are workaholics. You've got to admire them for their tenacity really, their ability to be able to sustain the sort of life of facing up to pressure, giving speeches, try and work out a strategy.' Di Lollo (2008) recounted this story of what Kim Beazley said when he started working for him:

> He said oh, you know, 'I felt very busy then [when a senior minister]'. But then he became deputy prime minister. And it was actually when he was deputy prime minister the first time he told me this story, and he said 'I didn't think I could get any busier, but then I realised that in fact I could get busier and that I occasionally I used to get home on a Friday instead of a Saturday after a parliamentary week, but that never happens.' Then, a couple of years later when we lost government and we went into opposition he said 'Justin remember I was telling you I didn't think I could get any busier? I actually can get busier, I can be opposition leader.'

Chalupa (2007) observed how, on the 2004 presidential campaign, Kerry 'was being pulled every single way'. When 'all of a sudden, it looks like you're going to be in the White House, then you just attract all these people and it gets overwhelming, and I think at that point it seems business expands so quickly from a town house to a 3, 4 storied building'. Thinking of the 2008 New Zealand election, Edwards (2009) remarked how:

> The politician is battered by this noise...you know? It's all this noise coming in...do this...do this...don't do that...do something else...Actually, at the very last session that we had, I remember Helen at one point saying *be quiet!*...And then she quietly sat down as she always does and made notes on what she was thinking. And that sort of...noise is the only word for it...terriblest thing ...

Summary

Marketing undoubtedly leads leaders and politicians to consider market research and public opinion more, but it does not dictate what they decide to do in response to this and advisors' input. As the rules of the game summaries for leading responsively in Table 3.1 suggest, leaders and their advisors are finding ways to use political marketing to merge pragmatism with principle to achieve broader goals, including advancing change, and to provide them with options and choices.

Table 3.1 Rules of the game for political marketing and leadership

Balancing leading and following the market
1. Politicians often become out of touch and marooned on planet politics; overriding the market adversely affects popularity
2. Try to develop the product to suit the demands of markets as much as possible
3. Be prepared to reject 'good' policies that the market will never accept
4. But be proactive in response to market analysis and adopt some kind of position – do not just follow
5. Market-led campaigns don't work, but neither do leadership-led campaigns
6. Focus on achieving a few changes and use market analysis to help identify how to change opinion
7. Get unpopular positions checked internally
8. Don't give up on new ideas at first sign of a crisis, especially in the media
9. Manage anti-market positions: continue to conduct market analysis; show awareness of and respect for opposition; and conduct listening exercises to get back in touch
10. At the end of the day, leaders still have to make the decision – marketing cannot do that for them

The advisor–leadership relationship

Advisors need to:

11. Build a good relationship with the leader over time to be effective and influential
12. Believe in the leader, but be able to be frank and offer long-term strategic advice
13. Provide leaders with a sense of support – they're always getting negative feedback
14. Have good political antennae and gut instinct, but back up advice with more than gut instinct
15. Support outside consultant advice – if internal advisors – so it is listened to
16. Build a good relationship with MPs
17. Accept managing mess even if it occurs after a leader has acted against advice
18. Avoid being egotistical or too important
19. Avoid micro-managing the leader/candidate; give them options
20. Work around the leaders' capabilities; can't control them
21. Help keep the leader focused on the strategy

Leaders need to:

22. Get a loyal team ready from the start
23. Avoid being too sensitive to take honest advice
24. Ensure advisors/consultants can still get access to the leader when in power
25. Don't expect consultants to drop everything and work on planet politics' time
26. Give the advisor space and time to make real change
27. Use good gut instinct and judge advisors and advice carefully
28. Remain strategic and keep mission in mind

4
Marketing the Party

> That's a whole different ballgame, because now I don't have to go 25 miles away to some Obama campaign office or even to another state and volunteer there. I can volunteer from my own home. I can download a list of those people, their names, their addresses, their age, and their telephone numbers; I can print a script of what to say, I can print flyers with information about Barack Obama's position on issues.
> —Mehta (2009)

> You need to keep restating your values and immersing people in those values to remind them of why you're doing this.... it is always political ideas that are the currency of politics, if it becomes reduced to a tactical game, then you lose sight of the whole reason to be there.
> —Evans (2006)

The party itself can often be neglected in the push to conduct and use market analysis to create winning election strategies, raising concerns that political marketing alienates members or supporters and thus reduces participation in politics. However, as this chapter will show, having pragmatic goals need not remove concern for more principled ones, because practitioners argue that maintaining an active supporter case, considering internal demands as well as those of voters, and maintaining a sense of vision helps win votes. This chapter will explore the value of marketing the party, maintaining a long-term party organisation, managing and developing volunteer activity, marketing for money, marketing vision and ideology, and internal unity.

The value of marketing the party

Practitioners argue that members are important. Karia (2006) said 'we need advocacy – a tier of people to share messages with and for them to then share them with family and friends, work colleagues.' Lavigne (2009), from the Canadian NDP, said 'without them, there is no movement. Without them, there is no party.' Members carry out a number of functions. Lilleker (2005c, 572) argued that 'some give money; others give a great deal of their time to trying to get their parties elected. They are the parties' foot-soldiers, they will run local offices, organise and coordinate campaigning activities, deliver leaflets, canvass voters and knock-up supporters on election day: as such they are the lifeblood of the party' (see also Bauer et al. 1996, 152 and Bannon 2005). Thus parties need to respect and show appreciation for volunteers. Mehta (2007) said activists need to be given more credit: 'they're actually a very, very intelligent group of people.' Smith, M. (2006) argued that in New Zealand members are 'absolutely crucial. We won the last election in large part because of the effort of our members on the ground.' As Bannon (2005) noted, members are more complex than employees in a business, given they join voluntarily, can exit easily and cannot be dismissed for poor performance. Members are also customers in that they pay a membership fee and have expectations of the service they should receive, and thus it is important to understand, and try to meet, these expectations.

Maintaining a long-term party organisation

To achieve success, parties need to develop a strong, well-resourced organisation over the long term – even in a candidate-basis system like the US. Lynch et al. (2006, 83–86) suggest that taking a resource-based view (RBV) shows that some parties perform better in the long term than others because they ensure that they maintain superior organisational resources in terms of their people resources (leaders, supporters and staff), background knowledge, general organisational skills and management of party members. Resource-based views provide parties with a strong basis from which to strategise and secure re-election. Parties in governments often neglect their party organisation, focusing too much on daily government business, and then turn to consider re-election only to find their party organisation is in tatters. Wiser governments will ensure the party is considered a valuable resource, which can help them stay in power (see also O'Cass 2009). Mehta (2007) explained that when

Howard Dean was Chairman of the DNC from 2004 to 2008, he focused on building 'a permanent infrastructure so that we didn't just keep rebuilding the party every 2 years. So based on that he created what's called a 50 state strategy' where the organisation would be built up throughout the country, regardless of whether a state was part of the top target list. Mehta's job at the DNC was to work with the state parties 'to build a team of people who are committed, trained, experienced and are constantly organising to keep a presence of the party in place, so that when we do have elections there's a machine already in existence that just turns on'. Previously, once an election was over the campaign structure built by an individual candidate would all fall away and have to be built up again. This also meant there was 'a 2 year lull where no one's talking to voters about the issues, the values, the positions of the party', preventing the party from maintaining a long-term relationship with voters. This type of organisation helped Obama win in 2008:

> When Barack became the nominee of our party he had all the resources and all the infrastructure to execute a massive political machine. The elements in that machine were A – the field organisers that we had hired, funded, and trained, and put to work for three years in their states, and they knew their states backwards and forwards, and they knew their districts well, they knew their constituents, they knew the ground, they knew the turf...And B – we built a national voter file, which the Democratic Party has never had in a presidential election...that had every single registered voter in all 50 states in one place, and we were able to turn that over to Barack Obama for free...he had a really extensive network built in before he even became the nominee.
>
> (Mehta 2009)

The Democrats continued their organisational efforts after the 2008 election, re-branding it as Organising for America. As Mehta (2009) explained, this would retain the millions of volunteers involved in the Obama campaign 'so that it doesn't stop with this election, so that four years from now we're not starting from scratch'.

Party organisation should, therefore, be developed in all areas, rather than segmented. This enables parties to develop support in new areas. Lavigne (2009) explained how it was important to win new ground:

> We've done it in places that places said that you will never – they said 'Jack Layton, you'll never win a seat in Newfoundland, you'll never in

Alberta.' Alberta is the second most western province. It is the most culturally and politically conservative – it is like our Texas without Austin... we have the only non-Tory seat. We won that in '08, and we came in second in every seat in that province, and we won one of them.

Such methods also send a positive message to all voters that they are important: 'by having a 50-state strategy, Barack Obama made it clear to people in Massachusetts, and New Jersey, Alabama, and Texas, and even in Alaska, that you also have a role in this election, you also have a voice in this election. Your vote does matter' (Mehta 2009). Even though targeting still takes place, maintaining a level of organisation everywhere helps support all candidates at all levels, including governors and state legislators. It also has an inclusionary effect: it helped such candidates 'feel like they were part of this tidal wave that was about to happen'. In this case, implementing a principle paid off pragmatically, as Obama won in states where Democrats traditionally do not compete, such as Virginia, Florida, North Carolina and Indiana: 'Virginia is a state that has not voted for a democratic candidate for president for 44 years – not since Linden Johnson in 1964. Barack Obama won it.'

Parties need to maintain organisation at all levels. Beeson (2007), from the US Republican Party, explained how the federal headquarters of the RNC worked with the state parties and candidates: the RNC is 'the flagship for the Republican brand'. It helps not just with the presidential election but with Congress. Mehta (2007) said 'I just go across the street to Congress and I look at those 30 guys who won and I ask them, what do you think was the best thing that helped you in your election...? And they said the fact that I didn't have to build a structure. The fact that the DNC has field organisers. Before I even decided to run for office there was already somebody there, some young person there, some organiser there, who's already like, organising the vote for the Democratic base, exciting people about it.' Smith, M. (2006) went to see Howard Dean and the Democrats in 2006 and noted that 'there was an argument going on between him and the person who headed the House election committee and those in the Senate election committee who wanted him to put resources into their marginal seats' not through all of them, but the positive impact 'was that besides winning the Senate and the House they also made huge gains in the state legislatures'.

Given this, parties need to invest in staff and supporters in the long term, not just for the campaign. Chalupa (2007) recalled how, 'in the presidential Kerry campaign, I worked for like a year and a month, a couple of months non-stop, like my life I don't remember that year, other than the campaign. And afterwards, you're dropped. That's it, it's good luck to you.' There was a lack of transition from campaign to opposition or governing. Sparrow (2007) said the same of the UK Conservative Party: there are 'very few people around in any general election at the Conservative central office that were there during the last general election. So, you see, they're not, the lessons aren't learnt, because the personnel will change.' Mehta (2007) argued that parties need to see their investment as long term: 'that's not just for the next election, it's for the next 25 years.' From the civil servant perspective, working in Number 10 Downing Street, Humphrey (2007) observed that 'there's a lot of people who bounce around doing a fair job, but could do an awful lot better if it was better organised and better managed and people got better training.'

A permanent party organisation also helps support candidates' campaigns if they run out of resources. In the US primaries exhaust resources, but Bush didn't have a primary in 2004 and thus when Kerry won the nomination in March they had zero funds against a well-financed incumbent. Mellman (2007) explains the situation: 'so he's in a position to start advertising', but the Kerry team 'didn't really have the opportunity, the money at that point to fight back, and so a decision was made to wait and not use any money until we figured out exactly how much we were going to have and we didn't know how much we were going to have, if we were going to have 10 million dollars, if we were going to have 100 million dollars, nobody really had any idea'. In addition, Kerry's staff were burnt out: they 'hadn't slept in 6 months, they hadn't seen their families, they were exhausted and they were all kind of like zombies' (Mehta 2007). For 2008, the party built up resources so it could then step in to help the nominee. Dean created the Presidential Primary Fund 'so the minute we have a nominee, and the Republicans will attack our nominee, and though he'll be broke and won't able to respond, we'll be able to respond. We're going to go on the air before the Republicans and define our candidate before they do' (Mehta 2007). And so they did.

Managing and developing volunteer activity

Parties need to conduct market analysis on their volunteers and supporters. Wilson (2006) noted that 'we used to do quite a lot a surveying of our members just to make sure they feel that their opinions are valued. We often get them to rank the MPs on performance kind of measure and ask them several questions that we would normally ask in a larger focus group, mostly polls.' Then parties need to actually act on the results and make changes. Bannon (2005) reported how volunteers reported a feeling of 'they say they listen, they even do listen sometimes but they don't do anything about it'. Parties need to adapt to the public's desired form of involvement. Karia (2006) said that 'our 21st-century party report made the point that everyone has busy lives now. So few want to go to a party meeting on Thursday night but they would come out if it was to do with local education and schools or the environment.' UK Labour created the *Let's Talk* project for people who were interested in being involved without becoming formal members, and to give the party a way of engaging people on policy who might otherwise never participate in party politics. The project was not the usual question and answer session, but a more informal round table. This responded to the nature of the market (see Lees-Marshment and Quayle 2001), and such responsiveness can be extended to all stakeholders (Bannon 2005).

Just as with voters, parties can conduct market analysis and segment volunteers into different groups to develop distinctive programmes for each one, recognising that people want different forms of engagement with political parties now. Parties can also create a category of supporters, rather than official members. Karia (2006) explained that 'if you say to people would you like to join the Labour Party, they often say well not really, I'll carry on voting Labour, but I don't want to join. If you say, well would you like to join this Labour supporters club, they are more likely to say yes.' He worked with the local Reading parties on a project where they rang people who had voted Labour in the 2001 election and invited them to join the Labour Party, and while only a few did, the rest were asked to join the new supporters network instead, whereby they would receive 'regular communications, from the member of Parliament, they get invited to party events and have a chance to have a dialogue with the party and ministers in the area'. It is a new source of volunteers; Karia noted how one MP gained 'about 2000 additional people that he could communicate directly with, which was more than his party membership...it gave the MP a source of people to tap into in the general election to help in campaigning work'. During the 2005 election Labour used this strategy again, as more people were visiting the Labour website, and it attracted 200,000 new supporters. It gave the party 'a chance to reach a wider group than just our members', so has beneficial implications for political engagement.

Rather than everything being channelled through the local party, volunteers can have support to run their own events and activities, using the internet, in a way that suits them. As Mehta (2009) explained, in the 2008 US Democrat campaign they created a new model of organising called the Neighbour-to-Neighbour programme, whereby 'any volunteer who wanted to help Barack Obama get elected could go on their computer, and go to his website to my.barackobama.com, and on that website they could type in their home address, and Google, using Google mapping technology, could find their home, and that would find 25 targeted voters' using Google maps alongside the party's national voter file. In the UK, Carter (2007) observed how 'the internet...was used in 2005 not only to convey a message, but to try and mobilise the membership, to try and give them a unique way of understanding where could they help, how could they play a part, what their role could be.' This not only helped candidates and parties, but increased participation in politics. Mehta (2009) recalled how, after the 2008 US election:

> I heard David Plouffe speak at the staff ball last week...one of the things he said was that there were 13 000 000 people that participated in the Obama campaign, whether it was by raising money, giving money, volunteering their time, working on the campaign, travelling to other states to help get other votes. 13 000 000 people. More than half of them had never participated in politics ever in their lives.

Parties need to understand what members seek from their involvement. There are different motivations for volunteering. Granik's (2005a and 2005b) research into members of a UK party found that members scoring high on certain motivations – such as social (political party membership is seen as a means of gaining approval), enhancement (political party membership boosts the self-esteem of individuals) and understanding (membership of a political party is seen as a way of learning more about politics) – are likely to experience higher levels of satisfaction with their role. By letting volunteers take control of their own activities, this helped them gain enhancement as well as understanding. The volunteer movement under Dean, Kerry or Obama did not just get involved virtually; rather, the internet was the means to reach people to stimulate face-to-face contact, thus fulfilling the social need. Parties then help create networks. Ubertaccio's (2008) study of network marketing explored how the US Republicans managed and trained volunteers to get out the vote (GOTV) and get the message out. The volunteers were given specified tasks, but the system was overseen in 2002 by Karl Rove and Blaise Hazelwood at the RNC and local volunteers called Bush Team Leaders. As Ubertaccio (2008, 514) observes, 'network marketing merges old-fashioned grassroots methods with sophisticated modern messages' but also uses the information available from voter profiling and segmentation. Participants were recruited one neighbour at a time.

The personal aspect is still important, and practitioners said the one fundamental rule was to ask people to join and build a relationship with them. Smith, M. (2006), who has presided over unusually high levels of party membership, said 'the thing I know from my union background, is that the most common reason that people don't join a union is because nobody asked them to. So we go and ask them...your chances to get a good response increase exponentially.' Smith, M. explained how he used volunteers who were particularly skilful and comfortable at being an 'asker' and effective at building relationships with people. Billot (2006) also noted the importance of one-on-one recruitment, particularly for a very small party: 'we're attracting members...by a one-by-one method.' This is also true of campaign volunteers. Boscawen (2009) recalled how he succeeded in building a new campaign team under great time pressure:

> You have to actually get on the phone and ask for help. You can send an email and say please come and somebody will come, but it's quite personal if someone is ringing up, it helps. So one of the things you do in politics is ask for help.... I was asked to be campaign manager one Saturday and by the following Saturday we had our building, we had our call centre, we had our trestle tables and we had our first set of leaflets delivered. 8 days after starting I had 40 people come that Saturday; over the course of the 6 weeks we had over 200 volunteers. So don't be afraid to ask people to volunteer, you have to ask people.

When volunteers make the call themselves to get involved, research suggests that campaigns need to respond to offers of help quickly. Lebel (1999, 134–140) suggested contacting them within 24 hours of them offering to help to capitalise on their enthusiasm. Parties and candidates also need to make it as easy as possible to get involved and provide practical options for involvement. Bryant (2008) notes how Obama's presidential nomination bid in 2007–2008 offered potential volunteers a specific goal and date (e.g. '1.5 million calls by Tuesday') and made them actionable and realistic through easy-to-use online tools (e.g. 'click on this button and make 20 calls from this list'). In her bid to secure the nomination in 2008 the Hillary Clinton campaign tried to involve voters in various ways, most of which were accessible through the 'Online Action Centre' on the campaign website. These included: Join Team Hill, Make calls using the volunteer calling tool, Attend/plan an event, Start a blog, Join/start a group and Send a fundraising/recruiting email to a friend. Online videos were also posted on the campaign website showing Clinton supporters in action. One humorous video showed famous movie director Rob Reiner giving volunteers tips on how to be more optimistic and convince more people to support Clinton when door-knocking and making phone calls (Gorbounova and Lees-Marshment 2009).

Effective management and training of volunteers is essential to make maximum, effective use of their skills and also maintain morale, but means they need to be promoted on performance not on time served. Chalupa (2007) noted how effective Kerry's campaign manager Mary-Beth Cahill was at making sure 'the staff were made strong, united and the morale was really up...she was a solid rock in terms of getting our spirit up...she listened to everyone'. Campaigns need to make sure a member of staff is assigned the task of managing volunteers to get the best use of talent; they need 'a very, very strong volunteer director, director of volunteers'. On the Kerry-Edwards campaign 'you had very talented people who came in there and they were just [put on] to data entry...it was basically first come, first served, rather than who's talented.' Lebel (1999, 134–140) suggested elites need to consider not just their attachment and commitment to a candidate but match the volunteer's skills to the set task. Parties train their volunteers to develop significant activities. The US Republicans provided extensive training. Beeson (2007) explained that they 'do campaign management schools, campaign finance schools, campaign field schools' for activists, staff and campaign managers at all levels – 'so you've got activists who know how to go door to door, who know how to do a survey, who know how to print out a phone survey and get on the phone, do the phone survey and enter it right into voter vaults.' This is true of smaller parties also; Ranger (2006) observed that because smaller parties relied on volunteers this made training even more important and thus 'probably a third or more of our time is spent on our training programme'.

When training volunteers, parties have to manage their stronger political views and attachment to the party as it stands. Mehta (2007) said that volunteers need to 'stick with the party line, because even though they hate it and it feels so constraining, it's not necessarily their voice; I need us to repeat the same message again and again'. But he would also train to them how to speak from their own hearts. Activists may protest that 'this message doesn't resonate with me and I don't understand why you think we need a new direction, I hate that message', and while he would concede and accept their view, he would argue that at heart their loyalty was to one party and they needed to do what would work. He would also explain that 'these messages were not crafted for you. We already have you. We love you, we appreciate you, we're going to get your vote, we thank God for your vote. But these messages are not being crafted for you; these messages are being crafted for that small, narrow group of voters who are truly independent.' It doesn't always work. Borrowman (2006) lamented that 'you can lead all the horses to water but you can't make them drink. It's very easy for people to dismiss you as being some bureaucratic thing sat in central London: "it's different here" is the one phrase that really makes us cringe.' They overcome this by being able to demonstrate previous success: 'it helps if you give them a reason, and if you can say we won using this method in a previous election'. Parties also test the volunteer force to make sure it is effective: Beeson (2007) explained 'you can't just recruit a bunch of volunteers and expect them to go out and make 20 million door knocks and phone calls around election day.' Nelson (2007) observed that this meant the 2004 Bush campaign 'had a very large volunteer organization, and by the time we got to Election Day it was well tested. It had a very large...it had an ability to contact very very large numbers of people.'

Elites should recognise the growing capacity of volunteers and give volunteers leadership positions and access to resources and information. As Mehta (2009) explained, 'grassroots have for a long time felt disconnected and very disenchanted by the Democratic Party', perhaps partly because the party used them for electioneering but not leadership; 'there has been no promotion system within the Democratic Party.' More recently, the party became more respectful towards volunteers and, in structural terms, more decentralised, giving their activists access to their new database for the first time. This helped keep the database up to date – 'the only way the voter file is going to stay accurate and current is if you constantly update it' – something which needs continual on-the-ground activity and needs volunteers to have the ability to go into the system in their local area and input such updates.

Involvement of volunteers in policy discussion is important, although not always straightforward; as Carter (2007) said, parties 'are organisations that reflect lots of different, competing interests. Sometimes everybody doesn't get what they want. Sometimes what happens is what nobody requested.' But feedback from volunteers shows that they always ask for more involvement. Karia (2006) recalled how, when UK Labour went through a review of their party organisation, 'the main issue that came up was with party members that we weren't dealing as much as we could have [with] topical issues... so we did this with the School's White Paper. When it was due out we did a conference call, with the minister, with party stakeholders, and then Jacqui Smith did a conference call for the 120 parties. So in addition to giving a paper submission they were able to have a discussion with the Minister and some of the comments were taken on board.' The party also reported back on areas where they could demonstrate that participation via policy commissions had an effect.

Parties can now use the internet to provide a forum for internal debate. Krohn (2009) described how they created an online version of the Republican Party platform, which is developed by the party every time a presidential election is held:

> A website where anybody, regardless of party affiliation could create an account and tell us what they thought the Republican Party should represent... if you go to gopplatform2008.com you'll see an example where we had over 13 000 submissions. We incorporated those entries into the platform document, and now you can go and you can access them. And, we've actually introduced individuals' comments into the party platform which is the first time that's ever been done, one, on the internet, but two, in such a way that somebody from South Dakota makes a comment about wind energy, and that shows up in the energy section of the platform, and instead of reading the party's decisions, actually read Americans' thoughts on it. That's pretty profound.

His prediction was that this would be more developed in politics over time: 'you're going to see some interesting activity from the Obama administration that's going to push the envelope in terms of governance' and engagement.

Nevertheless, there are limits to how involved the grassroots can be. Johnson (2009) noted that campaigns have recently seemed to have become bottom up, led by events on the ground, but 'ironically, the more blogging, external independent groups, social networking, and others join in through electronic sources, the more is the need for control. Message discipline, focus, clarity, definition – all are required in a modern campaign, and only professionals can give it.' This reflects issues of balancing internal and external demands, which will be discussed in a later section.

Marketing for money

Marketing can help fundraise. The first principle is to understand donor behaviour – understand who might give and why. Steen (1999, 161–164) observes that a number of factors can determine a propensity to donate, such as affection for the candidate, agreement with the candidate's stance on issues or policy and the candidate's power to influence legislation. Parties and campaigns should avoid asking for money all the time. Bannon (2005) interviewed 47 individuals from various political organisations in the UK and found that parties ask for donations all the time, which can leave members feeling used and damage the relationship. Requests for donations should be related to outcomes or offer benefits to the donor.

Candidates should market for individual small donations as well as big ones. Discussing the 2008 Democrat campaign, Mehta (2009) noted that 'Barack Obama raised $500 000 000 and he did it in $20, $30, and $40 increments.' This has democratic implications not just pragmatic ones: 'in the old days we would go to a small group of very rich people and ask them to write $28 000 cheques to the DNC, and they seemed to feel like they had ownership of the Democratic Party' but Obama decided to take a different path:

> The day that he became the nominee for our party, I remember every DNC employee got an email from Barack Obama saying 'As of today, not only will I not take lobbyist's money, but neither will the Democratic Party.' That's a huge thing, because he could have easily justified to the media that 'Listen, I'm on the Obama campaign, I have no control over the DNC. My rules are for me, but the DNC can do whatever they want.' And the truth is that the party can raise much more money than the candidate. The candidate can only raise $2 300 at a time. We could raise almost $30 000 at a time. So, we couldn't really raise money from these wealthy donors, and these packs, and these lobbyists. But Barack said 'It's the right thing to do, because if we're about changing Washington and reducing

the influence of powerful interests, then we have to begin at home. We have to start in our own house.' And we felt on that decision, I remember we lost $100 000 just that first weekend, and we lost millions of the course of the campaign... But as it happened in the end it inspired so many people that had become cynical about politics to give money to this candidate, and he ended up raising half a billion dollars. That's more than triple what anyone had ever raised before. That speaks a lot about when you do reform, it actually can have the opposite effect that you think it's going to have.

Thus, politicians can fundraise democratically – and still make money.

Marketing vision and ideology

Furthermore, practitioners argued that not only is vision and principle important democratically, it is needed to win. One of the common criticisms of political marketing is that it will lead to parties converging in the centre. But practitioners argue that being in the centre ground is not about all parties being the same. Bryan Gould (2007) argued, regarding how Blair changed the UK Labour Party in 1997, 'believe me...no one, and certainly not I, argues that the party didn't need change...the party needed to get rid of a lot of its baggage and adapt to what people wanted. But without saying we're no longer the Labour party.' Sparrow (2007), who worked for the Tories, argued that 'you've got to talk about the things that are important to our people and that means the centre ground, but the centre ground isn't just a place where you just end up like the others, there are lots of ideas in the centre ground.'

Using party values and taking ideological positions can also yield support. The UK Lib Dem position on the Iraq War was, Borrowman (2006) argued, 'a combination of ideology and gut instinct. There was some reluctance to completely wade in the way we did...such as the big march in London, where we eventually had a big formal presence...there was a danger we might seem like Trots as there was a big left wing element in the march. But it did us a lot of good. It's done a great deal of good for the morale in the party; people like to see us taking a stance.' Over the long term it is important for the party organisation to talk about values continually. Mehta (2007) recalled how the Democrats had 'people on the ground talking about these elections long before we even had candidates for these races, and certainly before we had a nominee for our party, because we needed to tell them what our values were'.

This meant making it clear that 'the first is fundamental fairness.... the second pillar of our party is the idea that we have to fiscally responsible... the third pillar is when it comes to foreign policy... we have to be not only tough, but we have to be smart.'

Parties need to link the new product to party belief/tradition in some way to get support internally. Changing parties to suit the external market will usually encourage opposition from members, because they think it threatens long-standing party beliefs. As Lees-Marshment and Pettitt (2010, 123) note, Cameron's strategy to change the UK Tories from 2005 onwards led to signs of discontent, with criticism that the party ceased to stand for anything. Carter (2007) argued that under Blair 'what has made Labour distinctive is that it has built a foundation, a very firm foundation about what its values are and how they can be applied in the modern world... once you have that foundation, it means that when you are looking at any one issue, you will do so from a firm set of values, a firm set of beliefs'. He argued that the weakness with Cameron's focus on the environment was that he had not tied it logically to the party ethos: 'it may be a good issue, it may be populist, it may be some of the focus groups tell David Cameron to focus on it. But what nobody in the public can understand or has yet had it articulated to them, is why that is a key aspect of the Conservative agenda.'

A means of succeeding pragmatically is key – you need a vision to win and achieve goals. Knuckey (2010, 106) observed that this was one of the reasons for Kerry's failure to win the 2004 US presidential election. The Democratic convention showed 'the inability of the Kerry campaign to provide a specific vision' with no obvious theme other than the candidate's war record. Harris (2006) argued that while oppositions need to see the incumbent party fall down, 'the first thing is that you need to create an overall vision, which is based on a set of beliefs, and people will think they will be better off under you.... Howard never ever created a sense of belief in what his overall vision was and all he did was get stuck into the negatives, and then with IDS he also had no clear sense of purpose. I think that without a noble purpose you're sunk.' Bryan Gould (2007) claimed:

> My criticism of Tony [Blair] has always been not that he lacked principle... he lacked politics.... he took the view, I think, that the job of a democratic politician was to persuade the voters that the persuader was a good person, a competent person, could be trusted with political power. So Tony's pitch very much was trust *me*, not: here

is my analysis of society and here is my prescription.... the party he felt was a burden, the ideology was a burden.... when we come onto the marketing, he wasn't marketing politics, he was marketing himself.

Can marketing help achieve vision? Evans (2006) said 'yes very definitely, as long as it is driven by a vision and a set of values. As long as it is about political ideas and doesn't become reduced to a tactical squabble for power. Anyone involved in that game will get outflanked. Another party provision will come along and will get traction with vision as to where people want to get next.' Thus, Carter (2007) comments that 'politics is an organisational battle, but it's also a psychological one. It's very important that you know what you stand for, you have a clear sense of values and you go out and articulate them.'

Internal unity

Internal unity is an important part of party marketing. Without it, marketing plans for strategy, branding, product development and communication can fall apart. The party has to be on board and aligned. Smith, G. (2006, 9–10) noted how factions destroy parties, as has been seen in the UK Conservative Party during the leaderships of John Major, William Hague and Iain Duncan Smith. Paré (2009, 52) notes how in the 2004 Canadian election, the Conservative Party 'had problems with candidates going off message', so they worked to adopt 'a more cohesive and disciplined approached to delivering the party's message' to win in 2006. Jones (2008) observed that with the UK Tories in the 2003–2005 period 'a sense of alignment, strategic alignment was always lacking and is a big issue'. He said that when Lynton Crosby came on board for the 2005 campaign he retained focus on the five pledges – more police, cleaner hospitals, lower taxes, controlled immigration, better schools – which had already been revealed at the party conference, arguing that 'our best chance is staying consistently on course with this, rather than a lot of personal interpretation and a lot of sort of personal indulgence'. Although the party lost in 2005 it increased its seats and may have not done so had it been disunited.

Parties need the desire to win to maintain unity. Rori (2008, 318) observed how the desire to win helped achieve change in the case of the Greek party, Pasok: 'as PASOK's change coincided with the campaign period, the vast majority of party actors and major party officials accepted all the changes introduced by the leader. Electoral prospects unified intraparty forces, even if the leader's innovations shocked a large part of the party elites.' Lavigne (2009) said 'we're incredibly stubborn not to lose the focus, and not to go back to where [we once were with few seats] – because we've worked too hard. It has been six years. There's nobody here that wants the party to go back to its lows. We've tasted what it is like to have authority – to have influence over the decisions. It's a great incentive.' Even natural dissenters need to be willing to play the game, and Sparrow (2007) tells an amusing story about the UK Labour Party under Blair's early leadership before they won in 1997:

> There were lots of people behind Blair who didn't agree with what he was saying... but what you had was a determination to be in government and a hatred of the Conservatives... The joke told by Denis Skinner, an MP... [was that] during the '97 election campaign, this TV crew were desperate to get somebody to say something, a Labour MP to say something negative about the Labour leadership. Denis Skinner, he's the man. So they set up all the cameras and everything and started filming him. And they said what do you think about Labour's plan to match the Tories' spending proposals for the next two three years and so on? And he said: 'very interesting.' And it just went on and on like this. And they thought right, get him to say this, you know, what about the Blair and Brown you know, and... 'Very interesting.' And what about the plans to curb the power of the trade unions? And so he, 'very interesting.' And every question they asked, he just said 'very interesting.' And they said look, stop, you know, we can't film anymore, this isn't giving us what we want. Every question we ask, you just say very interesting, why is that? He said, well the camera's off, isn't it? And he said well, I got called into the whips' office and they told me that when I was talking about Labour's leadership I had to stop saying bollocks and start saying very interesting!

In contrast, the Conservatives in 2003–2004 lacked the same discipline: Harris (2006) observed how 'they have a very nice life as MPs and shadow ministers, but they're not hungry for power, they're not hungry for power in the way that Labour were. They don't feel a yearning sense of injustice that they have to go in and correct.'

Parties can try to build unity into party organisation. Mehta (2009) noted that, in the Democratic Party between 2005 and 2008, they 'rebuilt a lot of broken political relationships. We're not the most disciplined party in the world... it makes it hard for us to work together as one cohesive unit, because you have people who have different positions on issues, different value systems, different ways of organising.' But parties also need to balance unity with room for internal participation. Smith, M. (2006) said that, while unity was important, 'it's a question of how you do it.... You've got to build relationships so that people trust each other, you've got to identify who does what so that you don't have people fighting each other over their roles and then you've got to provide opportunity for discussion.' In 2006 'they asked every organisation in the party what were the 3 key themes for policy. Sustainable environment policy was the number one thing people raised in the party' and the leadership took this on 'so you get a kind of a synergistic process going that actually makes people feel yeah, we contributed to that'. This created a 'process going where people feel they are engaged and they are, you know, it's not unreal. That's what builds good organisation. Then they're prepared to go out and do all the other things you want them to do in an election campaign.'

Campaign teams also need to be unified. The Bush–Cheney 2004 team was, as Beeson (2007) commented, made up of 'a lot of us that had been together for years. So it was one group... and we had one goal and that was to re-elect the President. Nothing else was more important to that.' Unity is crucial – it can 'make or break a campaign'. Insider comments have already suggested there were problems in the Kerry campaign; from the opposite side Beeson (2007) observed that they 'had people talking in the press about one side and they had different people talking to different parts of the press'. Noble (2009) said:

> A friend of mine said it best once, he said 'You know, in so many campaigns, if somebody trips and falls and makes a mistake, the vultures are all there trying to step all over him and get ahead.' In the 1995 campaign, somebody tripped and fell – everybody around the table was picking them up. That's the difference between winning campaigns and losing campaigns. Winning campaigns have this desire to all be together and walk through the wall of fire together. Losing campaigns have a stink about them, they're not fun, and you're always wondering who is going to get you.

Unity helps sustain a clear message to the public. As Lawrence (2008) said, 'everyone's got to sing off that same hymn sheet.' Speaking of the

2007 Australian Labor campaign, he remarked that 'it was an incredibly disciplined campaign. Rudd and his people understood the need for message discipline and we were good at doing it.'

Political marketing can, however, make unity harder to achieve, because elites respond to their stakeholders in developing the product and don't follow their members. Activists tend to have divergent views to political consumers. Wilson (2006) noted how they 'used to do quite a lot a surveying of our members just to make sure they feel that their opinions are valued.... we could basically see what our members said, which was extreme, what our current voters said which was a lot less extreme. And then people who would consider Act as second or third choice, as a target market and they were very very different.' Parties have to try to reconcile these differences or to ensure that the membership is representative of the electorate so that their goals and interests will be similar. Internal supporters tend to have a greater ideological or emotive attachment to the party, which makes it harder for them to accept new ways of operating. Mehta (2007) noted the need to explain to volunteers that changing the branding communication did not mean changing ideology: 'it's not that the founding cornerstone principles of the party are different, it's the brand, it's how we message, it's how we talk about it.'

The elected members or parliamentary parties can also be out of touch and marooned on planet politics and thus unwilling to support a new strategy. Lees-Marshment's (2008) analysis of the UK Conservatives under William Hague from 1997 to 2001 showed that just because leaders want to adopt and implement a market orientation does not mean that it will be successful – they have to get support from the majority within the party. Duncan Smith (2006) discussed how, after losing substantially, parties go into a first phase where they think ' "it wasn't our fault it was the electorate's fault, so steady as she goes and they're bound to recognise it's a mistake..." So the first phase that William Hague was in covered that. William at first tried to make some changes but ran up very hard against the party.' Duncan Smith explained that 'there is resistance to change until you understand what the changes are and whether it's going to be beneficial.' There is also resistance to political marketing itself. Wring (2005a, 16–17) analysed the emergence and development of marketing in the UK Labour Party and noted how the party had previously held electioneering approaches which did not fit a marketing approach. Instead, they followed the 'educationalist' approach, where 'campaigning was primarily about converting people to their cause...dedicated to overcoming ignorance and emancipating the dispossessed' and the 'persuasional' school of thought, which was 'designed to provoke more of a short-term emotional response and drew on Plato's contention that the Aristotelian ideal of democracy was an imperfection vulnerable to the tyranny of the suggestible mob'. Tension in the party between doing what was believed to be right, and winning elections, continued through Tony Blair's victory in 1997 and beyond. A comparative study by Lees-Marshment et al. (2010, 285) found that the internal party area can be a big barrier to marketing in a range of parties, including the LDP in Japan under Koizumi's leadership and the KMT in Taiwan.

Lees-Marshment (2001, 37–38) argued that leaders need to create a feeling that everybody in the party can contribute to the marketing strategy, by showing respect for internal as well as external views. A new strategy needs time to succeed and those within parties need to give it time. Mortimore (2006) argued how 'it does need time and in the meantime you have to manage vested interests who want to go back to the old product. And that's clearly what happened under Hague and Iain Duncan Smith. They both tried to change, and it wasn't bringing instant results, and so people wanted it to go back to how it had been.' Duncan Smith (2006) said the same himself – 'the problem is that the party here in Westminster needs a much quicker success. They have a sense that it is a weekly cycle here week, if you're up, then you feel that the poll should be up two weeks later.' Jones (2008) added that 'you see this all the time... a lack of continuity around language, a lack of continuity around focus, a lack of consistency; you'll see a strategy that starts to become increasingly shaped by trying to keep everyone in the boat, a strategy shaped by trying to stay on course, to stay in control. And all of a sudden the strategy becomes fragmented between a leader trying to stay in power in his party, versus a leader trying to get in power in government.'

As Dean and Croft (2001, 1207) observed, 'the enigma for a political party is how to allow the diversity of party members, activists and elected members a say in the nature of the "product offering" while still maintaining a degree of apparent unanimity for the consumption of less-controllable groups' (see also Lilleker 2005c, 576–567). As Lees-Marshment and Pettitt (2010, 123) note, Cameron's strategy to appeal to both internal and external markets when re-branding the UK Conservatives was not always easy; environmentally friendly policies alienated the core market of business, while an attempt to change the policy on grammar schools led to a retreat after internal opposition. Franz Luntz, consultant, ran a focus group of floating voters on Cameron's first year as leader, and noted that 'there is an underlying fear of "spin" that could undermine your long-term success...floating voters believe you are actively engaged in a sincere effort to bring about fundamental change, and they appreciate it...[but] they are afraid you'll turn into the Tony Blair of 2006' (*Daily Telegraph*, 4 December 2006). Cameron himself said, 'what I say to traditional Conservatives is that we have lost three elections in a row, we have to modernise and change to reflect changes to British society...[but]...look at the centrality of what I am saying: social responsibility, parental responsibility – that the state doesn't have all the answers –...this is a profoundly *Conservative message*' (from http://www.telegraph.co.uk/news/main.jhtml?xml=/news/2006/12/01/utranscript101.xml&page=3, accessed 26 April 2007).

The difficulty in politics is that leader cannot just tell the parliamentary party what to do/what to produce. As Gillan (2006) said, 'it's not like a manufacturing process where you've got a model T. Ford and you know that there's new technology you can bring in and re-shape the body. It's not that easy with a political party!...the Parliamentary party is notoriously difficult to manage.' Leaders' power is dependent on party/caucus. As Brash (2007) said, 'in a company or Reserve Bank or whatever, the Chief Executive is appointed by a board, or in the case of Reserve Bank Governor by a Minister, and you don't have to worry about what people think about you personally, though you always like to have good relationships with staff and so on.' However, in politics, 'the leader owes his or her position entirely to the will of the caucus...as I discovered, you can get away with blue murder if you are riding very high in the polls...but once your own poll support begins to diminish you are much more beholden to the caucus, because they are looking at the polls and saying can you win the election for us?' Hide (2007) also remarked, 'you couldn't fundamentally stamp your authority on the party because you had a whole lot of rival factors and interests and concerns that were looking for any change: something that didn't work would be your fault. So I really felt the constraint of keeping the caucus happy, because obviously they can dump you as a leader.'

Leaders or party managers (chair, presidents etc.) need the ability to effect change but this is hard to find. Howard Dean who brought in all the changes to the Democrat Party organisation faced significant opposition. Mehta (2007) said 'he's a little bit ahead of his time....[the] 2 and half years has been very, very tough. We've been hit with obstacles every, everyday...it's very tough to get Democratic politicians to listen to voter logic.' Even party leaders can't use promotion/demotion to help supporters of the new strategy rise. Brash (2007) commented that 'the people you promote regard the promotion as the very minimum to which they were entitled by obvious merit. The people who by definition you demote, because it's a ranking process and when someone is promoted, someone has to be demoted, they are just hopping mad. They regard that as absolutely unfair and unreasonable, and as if it shows that the leader is not suited to be leader.'

The final argument is to make the case about the need for power to achieve moral goals. Lavigne (2009) discussed this with regard to the NDP, who were moving from being the 'moral conscience of the parliament in the corner' to a party with more power:

> We have a moral obligation to govern, or have our ideas adopted, otherwise we're not helping the very people that we believe so deeply in helping. Whether it be the unemployed, whether it be eradicating poverty, justice for first nations, equality issues, human rights, social policy issues; none of those things get advanced if we don't govern, or if we don't influence in a greater presence within parliament. When we have a greater presence, there is a direct correlation between the government of Canada regardless of whether it is Liberal or Conservative. We rewrote the 2005 Liberal budget, which is still today – I can point to you in many parts of the country the effects of that. Taking $4.5b out of corporate tax cuts that nobody asked for and putting them into building transit infrastructure, first nations housing, and bolstering education, as a few examples of what we did with that money. I can still point to the projects that we helped influence. So, now that people can see – wow this is what can happen when we have more seats, more responsibility, or more authority within the government.

As Mehta (2007) said, 'I want to do all the good things we talked about for the jobs, the education, the environment, for Iraq, for healthcare, all those good things. I can't do a single one of them until I win.'

Summary

The party is an important part of political marketing and interviews with practitioners suggest elites are not ridding roughshod over the party, or ignoring the democratic value of participation, but instead trying to find ways to combine the demands of internal and external markets, as shown in the summary of rules in Table 4.1.

Table 4.1 Rules of the game for marketing the party

The value of marketing the party
1. The internal market tends to be unrepresentative of the wider public socially and in terms of opinions, but can't just be told what to do
2. If you don't get them on board, strategy/branding, etc. won't succeed because of lack of unity and clear message
3. If people volunteer it has to be on their terms
4. Identify what volunteers want from involvement and develop the organisation to suit this
5. Don't target organisational resources according to segments. Maintain organisation in all areas/at all levels to ensure a long-term infrastructure is there when needed
6. Invest in staff and supporters in the long term not just for the campaign
7. Use internal marketing to make volunteers more motivated, active, attached and accepting of the organisational goals

Managing and developing volunteer activity
8. Find out what they want (market analysis): members seek social engagement and approval, self-esteem and political knowledge gain
9. Find out who wants what (segment): create different options for different groups e.g. supporters, rather than official members
10. Accept they can't always do what you want when you want: offer things to do to suit different lifestyles and times and commitments
11. Act on it: respond to suggestions and market analysis
12. Adapt: change to suit how they want to get involved, not how you have always done it
13. Ask people: to join, to come to a discussion, to volunteer for a campaign
14. Keep talking: personal relations, word of mouth/face to face is still important – don't just use the internet
15. Be quick: if they offer to help, respond asap to capture that interest
16. Help them help you even more: offer support and training
17. Assign tasks and promote according to skills
18. Trust them: give volunteers leadership positions, access to data, let them organise their own events, etc.
19. Involve them: create ways for them to discuss politics, face to face and online
20. Thank them: show appreciation of volunteer work
21. Be nice: reach out to those who favoured other candidates/leadership nominees
22. Set limits: let them be involved in policy discussion, strategy and the campaign and let them influence it – but within constraints

Marketing for money
23. Use marketing to understand donor behaviour
24. Make sure fundraising events are enjoyable for the prospective donor, and give something back to them
25. Market for individual small donations as well as big ones
26. Don't just ask for money all the time

Table 4.1 (Continued)

Marketing vision and ideology
27. Utilise ideology and internal views to create a distinctive position but also to win
28. Need vision to win and achieve goals
29. Link new product to party belief/tradition in some way
30. Balance need for unity with room for internal participation

Getting internal support for a new strategy
31. Explain that a new strategy needs time to work
32. Explain why you can't do everything they want
33. Thank them for their efforts
34. Make the argument about the need for power to achieve moral goals
35. Keep on track despite internal criticism
36. Remember that balancing internal and external demands is not easy

5
Communicating

> The objective for the strategic communications in a political campaign is not to deceive, it's to put particular parties that you're working for in the best possible light.
> —Scard (2008)

> As a marketer you should never try and change someone's deeply-held worldview, you should only ever play to it.
> —Jones (2008)

> Today broadband is facilitating greater use of video, so why can't the candidate knock on everyone's door virtually? And why can't the candidate create multiple video messages based on the precinct they're going to and the issues they know that precinct cares about and electronically deliver that personalised message digitally?
> —Krohn (2009)

> In this transaction the cards are not dealt evenly, of course, and nor should they be. The basic commodity being traded is information. And one person, the subject of the interview is in possession and you try to acquire it from them in view of passing it onto the audience.
> —Paxman (2007)

Communication is an obvious area of political marketing, but it also crosses over with other areas such as targeted communication, communicating product change and e-marketing. Politicians communicate continually not just in elections and not just to win an election, but to improve a candidate or political leader's image, make something clearer, counter negative attacks from the opposition, educate and inform voters, gain or increase support for a particular piece of legislation, place an issue on the agenda and increase support for a referenda proposition. Its purpose therefore dictates how it is carried out and when. This chapter will discuss overall strategy and communication; then, using communication to achieve particular goals, such as communicating complex policy, selling policy, communicating a leader, communicating product change or re-positioning and get out the vote (GOTV) and election campaigning; and then look at different tools and techniques, such as advertising, targeted communication, competition communication, receiver-responsive communication, e-marketing, the need for authentic communication, managing internal relationships, managing the media relationship, and communication advisors and clients.

Strategy and communication

Practitioners strongly argued the need to engage in strategic thinking in communication and campaigning. Campbell (2005) noted that the political/media environment is 'an utterly short-term world' but in government you've 'got to stay focused on the long-term'. Humphrey (2007) observed how when Campbell 'did bring in a lot more of the strategic thinking about how you position the government, branding, longer term reputation, try to use all the different media, whether it's using specialist media, women's media, the internet'. Munro (2006) explained how, as press secretary to a prime minister, 'at the start of the year you put in place a strategy, you work out what your key messages are going to be, what your key themes are going to be and then you try to group your activity around those themes throughout the year'. Campaigners also talked of the need to follow the strategy: 'what you're doing is creating a campaign which supports what the strategy is' (Carson 2006).

Given this, communication teams need to ensure there is time to think strategically and then stick to that strategy. Rogers (2009) said that it is all about planning: 'I used to have a phrase for it which was "The tyranny of the urgent." We will not be victims of the tyranny of the urgent. We will not all climb on the school bus and let the first person who walks through the door drive it this week. We're going to push our messages up.' Munro (2006) remarked that one solution was to ensure one member of staff has time to think strategically. He explained how 'the Prime Minister has a daily programme...and so you need people handling her daily needs and her daily routines and you need someone like me who's thinking about the bigger picture.' He chaired the group of

27–28 press secretaries and tried to 'make sure that they were following agreed strategies and agreed priorities and to make sure that all the government communication had a cohesion to it and was well-organised'. In a campaign, Carson (2006) said that 'the big thing is to have a strategy and to stick to it. And if you're going to deviate from the strategy you have to have bloody good reasons to be deviating from it.'

However, retaining focus is not easy. Stanzel (2007) described how this is difficult in the White House press office, which is why there is a separate communications office: there's 'not enough time to think, not enough time to reflect, and that's why, that's partially why we have say, the Communications Office, because they don't have to be necessarily on the frontline every day.' Krohn (2007), in charge of e-marketing at the RNC explained how events take you away from strategic thinking: 'I had a window of time when I first got here where I was in that honeymoon phase and thinking really optimistically about all the things that we need to be doing as an organisation. And then very quickly I started to get subsumed by the realities of elections... there's very little time to think about the future.' Reid (2009), director of communications to Canadian Prime Minister Paul Martin, conceded 'I became caught up in day-to-day fire fighting, and as a consequence we didn't contribute as much to the definition of agenda.'

Collins (2006) also said that any attacks on the competitor need to fit the strategy. He claimed that 'the Tory [2001] strategy lacked a coherent strategy overall for attacking Labour. They started off of what was probably the right strategy – the strategy of "you pay taxes but where are the police and the nurses?", by trying to tap into people's sense of we haven't seen the delivery yet.' However, when this did not seem to gain enough support, because people wanted to give Labour another term, 'they targeted on the very traditional issues, tax and Europe, the very core vote issues, and they used the advertising to create high Tory turnout in what they thought might be a low turnout election and advertising reflected that.' They then added a third strategy with 'slightly desperate burst the bubble ads', which aimed at cutting the Labour majority, even if they themselves could not win. 'The campaign was generally all over the place' and even included different creative styles.

Communication should not focus on or be directed by the media, especially its daily news cycle and pack mentality. Humphrey (2007), from working in Number 10 Downing Street, advised that 'governments always suffered from being obsessed with the media, especially the day to day media. It makes it very reactive... it's very easy to lose the agenda.' Lloyd, D (2006) conceded that 'the media have a lot to answer for the way in which they pump out material from Whitehall and Westminster and there is that village atmosphere about them.' Sticking to the general strategy and remaining focused on achieving a range of goals is thus crucial to making communication effective. In the next section are a number of communication goals politicians pursue will be discussed.

Communicating complex policy

One of the difficulties of communicating the political product is that conveying the policy aspect is particularly beset with problems. Green (2006) said, 'if you have a more complex policy that it's harder to get it over. There is less coverage of politics, it's short, snappy more and more visual, all those sorts of things; people do not sit down and read 2000-word learned treaties on tax.' From the media perspective, Butler (2006) noted that with television 'part of the problem is the nature of the medium. It's just not suited to doing policy debate.' Stanzel (2007) argued that 'some issues more difficult to explain than others just because I think they're more complicated by nature', and one of these is immigration: 'there's so many different moving parts, whether it's border security or making sure that employers hire legal workers, or making sure that people who come here legally have the ability to assimilate into our culture, or making sure that we have a temporary worker program that addresses the needs of our economy.' In addition, people's capacity to take in multiple complexities is limited, as Fenn (2007) explained:

> The public, they care about politics, but they're worried about whether their kid is happy in school or how their spouse is feeling towards them that day, whether they made love the night before, whether the garbage has been taken out, what's on TV that they want to watch, whether they get enough money in the bank to afford this or that... if you're trying to throw 10 things at them, then I don't think you'll be able to, you know, doesn't compute.

The first solution is to ensure communication is simple with only two to three repeated messages. Sparrow (2007) said that communication needs 'consistency, being concise and having an idea in your head of, perhaps, two or three messages only that you want people to hear'. Ranger (2006) recalled how the Lib Dems gained traction through this during Paddy

Ashdown's time as leader: 'a good example during Paddy's leadership was a penny on income tax for education. I'm sure that putting a penny on income tax wasn't necessarily the most important bit of the policy, but it was something simple you could repeat frequently, and it said to people the Liberal Democrats are concerned about education.' Pringle (2006), of the NZ Greens, conceded how although they won awards for their billboards in 2008, in 2005 they 'were really complicated... which actually required you to stop and read them and try to work out what it goes on about. Of course with a billboard on the side of the road, people driving past could be at 50 to 100 km an hour.'

Ulm (2007) said that campaigns don't have the opportunity to talk about everything a candidate 'has said, done, voted on, believes in... we get to talk about 1 or 2 or 3 things tops'. This may have been another weakness in the 2004 Kerry campaign: Mellman (2007) recalled that 'Kerry is a guy who is first of all very sort of substance-oriented, very issue-oriented, so he didn't really want to talk in sort of more generic message terms. He wanted to talk about the concrete, specifics of each issue.' Brash (2007) noted the same weakness with National's losing 2002 campaign:

> We were attempting to market far too many policies, as a consequence the electorate simply didn't know what we were focused on. It wasn't that we didn't have policies, or we didn't know what we stood for, it was that there was so much of it the public were confused by it. I still remember vividly as a candidate reading a policy email about six days before the election, which was the 54th policy email sent out.

Detailed communication needs to be targeted to those who want it, in a medium that can take it. Armstrong (2006) said that newspapers do allow that detailed policy discussion: 'in the major policy areas there is pretty extensive debate.' Online media, which can include newspapers' own sites, offer more detail, substance, room for discussion and interactivity. Inglish (2007) discussed how after a typical television show 'what you can do is to throw, for example to the News online site, where there is much more detail about the NHS, about what the report says, about what the costs of the NHS are and some background information' for the people who want to know more. Discussions can be extended after the programme has ended, and be related geographically to the reader's location. Politicians can similarly vary the detail level of their communication. Clelland-Stokes (2009) explained that when the mayor speaks at public meetings he will say something generic like 'we've got seven councils, seven bureaucracies, seven mayors. It's a waste. We used to be number three or four in the OECD. Now we're number 20. Auckland needs to change. The governance is sick and the only way to get New Zealand forward is to get Auckland to a single-governance city.' However, for the royal commissioner and other more informed stakeholders much greater detail was needed in the areas of the economy, government structure and accountability structure. The substance has to be there, 'it's just a case of not giving it to everyone.'

The media and politicians can identify ways to explain complex issues and make political coverage accessible. Bray (2008) observed how the successful politicians 'are more and more adept at taking very complicated ideas and making them very digestible' and helping the media in this task. Inglish (2007) said that at the BBC 'you have to have people who are both intelligent, clever, understand what the policy issues are, are interested in policy as well as politics, but critically that they can actually explain it to people.' The media can use devices to explain issues. Bray (2008) noted the need to make complex issues in current affairs programmes relevant to the viewer, and so once, on the issue of tax, 'we chose the idea of this sort of family captured by the top end of the tax scale, what sort of pressures were on them, and looked at it through their eyes.' Inglish (2007) noted that what 'the audience research...tells you is that you have to be quite inventive and quite clever about how you explain what is important about what's happening in parliament.'

Selling policy

Communicating unpopular policies is a key area for marketing but, of course, is not easy. Stanzel (2007) explained that 'there are positions that the President has that are not supported by 50 percent of the people, there are a lot of them, and that doesn't concern him, but that makes our communications challenge more difficult...So we have to do more work to explain why he's doing what he's doing.' Sometimes it is a case of modifying or constraining more ambitious changes: Macken (2008) recalled a time when 'the Libs sort of floated this idea about eight hospitals about to close...and we [the opposition] started running stories: this is terrible; we started running a big campaign. And three days later they announced that only two hospitals were going to close. So they ran this line, Six Hospitals Saved.' It showed responsiveness to some degree and even turned a potentially politically damaging policy into a winning one.

Market analysis can help parties understand public views and devise communication to change public opinion. Allington, Morgan and O'Shaughnessy (1999) discuss how marketing was used to sell privatisation in the UK, something which faced opposition from the Labour Party, the unions and the media. Communication was aimed not at typical shareholders but at the general public, many of whom had never been shareholders. The campaign to privatise British Gas built on the appeal to individuals with a slogan 'Tell Sid', the message being that 'privatisation represented good news for ordinary people because they could now get a piece of the action' (p. 634). It also encouraged people to spread the word themselves: 'people from all walks of life were shown whispering the phrase to each other – cleaner to dentist, dentist to patient, and so on.' It was successful because of the other marketing elements within it, such as reflecting the general mood of the time – success through individual entrepreneurship in business – and the mobilisation of culture myths, such as empowering the little guy against institutional organisations.

Gelders and Van de Walle (2005) examined how the Belgian government communicated large-scale governmental reform, called the Copernicus reform, to modernise the government and introduce new public management principles: economy, efficiency, effectiveness. Market intelligence was utilised both internally and externally for target groups after the proposal was devised. Internal target groups included civil servants, and utilised communication to disseminate information to them under a project called the *Artemis Project* in autumn 2000. Internal intelligence had found that civil servants saw the announced reform as criticism rather than constructive change and had not received enough information about it, so the federal government initiated leaflets, road shows, newsletters, monthly magazines and a website for civil servants to improve perception. In addition to external intelligence and communication with the public this helped implementation, even though it still took a long time.

Communicating a leader

Communication of leaders and individual politicians is obviously a key aspect in electoral politics. One strategy is to allow politicians to meet journalists informally to build positive relationships and overcome any perceived weaknesses. Munro (2006) recalled how he set up informal chats over coffee between Helen Clark and editors of metropolitan newspapers in Auckland, Wellington and Christchurch, and 'had dinner parties at my place actually, where I got a group of senior journalists together and Helen would come along and we'd just have a very social evening together. So it was a good chance just for them to get to know her a bit better and get to know her sort of values and her views.' Stanzel (2007) made the same point:

> Having that opportunity even in an off the record setting, maybe to just sit a bunch of reporters down who are going to cover the White House every day, and off the record just let them chat with the President and see what he's all about; providing that access is very important, because then they have a better understanding of where he's coming from. It's one thing for me to hand a piece of paper to a reporter and say this is our policy and let me explain it to you, it's wholly another thing to have them have the opportunity to talk with him and understand well, why do you think there should be testing in every classroom?

Marketing communications takes into account the popularity of the leader. Lavigne (2009) explained how they 'centred the campaign around the leader, because the research told us that one of our best assets was our leader, and one of the biggest deficiencies of the Liberal Party was their leader'. When politicians are unpopular they are de-emphasised. Macken (2008) similarly recalled how, in Australia, 'suddenly halfway through the election campaign [the minister] got pulled from the campaign. And they wouldn't tell us why, but we knew that... his image wasn't polling too well.'

Charisma becomes less important if you can demonstrate leadership skills. Harvey (2007) said 'charisma is fleeting and it's a male thing. By that I mean Tom Cruise, Paul Newman, Bill Clinton. It's like aftershave. Nice for a while but then wears off. Women have much rarer qualities. They have beauty and they have leadership and when that's combined in the political arena it's very long lasting.' As Reid (2009) said, 'people want to see this person looking like they're in charge and they're running things well in office, so you reinforce that image.' Newman (2001, 210–214) notes how, in 2000, 'Bush's behaviour began to change to reinforce the image of how a potential president should be acting... on his plane with the press... he stopped bantering with reporters with the fear that it would make him look less presidential.'

The communication of leaders also needs to make an emotional connection with people. Newman (2001, 210–214) observed that, in 2000, 'George W Bush did [this] naturally through his personality. In his acceptance speech, he billed it as a talk from the heart... [but] there was something missing in Al Gore emotionally that people kept looking for but never found.' The candidate's central vision needs to reflect their personality and be consistent; Newman (2001, 210–214) argues that 'Gore[s] vision statements never caught on, were never reiterated enough to stand out, and subsequently left voters unsuccessfully trying to define who their leader was and what he stood for.' Gore also 'struggled to find the right look to present to the American people. His look on the campaign trail went from the *CEO* look (pinstriped suits) to the *Nightclub singer* look (dark suit, dark shirt, loud tie) to the *Casual Al Gore* look (polo shirt and sport coat)... he perpetuated the image of a candidate trying to be all things to all people, and in the end, a leader unsure of himself.'

Communications staff need to look out for potentially poor visuals that could be linked to opposition attacks. Brash (2007) recalls a particular problem during his leadership when he was asked to meet people proposing to sail an attractive-looking high-speed catamaran around the world, which was fuelled with bio-diesel to promote bio fuels:

> What I didn't know until I got there, and I should have done, was that getting onto this craft I had to walk across a 20 foot plank about so wide, across the water, and there were two problems with that. One, it was at a time when the media was speculating would Don Brash stay on as leader, and so leadership walking the plank was a bad metaphor; secondly it was quite a lengthy plank and quite a narrow plank, and I could have damn well fallen in! I wasn't at all comfortable about walking across it. Staff should have never put me in that position.

When leaders get into difficulties, it is possible to do something about it: staff can re-present or re-launch a leader and reconnect leaders by dealing with problem issues. Carter (2007) reported how they managed Blair for the 2005 election after he lost support on the Iraq War:

> Self-criticism came to be known as the masochism strategy, which involved taking the Prime Minister to studios after studios and putting him in front of live audiences that could engage and talk with him and put their concerns. Those events helped to show that the Prime Minister had not moved off the key agendas that he had been elected on, but indeed remained very focused on them, even though there had been other things going on.

Blumenthal (2007) noted how Hillary Clinton's exercise *Let the Conversation Begin* for the presidential race helped refresh her candidacy: 'it's what she did in New York when it was, it was a somewhat similar situation, people were weary of her, they didn't know her, they believed in the negative stereotypes about her, and the way to dispel them was to appear personally in small groups that were open, so people could report on them.'

Communicating product change or re-positioning

As discussed in previous chapters, political elites can change their product and direction and decisions to gain public support, but for these to have any impact the change needs to be noticed. Duncan Smith (2006) said it takes a long time to get those changes across because people listen more to each other and word of mouth than they do to the media: 'if someone you respect or trust says to you that an individual in a political party is okay, you're more likely to accept that. If they tell you themselves on television, that I'm okay, nowadays, they don't accept that.' Whilst leader of the opposition from 2005–2010, before winning power to become UK Prime Minister in 2010, David Cameron, listed as his proudest political achievement 'Getting the Conservative Party listened to again' (http://www.davidcameronmp.com/, his site, accessed 19 February 2009).

Practitioners and academics suggest a number of ways to show the product has changed. The first is to use a fresh style. Lawrence (2008) noted how 'our campaign gave a very, very fresh view of the Labour Party. We started by redesigning the entire livery for the Labour Party, which was old-fashioned...the style of our advertising was quite upbeat, it was positive.' Symbols of the new direction that fit the strategy can be effective. Lawrence (2008) said 'Go Kevin '07, which became, as everyone remembers now as the Kevin '07 campaign....initially that was designed as the name for the website but once we did the T-shirt and a few of us saw that, the big Kevin '07, it just took off.' Lees-Marshment and Pettitt (2010) observed how the UK Conservatives adopted a new party symbol, a green tree and blue sky, used the slogan 'vote blue, get green' in local elections and redeveloped the party website with fresh blue-green colours, using pictures which conveyed a more mainstream Britain. Green (2006) said that 'the classic example of successful political marketing is David Cameron, on his bicycle, which let everybody know that he is serious about the environment....John Gummer who was a successful and green environmental secretary before said that

David Cameron, just by riding his bike to work, has done more for the Tory Party's green credentials than him for years striving away in government, because that's the image there.'

Unconventional forms of communication also help attract attention to change. When asked what made Ansell's 2005 billboards so successful, Brash (2007) replied 'well, they were very unconventional... National Party billboards are blue, and you would never see Labour Party billboards with me on it either, but here was National putting half the billboard in red and a photograph of Helen Clark.' Unconventional communication also attracts other free communication. With the Rudd campaign '*Kevin '07* clearly captured people's imaginations and became the moniker, and it's young, it's a modern kind of idea to tag something like that' (Lawrence 2008). Brash (2007) explained that with Ansell's advertising 'not only did we get the benefit of the billboards themselves, but we got a huge amount of television and print media coverage of the billboards, and that multiplied the effect of them enormously. I think every single billboard that he produced the TV or the newspaper reproduced it, in colour.' Ansell (2007) himself said he follows the rule 'make ads that make news.'

Re-positioning needs to be started early. Collins (2006) said that 'if you've got a big job – and the Conservative party has got a really big job to change perception or to win a general election – that's going to be a three or four-year project. You can't come in shortly before the election and expect to win for them.' When interviewed about his role as director of marketing for the UK Tories 2003–2004, and asked if the problem was that he came in quite late in the process, Harris (2006) said, 'so did Michael Howard to be fair. 18 months before an election is a tough call. Changing the Conservative party brand is a long slow process. I know when I used to say I was or had worked as a marketer for the Conservative party I used to get sneered at.' Part of communicating product change is the need to manage media questions when politicians change their mind. From the media perspective, Paxman (2007) noted that 'one of the truly prevailing idiocies of our trade [is] that people are expected not to change their minds... changing your mind is a sign of maturity. Of course you owe it to say Mr. Smith used to believe this and he now clearly believes something else. But you shouldn't be judgmental about it, you should find out why they changed their mind.'

Parties need to be unified behind any change. Sparrow (2007) suggested that one of the weaknesses in UK Conservative strategising was not really believing in the new direction, and thus politicians might think 'I know we've got to talk about these issues that we don't feel passionate about, but we'll talk about it, and OK, we'll do that. Then they'll talk about it a bit, without too much conviction... it's kind of paying lip service to things the research tells them they ought to be passionate about, but they don't actually do it.' David Cameron's attempts to re-brand the UK Conservatives after becoming leader in 2005 had to overcome objections from the party itself. Seligman (2006) observed how 'if his shadow cabinet and backbenchers aren't seen to fully back him, the public will soon disregard his policies as nothing more than posturing.'

Get out the vote

To get the vote out, parties and politicians need to individualise the communication and use volunteers to give the message face to face. Carter (2007) described how, in the 2005 Labour campaign, they tried to make the campaign 'more personalised, more tailored, more bespoke' and 'have individual conversations with every voter on the issues they're concerned about'. Not only did they make repeated contact with voters because they understood what voters' issues were, but if 'you could connect with them and you could explain specifics to them, you were far more likely not to only win their support, we were confident of that, but actually then to persuade them to go and vote'. Ubertaccio (2008, 512–517) argued that parties can use network marketing, whereby communication is sent via personal relationships and social networks: in 2002 the US Republicans created 'a new organizational level of activism, the grassroots network, complete with upline and downline participants'. Nelson (2007), who worked on the Republican campaigns, explains how:

> The most persuasive form of communication was person to person communication. So when somebody you knew, or your neighbour, or someone who shared the same interests as you – maybe you didn't know them, but you shared the same interests that they did – contacted you about supporting the President, that kind of communication would be very impactful.

Parties use community organising to get the message out. Mehta (2009) recalled how the Democrats' neighbourhood scheme got volunteers to have in-depth real conversations with people they already knew, so that:

On Election Day it no longer was about some random stranger coming into your house asking you to vote for Obama. It was about having the guy who lives three doors down from you, the guy in your apartment building who lives upstairs who has been reading with you and discussing these issues with you and talking about the change that we want to deliver to the country coming to your door and saying 'Hey, let's go vote today. Here's our chance to do something!'

Such contact should be carried out continually, just as local candidates should ensure maximum contact. Lilleker's (2009) study of a local MP in the UK found that 'central to his representative style and his campaign was making contact with as many voters as possible.' Nelson (2007) noted that 'we needed to continue to have a dialogue with voters who were likely to vote for us, but who needed to be reminded as they got closer to the election, why it was important for them to come and vote.' The contact with core voters increased by 2004, and a postelection study showed that while in 2000 the Republicans were in contact with something like half of their voters this was increased to perhaps 70–80 per cent in 2004. However, while parties need to conduct GOTV on core voters, they should not forget that non-core voters require even more contact.

Election campaigning

Academic literature suggests practitioners need to build a range of marketing aspects into the campaign. Wring (2002, 174–180) drew together an election campaign analysis framework, drawing on the traditional 4Ps in commercial marketing, which includes consideration of the product, and the place and price as well as promotion in the campaign, together with consideration of the market and overall environment. All of these marketing aspects work together in a campaign. Practitioners argue that they need to create different activities for different phases of the campaign. Carson (2006) explained that, whereas in the beginning communication may focus on the overall strategy, brand and positioning 'towards the end of the campaign it might be much more tactical'. Evans (2006) said that 'campaigns have ribbons and life cycles. You need to seek to peak at the right time.'

In terms of focus, campaigns can alternate positive and negative messages. Borrowman (2006) explained how he alternated leaflets: 'the one that goes to everybody every fortnight is quite negative about the Conservatives, on council tax... it's a good message for our supporters and it's a good message from us to their supporters. The other week, in an envelope, with a letter in it, is a touchy feely aimed at our supporters... reporting back on grass roots issues we are dealing with.' Campaigns can also talk about the future. Collins (2006) observed how, 'in nearly all campaigns there is a party which is about the future and there is a party that is about the past. The party which talks about the future is always the winner... people vote for things... the problem with the [UK] Conservative party [in 2001 and 2005] is that they failed to establish what they stand for clearly that is positive in the eyes of most people... And Tony Blair has been good at persuading people that the government has been a forward-looking government which talks about the future.'

There are always uncontrollables and unpredictables in campaigns that throw all the best strategy off beam, despite efforts by staff who have spent months planning and know the rules of the game. Mellman (2007) explained how, in the 2004 Kerry campaign, they lost ground on the Iraq War issue because the Republican convention 'was reconvened during a major worldwide terrorism instant, where people were watching children get shot in the back in Beslan, it's like everyone's nightmare', so the Republican tough terrorism message had much more impact. While this was a random event, 'all those sort of real world dynamics were really working in Bush's favour.' As Taylor (2008) said, 'you might be pushing a great issue and the news decides to cover something breaking and your best effort didn't get a lot of play', while Fenn (2007) noted that 'campaigns are a lot of moving parts. You've got candidates, you've candidates' spouses, you've candidates' relatives, you've got people fighting for influence within the campaign. So to get everybody on the same page is like herding cats.' Reid (2009) recalled that, in the 2006 Canadian election, the RCP leaked that it was launching a criminal investigation into the government and cited the Liberal government's finance minister. This was not normal police practice and 'was an externality that was impossible to see coming, and it was vicious in its impact... Prior to that [we were] 18 points ahead in the province of Ontario which is the largest Canadian province. Three days after that letter came out, we were tied.' Thus 'some things are invulnerable to anticipation; you simply have no notion that they're going to happen.' You can react well 'but, there are instances where you can do everything right and you still don't succeed'. And, of course, the candidates are unpredictable: Mellman (2007) stated simply 'had he [Kerry] never said I voted for the 87 million dollars before I voted against it, well, we wouldn't have had that big problem. But he did.'

Advertising

Advertising is the one time you control the message. Ansell (2007) said that 'advertisements in the political system are the equivalent of lawyers in the legal system. They let a party put across its point of view. This view can be opposed, but not blocked.' Carson (2006) explained how, with other pieces of communication, the media interpretation gets in the way: 'one newspaper might pick up that speech and say it was a positive message about privatisation and say the audience lapped it up and a different reporter would say that there was a message which did not resonate with anybody and people just didn't like that message. The point about advertising is that you get precisely the message that you want to get across.' It is the one bit of marketing communications that can be planned.

As for what works, practitioners argued they could utilise negative advertising, but carefully, with humour. Ansell (2007) said he uses 'irony and humour rather than the full-on negative sledgehammer', but that arguing against the opposition 'is one of the cornerstones, indeed one of the safeguards, of the democratic system. When you don't have that argy-bargy, you have Mugabe.' Ansell wrote a song spoof *Taxathon* for the 2005 New Zealand National campaign using a popular tune called *Thank You Very Much*, which is used in television telethons. In the spoof, Labour politicians were animated and depicted as saying thank you for public money in various areas: 'the result was an effective parody of a troubled government and the various ways it wasted public money.' This highlighted areas of voter concern but was not nasty. In another example, the Australian Labor Party criticised the Liberals, depicting the last five Liberal leaders as bowling pins – 'the bowling ball ad', as Roozendaal (2008) called it. He explained how 'there was Brogden at the front, because there was quite a bit of concern over Liberals that change leaders a lot...the agency said "Well why don't you try bowling pins?" And we did...we left Brogden as a wobbly bowling pin, and it really flattered the theme that Brogden was really not suited for leadership', thus highlighting a serious theme but in a comical manner.

Advertising that clearly expresses existing views and emotions works best. Collins (2006) argued that the famous *Labour isn't working* advert was successful because it reflected the fact that there was a sense Labour was unable to fulfil its expected social contract, as the party was failing to lower unemployment: 'it was a summary of what everyone was thinking...and gave them a licence to talk about it.' It 'was part of summarizing this particular problem, what people felt and believed'. Ansell (2007) said that his 2005 ads in New Zealand worked because 'the emotiveness was just reflecting the way a lot of parents were feeling.' Advertising also needs to focus on positive future policies. Lawrence (2008) noted that, in the 2007 Australian election, 'Kevin was out there consistent in pushing future agendas', such as the Australia Day 2006 advert on education, where he said that 'the future of Australia absolutely depended upon being able to compete internationally and we couldn't do that without a serious change in our educational standards...it was all about the future.' Politicians also use advertising to reach people less interested in detail. As Ansell (2007) explains, people are 'too busy with the day-to-day problems of governing themselves and their families...they're open to persuasion by anyone who can boil down the issues for them.'

Advertising's impact is obviously contextual and limited. Ansell (2007) conceded that 'so far, my ads have won one Ad of the Year award three times in four elections. Sadly the party has only won once.' On the other hand, Reid (2009) recalled that, in the 2004 Canadian election, 'you can lay out graphically media rotations and public support...when they took out their hard hitting ads against us you could see our poll numbers dip, when we took ours out against them, you could see their numbers dip...it's incredibly powerful.' Collins (2006) conceded that 'you can have the best research, the best ideas and advertising, but if for the rest of the year, the party leader isn't delivering and speaking on message, it's difficult to know what advertising can truly achieve'. Ansell (2007) uses legal analogy to explain this:

> An ad is an advocate. It's just like a lawyer in a court – there to put the client's best foot forward. Some advocates are better than others, but the profession is neither good nor bad. In its raw form an ad is just a space. The trick is how you fill it. Can an ad persuade people to vote for a party? Of course. Can it fail to do so? Yes again.

Targeted communication

Communication should also be targeted – not just in terms of who it is sent to but what the message is. Kartch (2007) noted that US parties 'print out separate literature on specific issues and it'll be handed out in Hispanic neighbourhoods' and 'will focus on positions clearly beneficial [to them]', including positions on Castro. Thus, 'for all those Latino neighbourhoods they just emphasised social issues'. Roozendaal

(2008) described how the Australian NSW Labor Party aimed various communication at the female vote, using the candidate Bob Carr's wife to do a voice over for an advert 'done specifically for daytime TV when we know there is a high female viewing audience'. McGough (2005) illustrated how the Irish Party Sinn Fein put forward a different argument to different targets in 2002, such as promoting a picture of their voters as barely free from the chains of conflict and still enduring sectarianism and intimidation from various quarters to Northern Ireland – Nationalist Catholics who were fanatically faithful to the party – and an alternative language focused on change and responding to discontent among the working class for the second standard transferable vote (STV) of the middle classes in the Republic of Ireland who had different views. There is one caution with regard to targeting communication: avoid sending conflicting messages to different target markets. Beeson (2007) said that 'you always have to stay true to what your candidate believes. So while it may be a specific message to a specific person, it cannot contradict something you're saying to somebody else.'

Competition communication

Communication should aim to define the leader as soon as possible before the competition. The most famous example several practitioners mentioned with regard to this was how the US Republications labelled John Kerry as flip-flop in 2004. As Collins (2006) observed, 'they used it to try and create an impression of what Kerry was like before voters had actually seen that much of him.' Reid (2009) also noted that 'there was no real pre-existing frame built around John Kerry I mean, people had known him in the senate for years, and in Washington perhaps he was immediately identified as this or that, but to the broad American public – whatever, the guy was a blank slate.' In Canada, the Liberal leader Paul Martin was called Mr Dithers at the end of a small article in *The Economist* magazine, and Reid recalled how 'suddenly buckets of media in Canada are saying Paul Martin is Mr Dithers' and, unfortunately, 'that label took, then our frame had changed, and we never successfully, by the time we left office, we hadn't remedied that frame. It was deathly.' As Lawrence (2008) states, Australian Labor learnt this lesson in time for 2007:

> What the other side had always been very good at doing was kind of painting the picture of, you know, any leader we brought out,

oh, Kim Beasley, he's got no ticker or whatever. And they would immediately try to do the same thing to Rudd, so we got in first. It's a ninety second piece to camera talking about his background, his childhood and how that influenced him and why he thought education was so important. And we just got him out there. It was outside the normal political, electoral cycle.

Politicians need to use research to understand how the market actually thinks and use this to inform their competition communication. Mellman (2007), talking about Kerry in 2004, noted how 'while we argued the economy was bad, the economy was really about the, objectively, was about the same place it was when Clinton was re-elected on the economy in 1996. It wasn't so terrible.' The public's view of Iraq was not as negative as the Democrats had hoped: 'at that point we still had more than 50 percent, you know, close, but more than 50 percent saying Iraq was a good thing.'

Parties need to convey how they differentiate themselves from the competition. Robinson's (2009) case study of minor New Zealand party's 2005 campaign openings suggested that failure to differentiate meant that most of them failed to achieve their goals with regard to the party vote. Their advertising needed to show differentiation from major parties and create new policies to replace their old ones that the major parties had now co-opted. Brash (2007) explained that the impact of Ansell's adverts was due to the fact that they 'starkly highlighted the difference between Labour and National...the one on petrol tax and roads – what is your petrol tax used for? – and on the red side there was Treaty lawyers, hip hop tours, etc, and on the blue side Roads. Very simple, very stark, and words that you could see driving at high speed past these billboards.' Collins (2006) said that 'it should be the ultimate summary of what makes you different from your opponents, what is it that you want people to understand about you.' Lawrence (2008) recalled how, in the last part of the 2007 Australian Labor campaign, they focused on the theme *what's the difference between Rudd and Howard?*, partly in response to criticism of 'me too-ism, that Labour was shadowing a lot of the Liberal' policies. This meant:

> There was probably a potential latent danger that you go well, if they're just the same and their policies are the same, why not go to the experienced guy, rather than the inexperienced guy? So what we really firmed up in that last week was I will ratify Kyoto, he won't.

I will have an education revolution. Howard won't. I will look after working families. He won't. So it was really just made in the simplest possible way what you were voting for and voting against.

Receiver-responsive communication

Both academics and practitioners suggest that communication needs to be responsive to the receiver. Robinson (2006) argued that political advertising needs to be market oriented and that it should:

1. Demonstrate a sense of and response to voter needs, with images of party and/or leader interaction with target voters, including images of listening and words of togetherness.
2. Reach target voters by showing images of target audience and environment.
3. Demonstrate the party are offering something new in policy and/or leadership.
4. Identify and target the competition, showing a concern to increase market share.
5. Maintain relationships with traditional voters, through evocation of party history and myth; acknowledgement of shared characters, themes and stories, images or words of care for core supporters; other texts recognisable to core supporters.

In the 2008 New Zealand election John Key, leader of the National Party, was pictured carefully in the campaign opening. He was shown among a group of multicultural children, with various other societal groups, and talked about his family and background (Lees-Marshment 2009c, 464). In contrast, the majority of Labour's opening was 'all about Clark on Clark, telling voters why they should vote Labour, without even looking directly into the camera, and was shot in a million dollar beach house' (p. 469). Rogers (2009) recounted a story where he taught staff how to recognise the importance of relevant visuals that can reach the target audience by playing back an announcement with the sound and then without. The first time, with the sound on, everyone thought it went well:

> We thought it was a big success because we weren't impeded, we didn't emanate protesters, we knew it was good in policy, we felt we'd made a great public policy advance in reforming the welfare system we had... when I played it back, played back the television

reports, I played them with the sound, and everyone clapped and we congratulated ourselves.

However, when he played it a second time without the sound they saw things differently:

> The announcement was done in what was called the Red Room of the Nova Scotia legislature. It's a room that has received at least four monarchs upon their visits to Canada... Our welfare reform announcement was a white man in a tie behind a podium in front of a gold frame. The visual was completely dis-consonant with the substance of the message.

The wider lesson from this is keep the communication suited to voters, not to planet politics. Emotional connection with people's concerns and dreams is important. Fenn (2007) argued that 'you do it with words and you do it with symbols.... Obama is extraordinarily powerful with his politics of hope... [Bush used] no child left behind, the clear skies initiative, compassionate conservative... at least when he was campaigning in the early years.' Langmaid (2008) observed, with regard to Hillary Clinton's presidential nomination bid:

> It's interesting, about 18 months ago we sat down with Sidney Blumenthal, who's one of Hillary's advisers. And we talked to him about what we thought Hillary might learn from the Blair experience. And of course we said over and over again that emotional engagement with the consumer or voter is absolutely key... She was much more concerned to remind [voters] of the Clinton years, which she called her experience... the bigger emotional picture wasn't addressed early enough. We suggested that this was a woman who'd stuck through a difficult marriage, and therefore was emotionally qualified to take America through a difficult relationship with Iraq. Because she had been there in terms of emotional difficulty, and maintaining, trying to maintain her dignity and prestige in the face of a foolish adventure.

Communication needs to retain the right balance, however. Duncan Smith (2006) warned against using patronising phrases: 'one [mistake] was helping the vulnerable was a title I didn't like... the concept was mine and a man called Tim Montgomery. But the title was someone else's and I thought for ages it was too patronising. If you keep calling someone vulnerable when talking about helping them it sounds very patronizing.'

The nature and method of communication needs to reflect the reality of people's knowledge and consumption of politics. As Humphrey (2007) said, when communicating with the public, 'never ever assume that your audience is anywhere near or as clued up or as interested or are taught in the same manner as you are.' Communication needs to be on the receivers' terms. Ministers will ask that communications people try and get a signed ministerial article in the media, but the reality is that 'no one has ever found what the public make of this. I mean, you can persuade the newspaper to run it sometimes, but you know, do people read it?... Do they react negatively to it?' Sparrow (2007) explained how focus groups could help:

> If you could get them to go along and just sit in on focus groups and hear how ordinary people talk, that could potentially be the best education that they could get, because they would realise that people don't spend all of their time poring over political news or wondering what the latest announcement is. They get their information via something that you might call a crackly radio, you know, they hear little bits and pieces, it's incomplete, it might be a fair reflection of what they've been saying, it might be completely distorted and so on. The very few times I've seen them do it, the sheer look of horror on their faces when they finish, when they realise that actually people don't hang onto their every word.

The content of communication needs to respond to research identifying what voters care most about. As Ranger (2006) put it, 'the object of your message is to deal with the things that are on the voter's mind. So if voters are worried about hospital, schools and crime, then you need to have a platform that addresses those needs... the market research is useful in grounding us in what the public are concerned about.' Communication also needs to reflect what people already think. Collins (2006) argued that 'the "tax bombshell" stuff worked for the Tories in 1992 because people had trusted the Conservatives on the economy more than they had Labour, and they didn't believe the Labour Party economic ads. All the ads really did was confirm to people that the difference was still there' – so it didn't try to create the opinion first. Carter (2007) recalled how UK Labour in 2005 ran on the slogan *Britain Forward Not Back* 'because we felt confident that we were still a party that was connected with the future in people's minds. When they saw Labour and then saw the Prime Minister Tony Blair they connected us with the issue to change the country in a positive way' and thus believed that supporting the Tories under Michael Howard might mean going back to failed Conservatism.

Another aspect of receiver-responsive communication is that it is two way and can be used to develop a relationship with the public. Borrowman (2006) said that 'the things that make us successful are if we enter into a dialogue with people, so we're asking them what they're concerned about, and we're then feeding back to them what we're doing about it and you stay open to two way dialogue to them. But it goes wrong if we started treating our infamous focus leaflets as gospel from high.' Jackson and Lilleker (2004, 512–514) explored how public relations can be used by local MPs in a symmetrical (two-way) or asymmetrical (one-way) manner. MPs often fall into the trap of only putting out asymmetrical communication and therefore failing to listen to and engage the public. However, they can choose to respond to feedback and build a positive long-term relationship with voters to help wither the usual crisis and storms that all elected officials face.

The public also generates its own political media, which enables the audience to be a participant partner. Mehta (2007) linked this to the increase in online communication where users generate the content themselves to suit themselves. He noted how 'Al Gore won an Emmy award because he created this new television station that's founded on the principle that it should be user created content. Rather than some TV studio in Los Angeles creating the content, let's let the people create it, because ultimately they're the ones that are going to watch it, let them create the content they're going to watch. And it's become hugely popular.' This relates to e-marketing, an online form of communication that should also be created to suit the receiver.

E-marketing

Atkinson and Leigh (2003) note how e-communication should focus on the needs of citizens/customers, use information and offer transactions with government that people want, rather than information the government wants them to have, be organised around the citizen's needs and allow interaction with government at a time and place to suit the consumer. Jackson (2009) argues, however, that, from empirical research, 'MPs appear to be ignoring the advice of e-marketers to view their website from the perspective of the visitor.' There has to be thinking behind the communication and interactive behaviour for this to work. Social networking, online communication or e-marketing has received substantial attention since it was used by Howard Dean in 2004 and then by Obama in 2008. This has been a big change, with Stanzel (2007) commenting how President George W. Bush had his first meeting with bloggers in September 2007 to talk about the new strategy in Iraq: 'there's a whole new constituency of people who are communicating out to an audience, whether or not you think they are a member of the media, they are communicating to an audience that they have and they can shape opinion, so it's important for us to engage those people as well.' A whole range of communication can now be carried out electronically.

Electronic direct marketing provides a high-yielding, low-cost method of voter contact. Lees-Marshment (2009a) observed that, in the US 2008 presidential nomination campaign, anyone who signed up as a supporter or interested party to the Obama site received regular e-mails asking for both support and donations. Often the attention-seeking element of direct marketing was utilised well, with recipients being asked to donate by a certain time to allow Obama to stop fundraising for one day, or before some other deadline. These e-mails used emotional appeals, such as one sent from his wife, asking for donations to give her husband more time to work on campaigning rather than fundraising.

Internet advertisements that pop up when the public is browsing are designed not just to reach them but they are tailored to the recipient in terms of content and time. Krohn (2009) felt that there was greater certainty that such communication would reach the voter, as it clicks in when they go online, whereas 'there's no assurance that when you purchase a television ad that the individual is viewing it, because they're either flipping the channels or getting up off the sofa, there's no assurance that when you send a piece of direct mail that it's going to be read'. He recalled how, in 'November 2008, leading right up to Election Day, one dollar – you could purchase three pieces of direct mail, 25 automated phone calls, 62 television impressions, or 142 internet impressions', so the RNC were able to increase voter contact at low cost. They were also able to gather market analysis at the same time:

> [In 2007] we had done the database with the voter file and publishers to identify voters by party affiliation across major publishers like AOL, Yahoo, Microsoft, and we saw some very positive results from those programmes in terms of click through and people clinking

on an ad, and then filling out a form and then providing us with better data because they had a particular inquiry, such as they were trying to find their polling station, and we found that we were able to track those users' behaviour in ways that we hadn't done previously.

The internet also offers virtual micro-targeting, GOTV and door to door. Krohn (2007) argues that 'the internet is the best medium to facilitate micro targeting, because of the amount of information you can extract from the web in terms of user behaviour, user geography, day parting, delivering multiple messages to multiple people at multiple times or maybe even simultaneously.' Internet targeting can be more precise and less presumptive. Krohn (2009) argued that 'you're going to be able to find people more readily with similar interests based on the types of content that they consume... their public profiles – that type of information. That's really what we're talking about when you talk about cloud computing and web 3.0.' Internet segmentation would pick up information based on browsing behaviour such as 'the types of articles I tag, or stories I read, or information I store', which might be less presumptive than assumptions made for TV or magazine advertising.

The internet could also enable the candidate to appear visually, which would also get over people's discomfort with having a stranger knocking on the door. As Noble (2009) observed, 'facebook, twitter, viral emails etc are all these techniques where you're actually face-to-face with a person in the privacy of their home or their Blackberry or whatever... people don't have any interest in some stranger coming to their house, invading their home time... so you've got to find new ways in which they're comfortable receiving information.' Audio-visual communication which can be seen by everyone is increasingly dominant now and can be used by individual politicians. Robertson (2008) described how they put videos online for his local campaign to be elected an MP, 'so that if you just Google me or put me into YouTube you'll come up with all my videos'. Krohn (2007) predicted that they would be able to take 'the human component' out of door-knocking, which is very resource intensive and is reliant on volunteers.

E-marketing can also be mobile, both in terms of delivery and in matching the message to what the receiver is doing and where they are doing it. Krohn (2007) explained that the US Republicans 'look at a mobile voter now, not a voter sitting inside a residence', and at reaching people 'anywhere, anytime, any device':

With a GPS enabled device you could deliver a targeted political message so succinctly that... wherever the individual is, there is a political issue that correlates to that geographic location... can reach that individual at the time on that issue when you know they care about it. I can reach a potential voter when they're on a webpage that pertains to financial matters at 5 o'clock on a Friday payday, about a tax message when they're looking at how much money has been taken out of their pay check for taxes. And that's a moment in time where an issue resonates... you're in a lobby of a physician's office and a healthcare issue comes up when you're waiting for the physician to see you and you've read all the magazines in the waiting area and all of a sudden you've got that component. So the implications are profound.

The trick with mobile marketing, as with other forms, will be to ensure voters are not overburdened with communication and to identify what will be most effective. Mylona (2008) notes how mobile phones and SMS could add to the public sphere (see also Prete 2007, 48), but practice so far has lacked interactivity and dialogue and has been purely one way. The RNC did enjoy some success with mobile communication: 'we targeted Spanish-only advertising on mobile devices to Latinos in Colorado, New Mexico, and Florida. The response rates were phenomenal. The individual would see an ad on their mobile device and it would take them to a WAP page on their mobile device' (Krohn 2009).

Like all marketing tools, the use of technology cannot guarantee success. Middleton (2009) discussed how Act 'seize[d] on the internet as a channel for delivering the party's message' and e-newsletters and the party website were used between elections to run a permanent campaign on a relatively low budget. They invested in a Customer Relationship Management database, customised it and used it to target voters in increasingly complex ways. This couldn't offset losing voters when the major party, National, re-positioned itself and attracted their supporters. The lessons from this were that 'as campaigns in the USA – notably the presidential primary campaigns of Howard Dean and Ron Paul – have suggested, technology empowers large-scale and low-cost direct communication campaigns.' However, in this case, it 'was not sufficient to sustainably direct voter behaviour' and, therefore, 'while technology makes it possible to run large campaigns effectively to niche audiences at low cost, it is not a sufficient condition for electoral success.' Instead, technology needs to be part of an overall marketing approach, and even by itself effective e-marketing requires a holistic/integrated communications approach. Jackson (2009) argued that e-marketing needs to be comprehensive: 'MPs should not just dip in and out of those bits of e-marketing they like or understand.'

When Krohn was asked what worked best in his work, he suggested experimenting with e-marketing. The speed of change is fast, and e-marketers need to think more broadly about the implications of technological change for other parts of marketing communications. Krohn (2007) noted how some elements of campaigning still followed very traditional formats which had always worked, but technology would potentially upset this as it would affect the way people read and consumed information about politics: 'I look at things like requesting absentee ballots and voter registration and get out the vote efforts and phone banking, and look at it and think all this is going to change.'

There is also a potential effect on participation. As noted in Chapter 4 on the party, e-marketing can help attract supporters and facilitate face-to-face activity. Stirland (2008) explains how the Obama campaign had this effect because the tools 'enabled a wide spectrum of volunteers all over the country to get together in self-organized groups to help their candidate'. He quoted Ian Davis, another Obama supporter and community organiser in Austin, as saying 'this technology encourages... community members to network, and to do all of the old-fashioned organizing that we would never otherwise have had the time or resources to manage.'

The broader potential of e-marketing lies in creating a dialogue and relationship between political elites and the public. Mehta (2007) argued that the point of Howard Dean's presidential nomination bid in 2004 was that 'he changed politics from being a one-way conversation to being a two-way conversation.' Other communication forms tend to focus on 'the campaign, the candidate, the volunteers and their surrogates talking to the voters. But what Dean realised is the voters would like to talk back. The voters would like to say something to us too.' Blogs, discussions and online debates give them that opportunity. Mehta (2007) explains:

> I remember my boss, Joe Trippie, who was a campaign manager, would sit in his office till 3, 4 in the morning and he'd be reading these blogs and I'd be like what are you doing? He'd be like I'm reading what these people are saying. I'm like don't read that stuff, there's crazy people out there. He said Parag, read this stuff, their ideas are brilliant. The best ideas we came up with in that campaign were never

from the staff, never from Governor Dean. It was what we read on the blogs. The ideas the voters were giving us on messaging, organising, strategy, tactics, fundraising, they had brilliant ideas.

As a politician, Green (2006) noted how even email alone had helped create such a dialogue: 'people will e-mail their MP, email makes it very easy for them to email you, it's on the website or whatever and you develop a dialogue, you develop conversations, which you couldn't do if you were just writing a letter. So it makes it more two-way.' Jackson's (2005, 159 and 2006) research found that websites can be used for long-term communication, offering a combination of direct marketing and relationship marketing, rather than just being used in short-term sales campaigning and one-off transactions. It enables elites to build up a long-term relationship with voters if they use it effectively, as Jackson (2005, 95) suggests. They need to use it continually, not just in a campaign; make sure it suits the receiver; and allow two-way not just one-way communication to build networks between an MP and their constituents. Carson (2006) observed that, because of the internet, 'you can often make some of the relationships and actually have a dialogue over the longer period of time.'

Authentic communication

Contrary to what might be expected, communication needs to be authentic and align with the candidate's behaviour. Bryan Gould (2007) said, 'you can only present successfully when you're reflecting your substance.' Collins (2006) said that 'the job of the advertising is to move the perception of the brand on, but the organisation has got to support what the advertising is saying... Peter Mandelson has mentioned this recently in interviews about his time as Labour's director of communications when he brought in the red rose and got rid of the red flag and did various things to improve the overall image of the Labour Party. But the policy issues the party struggled with were still there... if you want to use advertising to move the perception on of the party on it's got to be linked to things true about it.'

Negative or attack communication also has to be credible. Hyder (2009) observed of Hillary Clinton's presidential nomination campaign negative ad – the 3am phone call – that it 'took a role of the dice on a high-risk opposition and said "Who do you want answering the phone at 3AM?"', but backfired as people realised that they didn't have any issue with Obama answering the 3am phone call after all. Therefore, advertising 'has to be compelling, and it has to have a merit of truth to it'. Carson (2006) said 'the rule you should use for that is that it has to be fair. So in other words if I said you're a liar and you're corrupt and you're my opponent, then you need to know that enough people believe that or agree with that, otherwise it won't work.' Reid (2009) recalled how the Canadian Liberals were fortunate that when they used negative attack ads on Harper in the 2004 campaign they 'got lucky because you got that perfect world where your advertising and your paid media and your earned media moved into harmony. Because, just when we were saying shitty things about Harper, he started making a couple of mistakes that made him look like he was shitty.'

False or unbelievable claims backfire. As Hyder (2009) observed, 'you look at the Dukakis thing and the Willy Horton ad – it stuck right? That stuck with George Bush Senior as branding Michael as soft on crime. It worked beautifully. People had their doubts, and Dukakis got slaughtered. On the other hand, Clinton was able to make effective use of George Bush Senior's commitment to read-my-lips, right? Or, more taxes, and the Democrats were able to make effective use of that...there has to be an element of truth to it. If what you are saying is untrue, then it won't work.' Hyder gave, as an example, the time when the Canadian Conservatives tried to brand Stephan Dion as a poor leader with a website, www.notaleader.ca:

> Not-a-leader works against somebody only works if it's true.... if he starts acting like a leader, behaves like a leader, and is a leader, you can say all you like 'He's not a leader.' But, the people won't believe it, right? Any more than the people believed – the Liberal government here ran ads against the Conservative Party saying 'These guys will put soldiers in the street. They're like militia. They're like the right-wing militia. They'll run every part of our lives. They're like fascists.' Canadians said 'Rubbish. We don't believe for one second that these guys are going to put soldiers in the streets.' There was no plausibility.

Positive communication about the leader/candidate also has to be authentic. Ulm (2007) noted how 'voters smell bullshit a mile away...you can fool people for a short period of time. But by Election Day they figure it out.' Advisors have to take this into account. Callingham (2009) noted how 'Geoffrey Palmer was a brilliant man [who] came across dreadfully on television...they told him that you should be more friendly and animated so he ended up looking like the Eagle in the Muppets!' It can't be over-designed. Carson (2006) observed that, in 1999, the National Party tried to show how its team were 'real Kiwis who were involved in family and sport and their children's education...Jenny Shipley did this thing where she's on the lawn, in the garden, talked about being a mother. Actually she was going like this, she was talking about being a mother as if she was holding her breasts. I'm a mother kind of thing. And that was a deliberate thing to kind of say the other one's [Helen Clark's] not a mother, you know. But the execution of it didn't work in part because they made it so unreal.' As Lees-Marshment (2008) observed, the UK Conservatives brought in a former newspaper journalist with the *Sunday Express*, Amanda Platell, in March 1999, to help re-vamp Hague's image using communication aimed at less Westminster-based outlets, such as magazines, and towards young people. The party also used new-style party election broadcasts in the 1999 European elections, including the so-called 'Chris and Debbie' broadcast, which had a young couple in their IKEA kitchen discussing the issue. However, such communication attracted ridicule.

As Edwards (2009) said, 'make-overs are potentially very hazardous. The only make-over that works is the make-over that you barely notice.' Communication has to reflect the nature of the politician. This is different to commerce – 'you don't judge whether the Coke campaigns were good on the basis of the chief executive of Coke' (Collins 2006) – but, for example, as Ranger (2006) explained in relation to the former UK Lib Dem leader, 'you couldn't really do much negative stuff with Charles Kennedy, because that was not the image of his wider persona.'

Managing internal relationships

Marketing communications involves a range of political actors including volunteers, staff, candidates, politicians, government staff and journalists. They have divergent and at times competing interests but need each other to succeed. Carter (2007) explained that 'politics is a pluralistic business, that it involves lots of different interests, even within one party. Lots of different interests, and stakeholders.' It isn't a monolithic organisation with just one view, and thus 'how campaigns are shaped, where decisions are taken, how these things are put into practice' is much more complex. Internal communication is important to maintain unity. Smith, M. (2006) argued that 'we've got a plan that we want to implement and we're going around marketing it internally. We start with the caucus, then the electorate committees, then the sector groups and out and about and give everybody opportunity and options for them to pick up so they will do what they can do to fit into the plan.'

He also noted that when the party is in government it was particularly important to explain slower progress on policy to internal market:

> Helen's been very good at creating a sense of incremental change in the direction that people want. For example when the Engineers' Union worked for four week holidays to be introduced into law, well, she wasn't going to do it in the first term of the government because they were going to change the Employment Contracts Act so it became an election promise for the second term, which was legislated for then and implemented in the third term. So people can see we're on a track to get it done and that takes the heat it out of the agitation.

Staff in parties, government and campaigns need effective management. Jones (2008) recalled how, under Howard, there were a range of individuals all trying to influence the party leader, and there was no leadership of staff until Lynton Crosby came to take over. Crosby gave people a sense of direction and vision: he ensured there 'was someone providing internal leadership...the majority of people I worked with in the Conservative party were people who were like me, focused on fixing the brand, fixing the party, getting on with the job and trying to do something to get elected. And for them it was like oxygen.' Nelson (2007) criticised McCain's use of committees, as did Mellman of Kerry's: 'everything has to be done by committee up to a point, there's no dictators in these operations, but it should be a very sort of coherent, consistent strategy and campaign and that was less evident' (Mellman 2007). Successful campaigns communicate effectively internally as well as externally: Lawrence (2008) said of Rudd/Labor 2007, 'one of the reasons for the success of the campaign I think was that you had this great virtuous circle of learning and communications, and forming a virtuous circle...the ability for information to come in, be analysed and go around that group was pretty much instant.' Similarly, on the Bush 2004 campaign, 'everybody had worked together' before so 'you weren't kind of building relationships from scratch, and that make a big difference in any operation like that where it's very intense and very stressful.'

Within party organisation, the centre party organisation needs to make marketing resources available to local parties, candidates and leaders. Chalupa (2007) observed how the DNC planned early to build up organisational resources that the presidential nominee could then use, and they communicated better with nominees about what they had to offer, so there was 'a lot of communication that's being had right now between like the political director in all the campaigns to let them know at every step of the process what we're building and report back', which of course helped Obama in 2008. The plan was designed to correct the problems of 2004 when, as Chalupa described, she went down to Florida and found volunteers building a new Voter Protection Program in Florida, even though the DNC headquarters had already done it: 'they knew nothing about what the DNC was doing, they had no idea we had a headquarters list.' She found the same with the student co-ordinator there as he had not been given the DNC's student list: 'we were able to get the list through another method and send it down and he was like "oh my gosh," it's like Christmas for him, you know; but it was happening all the way around the country. And it was a complete mess...from the Voter Protection to that component, to everything else, it was actually quite shocking, considering that was Florida too and what had happened in the last presidential cycle for that state.'

Local and individual communication needs to fit within the overall party brand. Marland's (2009) research also argued that 'federal election candidates in Canada are encouraged by the central headquarters to promote all things party – the leader, the label, the manifesto, the key messages, the overall brand – regardless of local electors' viewpoints', while Mehta (2007) discussed how the DNC trained activists to get the phrase 'a new direction' into normal conversation so that this would then tie in with federal-level advertising:

> So I go to my neighbour and say I'm supporting Jim Webb...he's a Democrat running for US Senate, because he's the kind of leadership we need in the US Senate, he's a war veteran of the Vietnam War, his son is in Iraq, he's a Democrat, he served under Ronald Reagan, but he realises we need a new direction, that's why he's a Democrat, that's why I'm supporting him. I slip in that phrase, because if they hear nothing else, I want the voter to hear me say the phrase a new direction, because when they turn on their TV and they see our ad, we're going to use the phrase A New Direction for America. And when they open their newspaper they are going to see our newspaper ad that says A New Direction. They're going to see a billboard on a highway that says Democrats Fighting for a New Direction. So over, an echo-chamber, their neighbour says it, the TV says it, the radio says, the newspaper says it, the billboard says it. They hear it again and again and again. So eventually, after the hundredth time, it finally slips into their brain, hey, I know what the Democrats stand for, they stand for a new direction.

However, Lilleker and Negrine (2002) argued that national parties need to allow for locally divergent and relevant campaigns; as Lilleker (2009) explained, 'a central tenet of good marketing communication is to make the message relevant to people's lives, connect to their fears and aspirations and offer something that they desire.' Carter (2007) explained that 'people are seeing campaigning as a much more devolved process', not least because:

> It's no good me deciding in London that perhaps the message was going to be this, that jobs whatever, and producing 50 million leaflets to be distributed around the country. Our materials needed to reflect what was going to motivate and mobilise you to go and vote, maybe an issue that's peculiar and specific to your community and we needed to be able to build a campaign that allowed people to use their stories as a way of illustrating the bigger picture.

Governing parties can also use MPs and local party organisation to help communicate leaders' positions and progress in government. Pleasants (2009) noted how they supplied 'a skeleton local statement and fed in the local data', and then asked MPs to adapt it further to individualise it to suit their interests and views, making it clear they had the freedom to change the wording and use it in verbal rather than written communication if they wanted: 'a lot of the Maori MPs, for example, prefer to use the statements and the backup data that I would supply as the basis for a telephone conversation with relevant local media. Relevant Maori MPs are more keen on feel-good communications than media relations.' Government communication staff also made suggestions about further opportunities MPs might want to organise their communication around. Parties have to try to get the balance right between locally relevant communication, and ensuring it fits the overall brand. Borrowman (2006) said that 'candidates are quite accepting in the main to getting "look, these are core messages so please don't change them" but be free to change other things.'

Managing the media relationship

A strong theme that emerged from the interviews with practitioners was that political elites need to maintain a respectful dialogue and relationship with the media. As Scard (2008) said, 'it's a marriage of convenience.' Thus, although politicians and their staff want to use the media to achieve particular goals, they are also constrained and cannot control the media. Stanzel (2007) said, 'my credibility is very important to reporters and it's very important to me. So presenting accurate information that they can rely on...is very important to the relationship that I have with reporters.' If there is no trust there is no influence. Griffin (2006) said that 'spin works only if the person carrying the message is respected.' As Armstrong (2006) said, 'those relationships are built up slowly over a period of time', and Tyson (2008) explained, 'the more you develop that rapport and relationship, the more they're going to accept you at face value.' Each helps the other. Stanzel (2007) said, 'we serve 2 masters. We serve, obviously serve the President, we want to put the President's policies and positions in the best possible light for reporters and therefore for the public, and it's our effort and our job to communicate those policies, but we also serve the media.' Thus the amount of influence political elites can exert over the media is debatable. Munro (2006) said that 'you have to be careful that you don't abuse that power you do have over information and you must remember that at the end of the day politicians need the media and they need a good relationship with the media to get their stories across and get their message across.'

The other aspect to this relationship is that the nature of the media – both their democratic obligations to question and scrutinise elites as well as potential weaknesses, such as negativity – creates obstacles for political marketing. As Temple (2010, 268–269) noted, 'politicians can tell voters that they have delivered, but the role of the Fourth Estate is to scrutinize such claims.' Paxman (2007) claimed 'you should be, you should be prickly and difficult and original.' As Inglish (2007) said, 'we'd all be massively the poorer if we didn't have the Paxmans and the Humphrys of this world....They are asking the questions that an awful lot of people in the real world want to know the answers to, and those are questions like why is my local hospital being shut? Why are my kids' schools not getting better test results?'

However, the lack of balance, and bias towards the negative, creates specific barriers to political marketing. It's hard to communicate a changed product (party, candidate, leader) through the media. Duncan Smith (2006) observed, with regard to the UK Conservatives 1997–2001, how 'William at first tried to make some changes but ran up very hard against the party and also the media, because there was a media expectation of who the Conservative party should be and it is hard to change that – at least immediately.' The media's negative bias towards negativity makes it difficult to convey delivery progress or for voters to give the government credit for this. Munro (2006) remarked that 'it's a constant struggle to keep the media focused on your positive announcements.' The problem for delivery is that, as Campbell (2005) said, 'once it's worked, it's not interesting' and, furthermore, 'the media deliberately obstruct the link between government and hospitals/NHS.' Blumenthal (2007) recalled how, after 1996, 'Clinton then pursued many, many positive programs, but the press was still interested in scandals.' Riddell (2006) remembered that 'in *The Times* we questioned the populace as to their experiences of government services like health and education and they tended to be a positive. But they think that they're the lucky one, because reading the *Daily Mail*/tabloids it said the health service is awful.'

As Byrne (2006) said, 'now do I undermine trust in politicians and public institutions? Yes I do, and so I should – it's my job.' However, Inglish (2007) said, 'I genuinely don't have this view that politicians are corrupt or liars or lazy or incompetent. The politicians I meet are extraordinarily committed, thoughtful people who work very hard and have gone into it because they believe that they have something to contribute to public life.' Coverage is not universally negative. Armstrong (2006) said, 'it is incredibly annoying when academics say the media are always negative, when they make that blanket observation, when we can point to 6 or 7 news stories that we haven't covered.' In relation to his own famous, aggressive interviews, Paxman (2007) said, 'you're talking about a tiny minority of interviews.'

The media themselves admit there is the need for a balance: Butler (2006) remarked that 'we don't treat them like they're God's gift, but we don't treat them as criminals either.' The politician and journalist need not be in opposing roles. When asked *is there anything that you'd like to see changed?* Paxman (2007) said, 'while politicians are of course coming in there to persuade the public they're good, sound, confident, trustworthy people with coherent, intelligent policies, the journalist's often there to demonstrate quite the reverse, that they're charlatans who can't be trusted. I don't think that's really terribly productive.' However, journalists do not see their job as being one where they have to convey a positive – or at least balanced – assessment of government performance. As Butler (2006) explained:

> I don't know how you could construct news that people would want to consume that said everybody's doing a good job today...if you filled the six o'clock news with "everyone met their targets this year" people wouldn't watch the six o'clock News.

Consequently, political elites need to use as many different forms and mediums of communication over the long term to try to get their message out.

Communication advisors and clients

As with market analysis and leaders, the relationship between advisors on communication and their clients is important to success. The consensus among practitioners was that advertisers should work for a product they believe in. Ansell (2007) recalled how he ended up doing the advertising for Labour in 1993, even though he hadn't wanted to, and 'that was when I realised that it's no good advertising a product you don't believe in... your great ideas come from living and breathing the product, and it's hard to live and breathe something you're not sold on'. Lawrence (2008), creative strategist for Rudd in 2007, said that while it was possible to be neutral when developing advertisements for commercial goods in politics 'this isn't just applying one's technical expertise, as you would do on a can of soup; I think it's very different.'

In the area of communication, different staff, inside and outside the government/party/campaign, from media, policy, press secretary, leaders personal office, party and so on need to work together. In particular there is a strong link between policy and communication. Reid (2009) commented that 'the best communications directors are people who can hold their own at any policy table, and I actually think that the best policy people are folks that have a some horse sense for communications considerations.' Ansell (2007) said that the 2005 National Party campaign manager, Steven Joyce, was capable because of his ability to see the different perspectives of several roles: 'he was able to see things from all four points of view – the writer's, the politicians', the party's and the public's.'

As with market research, politicians need to give communication advisors room to do their job properly. Ansell (2007) recalled how he had felt he had complete freedom to do this in 2005 with the National Party but later found this was due to National's general/campaign manager Steve Joyce doing the internal selling: 'I thought the billboards and so on sailed through without any objection. Not so apparently! Steven told me at the function when we were picking up the NBR Campaign of the Year Award that he had to fight pretty hard to get some of those winning ideas through the team.' However, advisors should not have too much influence; Scammell (1995), Kavanagh (1995, 91) and Wring (2005a) all observed the increased use of professionals in UK parties from the 1970s onwards. Sackman (1996, 147–149) noted that there was a problem with a 'highly centralized system of market research, where both the commissioning of work, and its interpretation revolved around a small and unaccountable collection of professionals'. Advisors themselves said it is ideal if politicians have already done the analysis and are able to brief the advertiser. Ansell (2007) said the ideal client has done the research, knows what the message is, what the benefits are to potential consumers and who those consumers are. However, 'most creative briefs we copywriters get in advertising are neither creative nor brief. So we end up spending at least half the job trying to figure out what to say and to whom', which loses time and makes it harder to produce highly focused work.

Advisors also need effective access to the decision-makers to be effective. Ansell (2007) said that if there are too many people between communication staff and the key people, 'this restricts the chances of being able to capture the essence of the leader and the party.' Collins (2006) explained how 'in politics...there's a danger of vast committees of people involved in the decision-making. The chairman of the party, chairman of the electorate, the chief of staff.' Carson (2006) explains that parties are like the mafia:

> When you're dealing with a business you've got a hierarchical structure where you've a CEO say, and a board, and you've got an executive making decisions and so on based on a strategy. A definition of a strategy might be that it is something everybody in the organisation agrees with, that it exists in writing and that once agreed that's what they'll do. But a political party doesn't work that way... political parties are made up of separate agendas, there's many politicians that you've got, there's many agendas that you've got. And they only coalesce together in a party as long as the collective direction serves enough of their individual needs. So people will break ranks pretty easily if it doesn't look like the party's going to go in the direction that's going to get them elected... the person who's the godfather or the godmother is probably going to get a bullet in the neck from their own party before they get something from the opposition.

To help this process, good practice is to develop a relationship of trust between client and advertiser. Collins (2006) said that 'as relationships develop you get to work with each other and trust each other. You need time to build up a relationship where they're prepared to accept the advertising organisation's creativity and ideas.'

Summary

Communication is multi-varied and involves utilising many other aspects of marketing, including strategy and market analysis, to make the communication effective and suitable for the receiver. Communication is not a fail-safe tool by itself; it needs to be well researched, fit with the overall product and also be believable and authentic. As the rules summarised in Table 5.1 suggest, using marketing communication to achieve certain goals involves a range of organisations and individuals and is thus a heavily relationship-based activity. Successful campaigns and communication tend to occur when there are effective internal relationships with a clear strategy.

Table 5.1 Rules of the game for communicating

Strategy and communication
1. Ensure there is time to think strategically about communication and campaigning
2. Know and stick to your strategy
3. Don't get bogged down in the daily news cycle/planet politics/following the pack

Communicating complex policy
4. Communication needs to be simple with only 2/3 messages repeated
5. Keep detail for the experts
6. Online media offer more detail, substance, room for discussion and interactivity
7. Find a way to explain complicated issues

Selling policy
8. Use market analysis to help devise communication to change public opinion
9. Use marketing to help sell government policy and change opinion by conducting market analysis and getting the communication right to suit the market

Communicating a leader
10. Media advisors can help present a politician more effectively and overcome common barriers and biases in public opinion
11. Make popular leaders centre of the campaign; put less popular ones in the background

Table 5.1 (Continued)

12. Be the first to use communication to define a candidate, whether yours or the opposition's
13. Communicate leaders' skills
14. Re-present or re-launch a leader
15. Use one clear central vision which reflects the candidate's personality
16. Make sure the communication has an emotional connection with people
17. Use market analysis to inform communication of unpopular decisions

Communicating product change or re-positioning

18. Use unconventional, fresh or new style, colours, label, hinge or logos to convey change
19. Start early if you want to communicate re-positioning
20. Maintain unity if you want to communicate party has changed
21. Make sure communication fits the strategy, and is strategic
22. Prepare to answer media questions following a change in position
23. Maintain unity to convey the change

Get out the vote

24. Get people talking to their neighbours over a long period outwith campaigns
25. Individualise the communication as much as possible
26. Ask volunteers to use word of mouth, face-to-face contact
27. Conduct GOTV on non-core voters too
28. Direct marketing can be used in many forms, including mail/DVDs, direct telemarketing, and not just in campaigns but to boost membership and fundraise

Election campaigning

29. Campaigns are the one time the public may listen
30. Create a new campaign for each election and situation
31. Create different marketing activities for different phases of the campaign
32. Alternate positive and negative messages

Advertising

33. Advertising is the one time you control the message
34. Utilise negative advertising, but carefully, with humour
35. Reinforce views by using advertising that simply and clearly expresses existing views and emotions
36. Use advertising to reach people less interested in detail
37. Use advertising to communicate your distinctiveness from competitors

Targeted communication

38. Target communication in terms of medium and message
39. But avoid sending conflicting messages to different target markets

Competition communication

40. Moderate politicians' inevitable desire for attacking the opposition, as they may not be as unpopular as is assumed
41. Define yourself before the competition defines you

42. Propose an alternative product
43. Rebut attack

Receiver-responsive communication
44. Use voter-driven communication with visuals that respond to voters
45. Make sure it connects with and is relevant to ordinary people
46. Make sure it responds to the reality of how people get their info from politics/levels of interest/knowledge, even if this isn't what political elites expect
47. Focus on what voters care most about, as identified by research
48. Convey responsiveness
49. Use two-way communication to develop a relationship with the public and make them a participant partner not a passive one

E-marketing
50. Ensure the leadership involves and supports e-marketing staff
51. Use technological not political people and experiment with new ideas
52. Use the internet as a high-yielding, low-cost method of voter contact
53. Engage in virtual micro-targeting, and GOTV and door to door
54. Utilise audio-visual communication
55. Use mobile marketing to respond to where a person is and what they're doing as well as what they want
56. Effective e-marketing requires holistic/integrated communications approach to create a dialogue and relationship between political elites and the public

Authentic communication
57. Advertising has to align with candidates' behaviour
58. Negative or attack communication has to be credible
59. Make sure communication about the leader is authentic and reflects the nature of the politician

Managing internal relationships
60. Parties are not monolithic organisations and need effective management
61. Use effective internal communication to explain policy decisions and progress, especially in government
62. Staff involved in campaigns/the party/government need to be managed for them to be effective
63. Central/local, party/candidate organisations need to work together to maximise resources
64. Ensure balance between unity of the brand at central/local level leaves enough room for local adaptation
65. Utilise lower level party organisation to help communicate leader's position and progress in government

Managing relationships with the media
66. Maintain a respectful dialogue and relationship with the media
67. Utilise different forms of communication over long periods to overcome media barriers to communicating product change and delivery

Table 5.1 (Continued)

Communication advisors and clients
68. Advertisers should work for a product they believe in
69. Advisors should be independent but not have too much power
70. Ensure consultants have effective access to decision-makers in the party or campaign
71. Brief the advertiser effectively on communication goals, target and strategy
72. Communication staff need to work with other staff, such as those in policy

6
Managing Delivery

> I never have a conversation with a government now when they are not worrying about how to improve delivery.
> —Barber (2007)

> Nowadays an effective politician is someone who is good at getting stuff done, and also good at making sure people know that they're getting stuff done.
> —Clelland-Stokes (2009)

> It's important to keep the language of delivery in the mindset of the politicians and their staff.
> —Keneally (2008)

Political marketing in power is different to marketing to get into power. Firstly, political marketing by parties in opposition can only ever be hypothetical to a degree, whereas in government everything changes: the product has to become a reality and be delivered. Secondly, while many aspects of political marketing are used in politics regardless of whether a politician or party is in opposition or in power, once elected, the nature of government impacts on strategy. This chapter will discuss the importance of delivery, pre-election delivery, delivery strategy, making delivery happen, managing failures in delivery, communicating delivery and public evaluation of delivery.

The importance of delivery

Governments have begun to create specialised units to focus on delivery: Blair established the Downing Street Delivery Unit; Howard, the Cabinet Implementation Unit; and NSW created the Premier's Delivery Unit. As Hamburger (2006) wrote, 'it is no longer enough for those advocating major policy to have a good idea...the Government demands that that we think through our ideas and how they are going to be implemented.' Barber (2007), head of the first delivery unit in the UK, said that 'people want ever improving performance from their public services but they don't want to pay more and more money for them, that amount of money available is capped but the expectations are rising which again drives you down the delivery route.' Lees-Marshment (2001 and 2008, 28) argued that delivery is key to the long-term success of political marketing for both major and minor parties; even parties in coalition need to show the difference their part in government has made and give voters a reason to continue their support. As Lloyd (2005) argued, delivery is one of 'the tangible ways by which electors judge the performance of political parties.' Delivery success affects public support and re-election. This is true of all levels of government. As Borrowman (2006) said, 'unfortunately we have a bit of a legacy which is for the few years the Liberal Democrats did jointly control it we did lop council tax up, even though all parties were putting tax up at this time...we got tarred to some extent with that brush.'

It is not just the product that has to deliver, but the brand. Needham (2005) argues that for parties to maintain successful brands they need to be credible by delivering on promises. Cosgrove (2007) also maintained that 'branding requires promises to be kept and highly visible policy and personal failures to be avoided at all costs.' White and de Chernatony (2002, 50) argue that the UK New Labour brand 'came to be devalued when some of the important promises made were not delivered'. The brand promise in 1997 had been vague, 'aimed to reassure, to allay fears and to convince the electorate that Labour would provide a new kind of government'. Despite effective communication, the difference between government talk and public perception of reality created negative feelings towards the whole brand. Cosgrove (2009) contends that George W. Bush's brand failed in the end because of several factors (e.g. the war in Iraq, failure to find Osama bin Laden, problematic response to Hurricane Katrina), which 'led the public to feel that promises made were not promises kept...brand promises must be kept or else disaster can ensue'. Obama capitalised on this in 2008, but will also face the same need to deliver in the future: 'offering people hope and change will be a daunting promise for any branded candidate to deliver in the real world.' Similarly, a candidates' delivery reputation is affected by the party. Kotzaivazoglou (2009) observed that with an individual candidate 'his/her personal delivery is, however, usually influenced by that of his/her party. Poor party performance can have a negative effect on his/her own actions and image and lead to voter dissatisfaction', which makes it hard for candidates to respond effectively to the public.

Elected candidates and parties need to make delivery a priority. As Brodie (2009) recalled of the first Harper/Canadian Conservative government, people were surprised how quickly they delivered key promises. This was because they had worked out what 'what we wanted to do if we were elected, all that investment had been done in advance of the election campaign... and as a result people had their marching orders'. They achieved four of their key promises very quickly and it was 'because of the momentum on the big campaign issues that we were able to carry along on a number of other niggling bits and pieces'. This follows Barber's (2007) advice, that having a focus on delivery makes it happen and that delivery success comes by 'being clear on what you mean by delivery'. As he says, 'if Blair had got on to the importance of delivery sooner he would have achieved more.... delivery thinking and the concept of delivery and the drive that is involved in that, and the change in culture that is required... those things didn't get focus soon enough in the first term.'

Other countries learnt from Blair's delivery unit and experiences. The NSW state in Australia set up a delivery unit under Premier Morris Iemma. Keneally (2008) argued that Iemma did this shortly after getting into power because 'of the observation of the UK version that worked for Tony Blair, and secondly his experience as minister for health, where there was kind of a performance management group within the New South Wales health structure... to improve service delivery'. Iemma focused on service delivery throughout his government, with the goal of 'delivering measurable change and performance'. Having the leader's support made a difference: 'having that sense that it is the premier who is committed to this issue and wants to see measurable improvement, that does help crystallise the importance of it'. Delivery units 'can only be successful if they have a mandate from the minister' and are less located in the bureaucracy but rather linked to the leader's goals and mandate; thus linking administrative progress with electoral goals. Clelland-Stokes (2009) also pointed to the importance of focusing on delivery and how this affects the way in which politicians are perceived:

> Do you want to be seen to be delivering and actually producing the goods, or do you want to be seen as rattling the cage and asking for goods? There's a very big difference in perception. Rodney Hyde [leader of the Act party], for example, can be Minister in the cabinet

and can rattle and be good-for-Rodney. And, people think 'There's a fine brand, he's fighting for my rights' etc., or, and of course he can decide to do a combination of both, he can be the minister who says 'Right, I want to get on and deliver. I'm the minister of the local government, so I want to deliver radical change in Auckland that makes the most people happy. Cost saving etc., etc.' Or, what I think he'll do – he'll do both. So, it's never cut and dry in the political world. Sometimes you know it's not deliverable, but then you go out there and you demand anyway, because it's just what you need to be perceived to be doing.

Pre-election delivery

Practitioners therefore advise that candidates should think about delivery before they fight the election and create key pledges or priorities. Levin (2008) observed how 'in opposition the tendency, the wish to promise to do everything is very hard to resist. And then you come into office and you've go to deliver it and you just you don't really know how to do it.' In the commercial market consumers can be sceptical of goods that make unrealistic and apparently impossible promises regarding low prices, and the same is true of politics, given the cynicism of voters. Being delivery-focused can attract support from voters. Roozendaal (2008) said, with regard to the 2003 NSW Carr campaign, 'we began the campaign with Bob talking to the camera saying "In my time..."' That set the tone about Bob getting on with the job and delivering.' Lawrence (2008) recalled how the Rudd 2007 campaign sought to ward off previous criticisms that Labour's promises were too utopian by 'matching what you want to do with what you can do, responsibly within an economic framework'. Paré and Berger (2008, 57) noted that the Canadian Conservatives' product offering in 2006 included 'short-term actions (e.g. cut in the GST, child-care reform, reduced health-care, reduced health-care waiting times) and long-term policy objectives (e.g. expansion of educational programs for health professionals, new legislation regarding crime) that were not dramatically different from previous governments'.

Pre-election delivery helps maintain support and win re-election by managing expectations. Noble (2009) noted how, with a Canadian premier campaign, they said ' "Look, we'll give you a money-back-guarantee. If I don't do this, I'm going to resign." People made a big deal about that, and all of our candidates actually signed a pledge, so it's like – it made it hugely difficult to not keep your promises. You'd never be able to get another message out from the day forward if you actually broke your word.' She said that it was hard to get voters to believe a politician who said trust me, but that they might say they trust you the most or give you the chance to prove yourself. What it meant for the premier (Mike Harris) was that when it came to re-election 'the number-one characteristic was – he does what he says he'll do', which gained support even if they didn't like his other attributes: 'most people also said "He does what he says he will do, so I'll give him that." That was a great brand characteristic to have.' Muttart (2009) explained how the 2006 Canadian Conservatives' five priorities helped 'because we were able to say "We came to power, we promised five big things, and we have delivered five big things." ' He said that delivery can help re-election, but 'in order for delivery to be a political asset, the electorate needs to understand what your promises are and they need to have expectations of what those outcomes are.' This makes communication of prospective delivery before getting into power important: 'they have to be clear enough so that the voter links the outcome with the expectation or the promise.'

Pledges, contracts and guarantees can be used to define such expectations. Lees-Marshment (2009a, 200–203) noted how one of the earliest examples of this was the 1994 mid-term Contract with America put forward by the House Republicans in the US, gaining them considerable votes and also a degree of mandate to dominate Congress for the rest of Bill Clinton's time as president. Tony Blair's Labour Party in the UK issued both a contract and credit card-sized pledges in 1997. Pledges and contracts have been copied around the world: Helen Clark adopted them for her Labour Party in New Zealand in 1999. In the 2008 New Zealand election, the National Party launched a commitments card in the campaign, in response to voters' desire for a clear alternative product (Lees-Marshment 2009c, 75); however, it was extremely detailed and lacked the focus that such methods normally provide.

Like all marketing tools, pledges need to be executed carefully to achieve the desired effect. UK Labour's third pledge card was so vague as to not manage expectations at all, changing from a specific pledge in 1997, such as 'we will cut class sizes to 30 or under for 5-, 6- and 7-year olds by using money saved from the assisted places scheme' to 'your child achieving more' in 2005. In 1999 the UK Conservative Party launched a number of guarantees as part of its Common Sense Revolution. When it was first communicated, press coverage was potentially positive: it was seen as a new break with the past, a new way forward, and even likened to Tony Blair's abandonment of Clause Four.

However, as Lees-Marshment (2008) noted, by the time of the election the guarantees had all but disappeared following a period of statements from senior party figures that watered them down or abandoned them entirely. The Tax Guarantee was suggested to be aspiration not a definite promise to reduce tax; the Patients' Guarantee had exclusions added, and the proposed married couples' tax allowance was restricted to those who had children under 11. The Conservatives also created a *Timetable for Action* for the 2005 election, which was launched at the 2004 party conference, with Howard declaring in his speech that 'we won't have a delivery unit but we will deliver.' The party used 'ten words': lower taxes, cleaner hospitals, more police, controlled immigration, school discipline, which responded to current topical issues 'but suggested an over-simplicity which belied the maturity necessary to be a government able to deal with the complex reality of running the country' (Lees-Marshment 2008, 175).

In the US, parties and leaders can prepare for government before election and use the transition period. Mehta (2009) noted how Obama ran an effective transition; partly aided by President Bush who received staff from both the McCain and Obama campaigns before the election. Mehta said 'I have to give President Bush a little bit of credit here...he thought very clearly about how he wanted this transition to happen, and I think that part of that was his own transition back in 2000 was terrible, and...he really thought through the process by which both sides could really put in place a team that could hit the ground running on November 5th and start building a government.' Other aspects of a good transition process include getting the right staff. Obama recruited John Podesta who had been chief of staff to Bill Clinton and had written a book about the perfect transition. The transition team also made all documents regarding the transition available on the website: 'the American people could click on change.gov any day and know exactly what we knew and hear exactly what we heard.' This could potentially set the tone for the administration. Transition staff also conveyed citizen views gathered during the transition:

> We even created something really cool called the Citizen's Briefing Book. Every night the President receives a briefing book from his staff – that's like his intelligence for the next day – domestic and foreign policy. It gives him the best information about what's going on, proposal recommendations, ideas etc.... We thought that in addition to staff recommendations, we should let the American people weigh in on what they think should be the priority for this

administration. So, on our website we opened up for people to make any recommendation they wanted. If you didn't have a recommendation you could read other people's recommendations and vote on them. So, we took the top recommendations – the ones that got the most votes, the ones that were at the top, and that had the best quality, and we put them together and we gave them to the president, and we said 'This is the briefing book from the citizens of the United States. This is what the American people want you to focus on...' The things that people said were very smart, very well thought out [and] very intelligent.

Delivery strategy

Once in power, just as with other areas of political marketing, there needs to be a delivery strategy, which also takes into account the nature of government. Muttart (2009) noted how 'once you get into government it becomes more and more difficult because you've got the great responsibility of taking care of the state as well as maintaining a political operation... the key decision-makers in government, just by the magnitude of their responsibilities, cannot be fully focused on campaign planning.' It is important to decide on delivery priorities as this gives staff and politicians a sense of direction. This is something that is not about government targets and measurements, but has more of a psychological focus. Keneally (2008) suggested that the Blair government created too many levels of multiple targets: 'as they got deeper and deeper into it, they kept unpeeling the onion and getting the deeper and deeper layers and measuring that and then adding indicators and targets and so on', and the problem is that they lost a 'sense of what are ones that really matter', which is important for maintaining public support. As Levin (2008) said, 'a government can only pay attention to a few big things; everything else just gets managed as best you can. Implementation gets short shrift because government has so many issues to address at any time.'

Governments need to keep pressure on politicians to focus on delivery. McCully (2007) explained that once politicians get into government, 'you've got all these people in the public service who are trying to run their agenda, including their agenda with your diary, so ministers of the crown are getting their diaries chocka with stuff that's been put in by their officials that they believe to be extremely worthy, but which is designed to take the minister's eye off the political ball. So one of the things you have to constantly do is keep re-imposing, reasserting the claim of the political agenda...for the delivery of the outputs you need.' Real delivery is slow: it is easier to make progress on burning issues which have a sense of immediacy than on routine ongoing services. Keneally (2008) said that the 'government usually does really well when there's some kind of burning platform, when you've got to fight a war or ensure that an Olympics gets staged on times...when it's just simply about saying we've got to do better at emergency room performance or we've got to do better at the time running of trains, it doesn't have that air of crisis about it.' Kartch (2007) observed that 'if you go too fast on something and then it fails, then you could harm your long-term will' amongst staff, but you also need to keep moving: 'as long as you're moving in that direction'.

Elected politicians need to focus on what they want to achieve most of all – despite media and public criticism and any failure. From his experience as a state premier, Carr (2008) said 'you've got to have a notion of where you want to make an impact I think that's the clearance test...I'd focus on the areas where you want to have a legacy.' Campbell (2005) pointed to self-determination and focus: 'get on and do it.' However, the daily media cycle can work against governments' delivering: every new issue that emerges may be attached to the government and create a sense of crisis. As Robertson (2006) put it:

> You're responsible...Doesn't really matter what it is – George Bush invades Iraq and it's your fault. Ahmed Zaoui is found in New Zealand and taken in by the authorities and the public are highly excited about it and it's your problem. You have a programme of work that you're wanting to get through and achieved but you're quite simply having to deal with issues that are chucked at you from left field.... it can be very derailing...we had a year of it actually in election year in 2005 when we had David Benson-Pope and stuff just kept coming and I remember at one stage we were doing an audit, just looking back over a 6 month period and I couldn't find a week in which there hadn't been some kind of scandal or mini-crisis that wasn't of our driving...It's a huge challenge in government to implement your programme whilst dealing with every other thing that might come up.

Having a clear strategy can help, however. Keneally (2008) observed that state plans and Rudd's 2020 summit helped governing politicians to consider long-term goals, and avoid being subsumed by the daily media cycle, which also allowed the civil service to be free to focus on implementation: 'here's a very clear statement of what we want the strateg[y]... of government and agencies to be. And you can get on with that without us interfering too much on a day to day level with how you're doing.'

In coalition governments, the minor party's delivery aims and demands need to be considered. Minor parties need to think this delivery strategy through so that they have delivery success to claim at the next election; and the major party also needs to consider if they want their coalition partner to retain support and be able to form a government with them again. Rudd (2005) notes how the New Zealand Labour Party gave credit for delivery of certain policies – such as the establishment of the 'People's Bank' as a subsidiary of New Zealand Post and introduction of paid parental leave – to its junior coalition partner, the Alliance, during 1999–2002. In contrast, Lederer et al. (2005) noted that when the Freedom Party of Austria (FPÖ) entered coalition government in 2000 they were unable to maintain opposition to the government which FPÖ's supporters wanted it to, and the party was also unable to deliver their promises, as they were inexperienced in bargaining. Although entering coalition government gives minor parties the potential to get some of their policies delivered it can also constrain their positioning options and reduce their support.

Making delivery happen

Practitioners advised that one should not just assume that because the leader has given the order it will happen: government is about management. As Carr (2008) explained, 'you have got to get used to giving orders and finding out nothing happens' as well as not being told delivery has not worked. Once a politician is elected, other stakeholders take more notice of their policies and how it might affect them, and thus hinder or help the policy being implemented. George W. Bush's attempt to push social security reform through in his second term of office is just one example where, despite appealing to the public for support, the nature of government and special interests blocked the change (Arterton 2007, 155–157). Another case of failed delivery was health care by Bill Clinton, whose package was blocked when it went through Congress, despite it being a visible part of the product that he offered to voters and won the election for (see Newman 1999, 99–101).

There are a range of potential solutions. Once elected, candidates' electoral promises need to be linked to the government apparatus.

Robertson (2006) recalled that talking to civil servants about the product promises works:

> One thing we did do after the 2005 election is that I actually sat down with the Prime Minister's departmental officials, the bureaucrats and we actually went through the manifesto and said what are we going to be able to do to implement these things. And of course a lot of them said oh we're already doing it or whatever but it wasn't an exercise that happened after 2002 or 1999, as far as I can tell you.

In contrast, between 2002 and 2005, Robertson felt that 'much of the time officials didn't even seem to really know that the government might have promised to do something in their manifesto.' Muttart (2009) discussed how the priorities of the Canadian Conservatives under Harper helped ensure success in delivery in their first term in government: 'what we never anticipated was that it would be so effective, once we won government, of pointing civil service in the direction of delivering a few key urgent priorities of the government... it ended up being a very effective tool for the general management once we were in government.' Brodie (2009) recalled how the prime minister made it clear within the party, cabinet and bureaucracy that he remained focused on delivering X,Y and Z, and while it took a while to convince them, after that 'then everybody said "Oh, OK, they're serious about the GST thing, and they're serious about the childcare. OK, alright, that's fine".'

Relationship building and compromise are needed to get legislation passed through parliament or Congress. Robertson (2006) noted how they worked to get the votes needed to pass Labour's policies: 'on an ongoing basis too, Labour needs 61 votes to get legislation through parliament... you've got 51, you need another 10, you've got to find them from somewhere... So that relationship management role, those skills are absolutely critical.' Similarly, Griggs (2008) said that 'if you treated very bright people with respect you got a lot of help in getting good legislation drawn up and you'd go to them and say I'm in big trouble, I need to get this through, what's a compromise?'

Once the legislation is through, politicians need to work with not against staff and offer help. As Keneally (2008) said, 'it's a highly relationship-driven thing', and politicians may need to change their attitude also. Levin (2008) remarked that 'when new governments come in they don't much trust the civil service, because those are the people that they think have just been screwing everything up for years.' Keneally explained that Iemma's approach was 'about working with the director generals responsible, not about sort of doing it *to* them', and thus the role of the delivery unit was 'not to go in there and sort of kick heads and take names, but to actually go in there and work, provide some additional resource and some additional support, work with them so that they have a plan that they're signed up to that will deliver that sort of measurable performance improvement'. Thus, instead of being negative after identifying a problem, they would offer support. He recalled the difference this had on the relationship between the unit and civil servants or public sector staff:

> I remember one meeting early on with one agency, where it sort of dawned on them that I was saying I'll bring four or five people with me... we'll start doing some extra analysis and some work for you and help... when that penny dropped, suddenly we sort of got a whole lot more collaboration and cooperation and actually ended up doing some quite useful things at that agency... it's additional support, not punishment. We're going in there to help.

Instead of assessing performance, the unit acted in more an advisory capacity. Similarly, politicians need to trust civil servants more: 'the civil service has lost a lot of its confidence, a lot of its ability to deliver' (Humphrey 2007), so politicians needed to listen to their staff more, allow two-way communication, and act on their ideas so as to make them work more effectively. Humphrey argued that 'if you can get that kind of relationship going, your organisation will improve', and 'if a political party could find a way of engaging with the public services in a more positive way, once they're in power... you would both deliver for the public and you'd win a lot of advocates.' Griggs (2008) agreed, noting how he tried to have 'a good relationship with the bureaucracy, otherwise you get killed', and that any political staff who were rude were sacked – 'you have to make the bureaucracy work for you.'

Given this, politicians also need to communicate with those doing the delivery. Barber (2007) recalled that 'we didn't communicate enough to the people working in the front line of education or health what we were trying to do, so instead of being advocates they tended to be critics.' Humphrey (2007) explained that Blair's comments about bearing the scars on his back because of public service reform is 'going to hit the same audience and negate a lot of the beneficial impact', and that public criticism of staff would backfire: 'that is not how staff want to hear about what you think about them.' Levin (2008) puts it simply: 'generally calling people incompetent is not a strong incentive for them to improve their performance!' Humphrey (2007) recalled that, when working at 10 Downing Street, a cabinet minister went to the Cabinet just after 9/11 and complained how her civil servants were letting them down. The problem was that word got back to the minister's staff, and 'if all your officials in your department hear that you've been in Cabinet slagging them off, are they going to go the extra mile for you? Are they going to stop leaking? Are they going, you know, to produce the policy things that are going to make you individually a success in the future? Now that minister, she survived for quite a while, but she had a pretty ropey time with a lot of her senior people.' More co-operative communication is effective. Humphrey (2007) recalled a positive example from Blair:

> Tony Blair would go, for example, to a staff conference, go talk to them, no cameras, and he would be there because he wanted to engage genuinely with staff and be seen to do that. And staff would respond extremely well to that and he would go, for example, to a conference of police superintendents, and, you know, he would take questions, and, you know, because at those kinds of conferences people fill out the forms, what do you think about each of the speakers, he turns up unannounced and spends 20 minutes taking questions, that gets an extremely strong response. And is very valuable – Prime Minster's time is precious, but it's a valuable use of his time. He was completely convinced that this was a worthwhile way to spend his time.

Giving examples of delivery success helps create support for change. Barber (2007) said that 'there are enough examples around the world to show that these things can be done and I do think that cultures can be changed. I think you can change them by bringing in or changing the way leaders lead, by giving demonstrations of success.' Norquist (2007) noted how, in the US, 'if something works in a state, it's easier to sell to other states; it's easier to sell it nationally. If it doesn't work at the state level, it's not going to sell.'

Working across institutional divisions is important. Brodie (2009) observed that, in their coalition government, 'in almost every minister's office, we had somebody from the opposition in the staff organisation at some relatively senior level, which was a big help, again in terms of facilitating the personal relations to make the thing work.' Keneally (2008) talked of the importance of effective discussion between the relevant actors: 'often bringing the right people together with the right facts in front of them at the right time is sort of orchestrating, that is as much the key element as anything else.' Campbell (2005) said that the UK delivery unit helped because 'getting cross-departmental co-ordination in communication let alone policy delivery was very difficult.' Levin (2008) said that 'you've got to be talking to people all the time'; governments need people to have the will to do it. At the ground level, policies also need to be linked. Keneally (2008) remarked that 'in some locations we were doing this work to try and improve, reduce the level of assault in a handful of locations' and one way was 'changing bus timetables so that they were aligned with closing times of hotels and people weren't standing around on the street, they were getting the bus and going home' but this involved cutting across different policy areas. Governments need to facilitate networks, relationships and conversations to deliver – something that could relate to relationship marketing, although the academic literature on political marketing has yet to consider this.

Managing failures in delivery

There will always be some failures in delivery that threaten the chances of re-election. Government throws up unpredictable issues such as war and economic turbulence, which constrain the ability of politicians to carry out previous promises. Bill Clinton, elected in 1992 in the US as a New Democrat, tax-cutting middle-class-targeted president, found, once in office, that the actual deficit was far worse than they had previously been informed and what they had promised to do was impossible. After 9/11, George W. Bush's compassionate conservatism agenda was pushed to the background in favour of the 'war on terror' and more right-wing social agendas were revealed than were evident from his 2000 presidential campaign. As Arterton (2007, 147) notes, in the US presidential structure 'the government can neither dictate nor assume legislative action.' In business this is known as the service delivery gap; as Newman (1999, 37–38) explored, different constraints stop candidates from delivering even when they want to, and 'politicians are much more vulnerable to this gap than are other service industries as a result of the unexpected situations to which politicians always must respond.'

Given this, both academics and practitioners suggest being honest about problems in delivery. Patrón-Galindo (2004, 116) studied the first term of Peruvian President Alejandro Toledo after he won power in 2001. Although most election promises were achieved within a year or so of getting into power, people's expectations were not satisfied and his popularity declined, something that was not helped by a personal scandal that he avoided admitting to. Patrón-Galindo (2004, 122) observed that 'it was a mistake on his part to take so much time' to decide to be honest. Edwards (2009) said that their advice is 'straightforward, tell the truth and admit your mistakes... a sensible politician knows that it is counter productive to tell lies and get found out'. Reid (2009) recalled that, under the Martin government, there was a sponsorship scandal caused by their predecessor, and one suggested 'posture was "You know what, this isn't a big deal, don't make too much of it." ' but 'to maintain that would have been disastrous.... I believe that if the Prime Minister had taken the posture of saying "You know what? This isn't that big of a deal." you would have failed the fundamental test of "Do you get it?" And, we would have been incinerated at the polls in 2004.' Getting it is a way of showing that the politician understands the voter. Tyson (2008) observed how 'you cannot keep beating up someone who's concedes weakness, and some politicians in this country [Australia] abuse that masterfully.' Peter Beattie, the QLD premier, had any number of disasters in his government and he would just 'fess up in front of the media, say "Sorry, we'll do better next time," and the issue will go away.' Evershed (2009) said that voters will say 'show me your progress, but don't just tell me about your successes. Tell me about some things that haven't gone as well as anticipated. Tell me about things that have gone badly, because then I'll believe you.' It helps to build a more trusting relationship with the public.

Politicians then need to take action to fix the problems. Fitzpatrick (2008) said that 'as long as you are able to present a solution, which is what you are obliged to do as a government, I encourage governments to come forward and put their foot forward – announce problem and solution all in the one hit.' Levin (2008) provides a clear example of this:

> In Manitoba the changes to the Grade 3 Assessment were an election commitment in 1999. We didn't do these changes very well at first. Teachers were very unhappy with it and they told us so in no uncertain terms that it was too difficult for teachers to do. I remember saying at one meeting, OK, I hear you, we're going to change it, we're going to fix it. And we did. The interesting thing is that we actually got more goodwill out of getting it wrong and fixing it than we would've got out of getting it right in the first place. People saw was that we actually listened to their concerns. If we had got it right

in the first place, no one would've said anything. But because we got it wrong and then fixed it people said they actually listened! You get double marks for that.

Fitzpatrick (2008) suggested a three-step approach, which was to communicate that you have:

1. Recognised and spotted the problems straight away
2. That you're doing something about it
3. That you're doing something to make sure it doesn't happen again

Communicating delivery

While most communication focuses on what to do to get elected, communication of delivery once in power is crucial for re-election, but has to overcome obstacles from the media's mission to identify problems rather than progress. Blumenthal (2007) reflected that 'the Clinton White House had enormous difficulty in its first 2 years in communicating. Especially on positive programmes... when it succeeded in passing an economic program that turned out to be the most successful economic program in decades, it took a long time for that program to work its effects on the economy and therefore [it] really [was] not felt until years later in the 1996 re-election campaign. The national press and the Washington press corps were much more interested in scandals, really pseudo-scandals involving the now much-forgotten but momentous scandal called White Water.'

Nevertheless, government can use a range of tools. These include annual or progress reports, newsletters within each electorate/constituency/branch or ward, talking about delivery in interviews and speeches, and online communication. Hughes and Dann (2009, 88) observed how, once in government, the Australian Labor Party under Kevin Rudd placed emphasis 'on early delivery milestones as means of reaffirming commitment, demonstrating performance to enhance trust, and producing evidence of the reciprocity of delivering reform in exchange for the votes received to take office'; producing a document on their first 100 days in office.

Delivery needs to be demonstrated not just claimed, however. As Lees-Marshment (2009c, 468) notes, in the 2008 New Zealand election Labour had a picture of Clark on their campaign website (Labour08.co.nz) with the quote 'I believe that we have shown in government that we deliver on our promises and we keep our word to voters', and the phrase, 'this election is about trust. Vote Labour. A team you can trust to deliver for your family.' However, what Helen Clark believes she has done is not the issue. Clelland-Stokes (2009) said, 'I can't just have John Banks saying "I believe in affordable progress" because it's a hollow thing.' They thus focused on certain issues, which took place in the public eye, to back this claim. For example, he engaged in public consultation about heritage rules versus property rights in the city, which generated intense debates and produced 'for the first time ever, a negotiated outcome. You have him being seen to have championed that, and then you have John Banks being seen as the person taking of Auckland's heritage and Auckland's colonial past – taking care of Auckland.' This then supports the message of affordable progress. More direct communication of real-world great cases of delivery to voters can be effective. Mellman (2007) suggested that the solution is to identify actual examples. This helped an incumbent in a governor's race in Michigan in 2006 receive credit for the work done to get new jobs created. The auto industry, which the state was dependent on, was declining and so 'people said well I don't see jobs', so advisors found that they had to give specific examples of what he had done: 'he went to Japan, got 10 companies to come and... they came and invested money so we're going to build a plant here... and Google opened their East Coast place in Michigan, that's going to employ 1000 people.' When 'we told these individual stories and they were able to get a lot of traction, they were where we were able to get people to sort of nod their head.'

Another tactic is to create signature moments. Mills (2009) noted how 'voters, with low levels of interest and awareness of politics, tend more to seize on signature moments rather than tot up policy achievements. The previous [NZ] Labour Government had a few of these such as the slaying of Muldoon, dramatic economic reforms (both a plus and a minus) and nuclear policy. The last Labour Government [2002–2005] didn't have many at all. In their heyday they were seen as exceptionally competent managers. The closest they got to a positive signature moment was Helen Clark not sending New Zealand troops to Iraq.'

Delivery communication can be personalised or micro-targeted. Keneally (2008) explains how 'people don't live in the state on average; they live in locations and they experience services in locations' so governments need to convey 'here is what state government has done and achieved for this region, this is where we want to focus our efforts over the next couple of years in terms of improving outcomes and results.'

Carter (2007) described how, in 200,5 UK Labour's online 'manifesto had a personalised section where you could type in your address, your age, your family status and your working status and you would get not only the benefits that you personally would've seen, benefits in your local community: more police on the beat, more teachers in your local schools, more doctors and nurses, the impact on the economy in your local community; but then what our future commitments would be to you personally.' Keneally (2008) noted that an academic in the US re-analysed police commission reports on their performance, which were very key performance indicator (KPI)-driven, and instead 'applied it to a whole of city level, so it's everything from roads and potholes, to rodent eradication to, everything that government deals with, to education and so on... driven by the mayor, driven by the first minister'.

Some parties use their own media to communicate delivery. At the presidential level, Blumenthal (2007) reveals that during Clinton's second term he engaged in his own investigative journalism to show a right-wing conspiracy. Although 'the press wasn't much interested in it, the public was. And it provided a kind of counter-narrative... the lessons to learn from the Clinton White House... [are] communicate directly with people.' At the local level, politicians can communicate their own delivery. Interviewed only a few months after being elected, Robertson (2008) was asked *have you thought at all about how you are going to try and communicate and demonstrate delivery*, and he replied 'we actually had a meeting on Thursday... to talk about that... I'm certainly going to try to use the net a lot... I want to do more face-to-face stuff between elections... I want to set up some contact groups with youth, seniors, and the community... I've got reference type groups that I'm meeting on a regular basis.' Such methods give minor parties the opportunity to convey delivery even if they are not in government. Lavigne (2009) noted how the NDP would emphasise what individual members gained for their particular constituency: 'we work harder at getting deliverables for the local constituency – much more than others.' Central government can provide local MPs with local stories, so that they can communicate delivery. Pleasants (2009), who had worked in the New Zealand prime minister's office, noted how they collected and supplied local data on national developments to go to local MPS to use. For example, if they had administrative articles about school funding or early childhood education grants being given out this would normally be announced by the minister but not get any interest in local media: 'the *Gisborne Herald*'s not going to be interested in that. The *Manukau Courier* isn't going to have interest in that at all... so, what I [do] would be to follow the local stats, numbers ... and make up a whole lot of local media releases and fit those out to the local MPs.'

Academic research also supports the importance of politicians communicating local delivery: Lilleker (2009) found, in a case study of one MP, that there was a strong correlation between positive perceptions of Knight as MP and recalling being contacted by him. MPs also issue annual delivery reports on their websites and send these, in hard copy form, to residents. Local delivery can offset national weaknesses and help protect individual MPs (Lilleker 2005b, 2006, 212–214). Butler and Collins (1998) noted how Irish MPs can help represent and support constituents in bringing complaints to government departments, and in fighting for state benefits and services. This is also true for Congressmen and women in the US. Steger (1999, 668–669) observed that they can also get credit for fixing funding formulas to the benefit of their market, securing tax breaks for their constituents and opposing potentially damaging regulatory legislation.

Delivery communication, like all other messaging, should focus on key priorities. Reid (2009) explained that while government is obviously involved in managing all issues, electorally 'it won't live and die on a wide number of issues' and thus any prime minister 'can only afford to identify his or her time with a small number of issues'. With Canadian Prime Minister Paul Martin they were unsuccessful in 'narrowing that agenda down... we could tell people that the government was going to execute 112 fronts, but we needed it to be clear that the Prime Minister did not have 112 priorities.' In contrast, Clelland-Stokes (2009) argued that he actively tried to make sure all communication supported John Bank's message of affordable progress, 'so at the end of the day, what I want the public to think, over time, like at the end of a year, what I want them to think is John Banks equals affordable progress'.

A sense of progress over time needs to be conveyed. Griggs (2008) describes how, in the Carr NSW government, 'we were ticking things off month by month or at least having a viable position to say to the media we're not finished yet, but we're getting there.' Fitzpatrick (2008) recalled how they drew up a NSW state plan, which was put on the state government's website, and which 'played a big part in being able to articulate and demonstrate to people that we are about services' as well as having a long-term perspective.

A final word of warning, however, is not to focus on communicating delivery at the expense of actually delivering. Sometimes policies naturally lend themselves to communication. Keneally (2008) cited an example where 'we were able to offer up and say look, here's a little story you can tell about how we're fixing the problem of late-night drunken street violence by better aligning bus timetables with pub closing times. The media can get out there and do a little story about it.' However, at other times delivery communication can actually hinder good policy:

> There's always a pressure for a public communications dividend from this sort of work and that has to be managed. There's a risk that because there's a sudden firestorm in the media about a child dying or something like that, that work that you're doing in that area suddenly gets held up as the answer or the five point plan that will solve it or something like that. I think it takes good small 'p' political leadership of a group like that to be able to understand and be sympathetic to political offices' need to tell a positive story about what they're doing and to feed the media beast; but at the same time to sort of insist upon the need for an evidence-based approach. You know, if you really want to [fix] this... we need to take an evidence-based approach that is more than just a whipped up five point plan over the weekend.

Humphrey (2007) tells how, during 'the Campbell years... media management was seen as the big all and end all', while Griggs (2008) reflected that, in the NSW government, 'managing the message became a bit more important than managing the policy product.' Keneally (2008) said, 'the point that I've tried to push on the political people is actually improving the underlying level of service is probably the best thing you can do. Yes... you've still got to keep arguing the case about why the system's doing really well and we have the, the best five year cancer survival rate in the world and it shows that the whole system is not in crisis as everyone's alleging. But, you know, you may never win that battle, but you've got to win the battle of people's own experience of the service being a positive thing.' Actual delivery is what counts the most; thus the nitty-gritty of policy implementation is as important as researched communication and strategy in a political marketing context.

Public evaluation of delivery

The last consideration related to delivery is how the public evaluates delivery. There are many problems with this that elites need to take into account. The first is that there is a gap between public experience on an individual level and perception of national government progress. Levin (2008) observed how 'people make a distinction between their personal experience with the system and the system in general. So people will say that in their experience the healthcare system is doing great, but they know the system as a whole is in a terrible mess, because they read about it in the papers or saw it on TV. Same with schools. My kids' school is great, but schools in general are felt not to be doing well at all.' In the UK, a poll in October 2006 revealed that voters thought that the NHS had become worse, not better, during Labour's decade in power, and that much of the government's huge extra investment in health care has been wasted. Nevertheless, the public's personal experience of using NHS services is overwhelmingly positive: 71 per cent of people say that their family and friends have had a good experience (Lees-Marshment and Pettitt 2010, 121). This increases the importance of focusing on delivery and communicating progress, because there is a barrier to conveying success to the public.

Another related issue is that political consumer satisfaction is determined by a mix of things – not just delivery. Gill (2007) suggested that it reflects or is related to the public perception of the leader: 'look at the Mori Delivery Index...when it first started in 2002, broadly all of them were positive. And then they just decline pretty steadily. [There's a] correlation between the job of the PM and...whether you're positive about public services...a lot of the concern with public services that you've seen over the last 2 or 3 years is actually just a reflection of the popularity of Tony Blair, the man himself and what his image is.... the latest polls show quite a big increase in optimism about NHS, schools and everything, because Gordon Brown's in power.' Another factor is voters' expectations. Sherman et al. (2008, 108) argue that 'political trust will increase or decrease depending on the relationship between citizens' expectations and their perceptions as to how well the government performs in order to meet those expectations.' Lees-Marshment (2009b, 212) claims that 'it is important to manage the expectations that the public have of a new government; if not during the campaign, then soon after winning office. Without clarity, voters project own aspirations onto promised product. This causes problems in government as voters possess different and unrealistic beliefs of what a party will do in power, stimulating demands that are unlikely to be satisfied.' Politicians also need to explain the realities of government and explain long-term strategy. Barber (2007, 369–371) noted that with delivery 'citizens have to see and feel the difference and expectations need to be managed.'

Political consumers want instant delivery. Campbell (2005) explained that 'it takes time to build schools and hospitals, and to actually deliver', and that voters 'don't believe it' when the government has delivered. The only way to really convince them is 'end delivery'; for example, good treatment when a new hospital is built. However, even when the public have positive perceptions, political consumers don't give politicians credit for delivery. Gould (2007) said, 'the public don't give credit to the government for anything much.' Mills (2009) recalled that 'sometimes in groups I've run through a list of achievements of Governments and you can see slightly rueful voters who had been rubbishing the Government start to change their minds a bit as the list of what they had forgotten is conveyed.' Muttart (2009) mentioned that 'there are governments that do a lot, but because what they do is so complex, or they do so much, the public doesn't really understand what they've done.' Barber (2007) argued that governments have got to be great, not just good enough, in delivery: 'I do think they could become more satisfied if you get to a real level of quality. I think you have to make big changes...we cut crime a lot in this country but people didn't think that crime had been cut a lot, in fact they thought it had got worse. But in New York City they knew it had got better because it had really fallen a long way.'

Even when voters accept success and credit the government, they still want more: demand will always be insatiable. As Humphrey (2007) said, 'in the minds of politicians there's a sense in which well, we'll do all of this and the contract means you've got to re-elect us.' But, as Mills (2009) said, 'that isn't of course how it works – the standard cliché of "thanks for all that but what are you going to do next" usually prevails.' Similarly, Edwards (2006) said, 'if you don't deliver on your policies, then you will get punished for that, and if you do, then the next question is what else have you got for me?' Roozendaal (2008) noted that this issue came up when undertaking training in the party:

> We used to do a lot of campaign training, and one of the skits we used to show is that snippet from *The Life of Brian*, you know 'What did the Romans ever do for us? Apart from roads, sanitation, and education, and law and order...what have they done for us lately?' We used to show that skit from *The Life of Brian* to our campaign directors and leaders, and MPs, because it's a bit like that. What have you done for me lately? And I think in some ways, that's the challenge of government, and in some ways the heartening part of government. It's always, what have you done for us lately?

In his last party conference speech in 2006 Tony Blair noted, 'I spoke to a woman the other day, a part-time worker, complaining about the amount of her tax credit. I said: Hold on a minute: before 1997, there were no tax credits not for working families not for any families; child benefit was frozen; maternity pay half what it is; maternity leave likewise and paternity leave didn't exist at all. And no minimum wage, no full time rights for part time workers, in fact nothing. "So what?" she said "that's why we elected you. Now go and sort out my tax credit".'

However, practitioners did not always see this type of attitude as bad. They felt that the public should always want more progress. As Carter (2007) explained, 'the public are, at the end of the day, they are ambitious for themselves, for their society and country and whilst they do recognise and see improvement, they remain hungry for more change and for more improvement... it's not enough to simply have achievement – without future commitment people will be frustrated at your lack of ambition and your lack of desire for future change.'

Summary

Delivery is crucial for parties who get into power if they want to maintain support. However, being in government is different to being in opposition, and presents a number of barriers to continuing to use political marketing. Ideally, politicians need to start thinking about delivery management before the election. The conventional pattern after successful political marketing puts politicians into power is failure to meet public expectations, declining use of political marketing, and defeat by a new opposition who has researched the market and proposes a fresh hypothetical product. This cycle only deepens the negative relationship between the public and politicians. Inferior political marketing in power, therefore, not only damages the electoral fortunes of the individual party, it impacts on the state–citizen relationship. As Savigny (2008a, 2) said, 'there is also a sense that political marketing is not just confined to election campaigns, rather it has become a means of governance.' Thus, marketing needs to move beyond electoral strategy to handling this state–citizen relationship better, and Table 6.1 lists the rules of the game for the key issue of managing delivery more effectively. The next chapter will explore academic and practitioners' perspectives on political marketing and democracy itself.

Table 6.1 Rules of the game for managing delivery

The importance of delivery
1. Delivery performance affects future elections through public support when in power, re-election and the overall brand
2. Leaders and staff and local MPs need to make this a dedicated area

Pre-election delivery
3. Think about delivery before you fight the election
4. Create key pledges or priorities to build credibility
5. Convey management and governing abilities
6. Convey delivery at local council level or in office through regular reports at local level
7. Prepare for government before election
8. Manage expectations
9. Tangibilising the product does not always win support: it has to be well thought out and supported

Delivery strategy
10. Focus on what you want to achieve most of all – despite media and public criticism and any failure
11. In coalition/partnership, make sure all parties can show some delivery
12. Compromise carefully – coalitions, interest groups, crisises can distract you from your delivery intentions

Managing failures in delivery
13. There will always be some failures in delivery
14. Be honest about problems
15. Admit mistakes but then propose a solution
16. Don't always blame the civil servants for problems in delivery

Making delivery happen
17. Don't just assume that because the leader has given the order it will happen
18. Sit down with bureaucrats after election and go through promises & priorities
19. Facilitate networks, relationships and conversations to prevent fallouts, stepping on people's toes and so forth, and to get legislation delivered
20. Encourage the will of those doing the delivery to succeed: give examples of progress and success, don't blame them publicly, ensure tasks and goals are clear, work with not against them
21. Identify problems but then offer help to solve them
22. Focus efforts on certain areas only
23. Create a delivery unit
24. Real delivery is slow; it is easier to make progress on burning issues than routine ongoing services

Communicating delivery
25. Communicate real-world great cases of delivery to voters
26. Create signature moments to get voters to credit government for delivery
27. Micro-target delivery communication to make it personalised

Table 6.1 (Continued)

28. Use own media to communicate delivery
29. Central government can provide local stories for local MPs to communicate delivery
30. Use delivery reports at all levels – incumbent politicians can note their achievements
31. Focus on specific delivery areas
32. Communicate a sense of progress over time
33. Delivery has to be demonstrated not just alleged
34. Don't focus on communicating delivery rather than actually delivering

Public evaluation of delivery

35. Public assessment of delivery is tough and unfair!
36. Even when the public have a good experience they think the national picture is bad
37. They don't give politicians credit for delivery
38. Got to be great – not just good enough – to get attention
39. Try to manage voter expectations, especially if you can't deliver
40. Political consumer satisfaction is determined by a mix of things – not just delivery
41. Maintain all other marketing activities in power
42. This is harder in power than opposition, but re-marketing is essential
43. Make time to strategise and re-market
44. Adopt a learning orientation – be open to new ideas, keep doing market analysis and internal discussion, make time to re-develop and aim to improve performance
45. Demand is always going to be insatiable – this helps society progress

7
Marketing Democratically

> It's a legitimate criticism that someone like me has a particular kind of view... The answer to that is not to stop people like me doing research, but to have other sources of information.
> —Gould (2007)

> People's views evolve the more information people are given, the more considered people's views can be.
> —Glover (2007)

> As citizens we play a game electorally don't we?... we pretend that we expect governments to fix it for us, and actually there are just limited things they can do.
> —Pattillo (2009)

As well as considering what works in political marketing, this research aimed to explore the democratic implications of practice. There have previously been several concerns raised in academic literature, such as using market analysis threatens leadership and elevates voters' input in political decision-making through focus groups rather than formal elections, which works against citizenship; voter profiling and segmentation encourage focus on some voters more than others; and moderator bias prevents market research ascertaining voter opinion. Rather than just repeat them, as with previous chapters this analysis turns negative into positive, and thus the critique is re-presented as rules on what to avoid in order to practise political marketing democratically. The chapter explores perceived problems elites need to overcome and how they can do this, realising the benefits to democracy, and then, lastly, looks at the potential developments elites explore in their bid to create new ways to use political marketing democratically.

Overcoming potential problems

Savigny (2008a, 1) asserted that 'politics, as both elite-level activity and the dissemination of this to the public, has predominantly become a process of marketing... this use of marketing has played a key role in contributing to the existence of a political "malaise" as marketing subverts the democratic process and disconnects the public from politics' and there are strong arguments that political marketing can be used in a way which is negative for democracy. Thus elites have to take care to avoid such practice.

Practitioners acknowledge concerns with the quality of public opinion. Butler (2006) explained that 'we know quite a lot about people who watch our program [The Politics Show]...we had a focus group in Birmingham, where we met a lot of our viewers, and they tend to be retired, middle-class people from the West Midlands and they're bright people. But they didn't know nearly as much about politics as we all assumed they did.' Nevertheless, while the public may not display interest in politics in the way academics expect, they are interested in their own way. Humphrey (2007) observed how academic concerns are 'influenced by some sense of how people ought to behave'. Mehta (2007) explained that 'it's not because our population is somehow more stupid or less interested in world events than other countries...it's because these people have a lot going on in their lives, I mean, they're dealing with a lot of issues, some of them are working multiple jobs, they're worried about their kid who's failing maths or whatever, that their wife who's going to lose her health insurance, there's a lot going on in these people's lives.' Does this mean their opinion should be ignored? Hyder (2009) admits that prior to becoming a practitioner he 'was one of those that had that academic, cynical view of what do the people know? They're not as smart, they barely read the newspaper. They certainly don't pay attention to politics.' However, after more practical experience 'you realise – people do tune in. They do have the ability to decipher through all the rubbish, and all the hype, and all the newscasts, and go – what do I want? What do I need? Who's reflecting my aspirations, my hopes, my dreams, my vision? And, who best do I think can fulfil that?'

Although public opinion can change easily and weekly, it changes less on big issues and more on arcane issues. Ulm (2007) argued that inconsistency doesn't happen on big issues but on those that are less relevant to people 'such as campaign for finance reform. What mother wakes up in the morning and sends her child off to school and says make sure this campaign finance reform [gets passed]!...if you're talking about racially integrating a public school, they know all about that.' Mellman (2007) explained that 'on some things they are inconsistent, on some things they're consistent, on some things they're volatile, on some things they're quite stable, you know, it depends...on a lot of issues there are some basic views that are pretty consistent.' Carter (2007) said, 'voters tend to be pretty rational, rational in way that serves their interests. I think they tend to be pretty consistent.' McCully (2007) remarked that 'I've learnt in my time in this business that the public are actually pretty smart and you should rate them as such. You should look respectfully about what you can learn about [them from] market research and polling and focus groups and so on. Not slavishly follow the detail but understand the substance of it and demonstrate some respect for their requirements.'

Although the public judge politicians on their personality and have an emotional response to the candidate, rather than to the policy, there is some logic to this as 'judging the character of the politician is extremely important'. Despite the fact that politicians convey their manifesto before being elected, once they get into power 'nobody knows what's going to happen, and it's all down to the person, I think, character and values of that individual as to how they're going to respond...that means that if somebody says yes, I drank 14 pints a night, then that is a clue to what they're really like and how they behave and the vision they have of themselves and a bit of fantasy and a bit of trying to reinvent themselves' (Humphrey 2007). Thus the way the politician is perceived overall becomes more important. Duncan Smith (2006) noted that 'I always ask people when they say I saw you on television last week what was I talking about, and they can never remember.' But as Munro (2006) explained, 'they will always remember how you looked and what your demeanour is...it's very important in telling people just how you are dealing with that issue.'

Regardless of how to collect market analysis, academics and practitioners diverge on whether it is worth gathering it at all. Academic perception of voters is almost universally negative. For example, Coleman (2007, 181) takes issue with the suggestion 'that voters' views and preferences are sufficiently consistent to be suited to strategic reasoning. Most of the empirical evidence suggests that voters are promiscuous and rationally irresponsible in the range of inconsistent views they hold at any one time, and rarely think about long-term policy consequences in ways that politicians and their advisors are required to do.' A range of literature criticises voters for being changeable in their opinion; selfish, for example, acting in their own interest not that of the whole country; highly emotional, prejudiced and irrational; short-term in focus; lacking the necessary experience, knowledge and capacity to make appropriate judgements; and led by the media. Obviously there is the potential for elites to shape preferences and thus control the opinions they are listening to. Savigny (2008a, 38–40) notes that political marketing theory seems to omit any consideration of preference shaping that can be carried out by elites; whether by politicians or the media (noted also by Temple 2010), or by politicians influencing the media. However, evidence for these potential voter weaknesses is hardly clear and we have to be cautious of accepting them given the theoretical roots of most critiques and the dearth of empirical studies on how political consumers actually do behave. Notably, practitioners who have carried out work with the public offered strong rebuttals of public weaknesses:

> I spend a lot of my time talking with members of the public, and in fact I am a member of the public. And what you do, when you talk to people, is...they're just as smart as you or me. Sometimes even smarter, you know?...These people aren't dumb, or they're not stupid, they're not even fickle.
>
> (Utting 2008)

> I have a lot of confidence in their judgment...I think they're sensible, I think they're wise, they're understanding, far more than many people, you know, members of the political elite, who seem to me not so...the idea of irrational self-interest actors is nonsense...people vote from a pamphlet of reasons – emotion, values, sort of intuition is crucially important, a sense of right and wrong as well as self interest.
>
> (Gould 2007)

> There is something in it for them if there is something in it for the future generations, if there is something in it for less advantaged Canadians.
>
> (Evershed 2009)

An alternative argument is not to debate the weaknesses of public opinion but to use more effective methods to increase its value – Gould (2007) acknowledged that 'it may well be that voters are less than perfect individuals, but they are the boss, and we serve them.' Practitioners made a number of suggestions for ensuring higher quality feedback.

Politicians can consult citizen experts rather than the general public. Such 'experts' are those that have some knowledge of the issue through their experience of a service or local problem (such as people with a long-term health condition who use the health service regularly) and can therefore offer a more informed view. The Rudd government in Australia hosted a public consultation called the Australian 2020 Summit on 19 and 20 April 2008 (see http://www.australia2020.gov.au/about/index.cfm, accessed 13 May 2008) to help shape a long-term strategy for the nation's future. It involved a range of experts, rather than the public, looking at long-term issues that required addressing over a period beyond the 3-year electoral cycle. Participants came from 'business, academia, community and industrial organisations, the media'. The aim was not just to consult, but to gain 'ideas from the community that are capable of being shaped into concrete policy actions'. Consultations can also focus on professionals employed in a particular industry: Karia (2006) said that the UK Labour Party had created specialist networks 'designed to bring in specialist views. We have tried for example with the Labour school governor's network to get their views.' Consultations can also work at community level: Pattillo (2009) explained that 'the people who live with the problems or live with the solutions have information and data that won't be on any government database... engaging with the public certainly gives you the capacity to have richer problem definition... or to be able to create a richer, or more challenging kind of vision for the solution to a problem, or for an opportunity, or defining the way forward.'

Glover (2007) suggested that the public need to know the constraints governments face: 'you can either engage them in a very superficial way and just say "do you like it or don't you and are you happy to pay this for is, and this is the kind of thing that will happen" and on the issue it can be really quite superficial. Or you can do stuff where you're actually taking people through a process and informing them about some of the issues, giving them time.' He explained that they worked with 'a smaller group of people and we try to bring them up to a higher level of understanding so that they can make some meaningful decisions'. Karia (2006) said, 'the PM is quite good at setting some of this stuff out. You can't spend all the money several times in all areas – they have to choose.' Consultations also need to provide information in different ways to suit different needs and interests, making it accessible and relevant but also responsive to what people want. As Pattillo (2009) explained, 'really in depth information might be more available on websites where you can go and do your research if you're deeply passionate and want to know about something in a lot of detail. For others, having a touch of information, but relevant to them, might be sufficient for them to participate.' Gould (2007) also argues that 'they get it more the more information they're getting, and the more they can have deliberative debate, all that stuff is good'.

Furthermore, if consultation enables the public to see other people's views it leads to greater understanding and reflection, overcoming the potential issue of self-interest over community interest. Glover (2007) therefore argued that 'what sometimes happens in focus groups, depending which subject it is, is that people see the other point of view that they had never really seen before. Because they hadn't discussed the issue that widely, or they'd discussed it only with people who have the same view as themselves, then they might not have thought of the other people's shoes.' These participants can also be asked for solutions. As Pattillo (2009) noted, 'we need to do it well, so that in our busy lives we can capture what we need and then use techniques so that we are then part of constructing something rather than always just critiquing something... if you ask me to critique, then I will look for gaps. If you ask me to solve a problem, then you're going to get me in a different kind of state.'

Segmentation and targeting can lead elites to listen to some consumers and not others, disenfranchising the electorate. Savigny (2008a, 57) argued that 'the "product" is only targeted towards those groups who are in marginal seats, those groups for whom it is necessary to win the election' (see also Temple 2010, 271). Similarly, Steger (1999, 680) argues that in the US 'legislators are disproportionately attentive and responsive to those subsets of society that contribute most heavily to their re-election.' This threatens the democratic ideal of egalitarianism. Lilleker (2005a) claimed that segmentation and targeting 'are to some extent responsible for causing a division in society: those to whom politics belongs and those whom politics has abandoned'. Savigny (2008a, 54–55) argues that focus groups are not conducted 'in accordance with standard sampling techniques, which seek to ensure some kind of demographic equality, rather focus groups comprise tactically significant voters'. In consequence, any political responsiveness is geared to 'selected members of the electorate' (see also Savigny 2007).

However, elites can choose to use segmentation and targeting differently. It can be used positively to reach previously neglected voters: Nanos (2009) asserted that 'realistically, the voice of the silent majority, in any kind of nation, whether it's during an election or in between the elections, is revealed through public opinion research.' Mechanisms and services can be developed to identify, and help politicians understand the concerns of, smaller groups, which might otherwise be neglected, such as those less likely to vote and those who don't normally participate in consultation. Such methods can also help the groups' involvement in the political process. As Davidson (2005, 1190) noted, there is an argument that 'where levels of party identification and trust in the political system as a whole are in decline, simplistic categorizations of voters is an inadequate response.' Segmentation of the pensioner or retiree market has shown significant variation in the needs of those who have retired. Emerging minorities may be discovered earlier – and their issues addressed – because of organisations using market segmentation. Otherwise, they would just be left to grow over time until they were finally powerful and established enough to get their issues placed on the political agenda.

More broadly, consumerism seems to threaten traditional notions of citizenship. Lilleker and Scullion (2008, 4) explain how 'voting is implicitly an act with ethical values and morals attached as any individual choice will also take into account the broader impact on others of that choice.' In contrast, consumerism encourages people 'to be selfish, vain and individualistic'. Needham (2003, 7) argued consumerism has 'turned democracy into a marketplace' and downgraded citizenship, while Savigny (2008b) believes that it encourages self-interest (see also Walsh 1994, 67 and Slocum 2004, 744). Consumer and customer concepts ignore the big issues of politics, such as distribution of power, fairness and social justice (Aberbach and Christensen 2005, 236). Nevertheless, academics have also conceded that citizenship-type values can be integrated within consumerist behaviour. Consumers of commercial goods often integrate ethical and environmental factors into their purchasing decisions, as Slocum (2004, 767) notes 'personal wellbeing may be at the heart of much consumer action, but it is doubtful that people only think of themselves when they consider the safety of food, water, and other goods: they think of kids, family, and even community.' Similarly, Scullion (2008) suggested that citizenship and consumerisation can work alongside each other. People can take on 'citizenly roles' while in the market as consumers, and retain responsibility (see also Lane 1991, 1996 and 2000, Lilleker and Scullion 2008). Mark Penn (2007, xii) argued that V. O. Key's book on the rational voter that asserts voters are not fools was 'not only sound' but 'should be the guiding principle of understanding the trends we see in America and around the world'. Penn argues that (p. xii) 'people have never been more sophisticated, more individualistic or more knowledgeable about the choices they make in their daily lives.'

Conversely, Paleologos (1997, 1184) argues that 'the depressing and harsh reality of a poll-driven society' is that 'such a society ignores creativity. It overlooks new ideas. It prohibits change and true reform.' Political marketing may prevent emergence of new policies, which at first seem controversial but which are a necessary part of society's development, even if they are not yet part of mainstream market demands. As Jacobs and Shapiro (2000a, 11) observed, 'the proliferation and visibility of public opinion polling during the Clinton administration...led many critics of American politics to fear that poll taking of focus groups and the like has permanently replaced political leaders' (see also Newman 1999, 41 and Slocum 2004, 770). Paré and Berger's (2008, 58) conclusion from a study of how the Conservative Party of Canada was elected in 2006 as a minority government showed that using marketing does not necessarily result in meeting voter needs. The party revised 'its product offering with short-term and personal gain proposals in areas such as national unity, social policy, and economic policy that were aimed at appealing directly to the demands of voters', but then strategically chose to avoid 'engagement with contentious policy considerations that appeal directly to contending social values'. Paleologos (1997, 1183) argues that 'polling today...harms our democracy...Politicians are unwilling to take important leadership risks when immediate electoral gratification is so starkly visible.' Bernard Ingram, former press secretary to Prime Minister Margaret Thatcher, said in a debate held at the House of Commons in 2003 (quoted in the *Journal of Public Affairs*, vol. 4(3)),: 'politicians are there, or ought to be there, to do what is right by their country. They ought to have the courage of their convictions to do what is right and then they ought to employ the means available to put over that message and explain effectively why those policies are in the interests of the nation. If all we do is reduce politics to the art of analysing public opinion and going for that which is possible, then all we shall have is a bunch of measly, incompetent, useless followers.'

However, practitioners suggest that the way leaders use market analysis does not mean the end of leadership and doing what is right. If focus groups were wholly relied upon, this would be bad. But they aren't. As Carter (2007) said:

> At the end of the day, focus groups are not, nor do they intend to be, representative of 100 percent of the public. Therefore you can

get a level of response from focus groups which in some ways is misinterpreted when it's presented, because it's not representative. Nevertheless, I never felt that research was being used in that way. It's always a question of using research to help explain what are the right courses of actions and then using judgement as to how best to deliver that through specific actions.

Market analysis is just another market or source of opinion that is no different to other traditional pulls on the politician. As Utting (2008) explained, 'politicians aren't slaves to opinion polls because politicians are slaves to other more substantial interests like...the internal dynamic level in their party...what their support level is in caucus, what the attitudes of some of their big donors are, the cultural institutional things...they're the kind of real things that they have to sort of balance.'

There are a number of potential problems with marketing-informed communication. Academics argue that political marketing communication can increase distrust depending on how it is used. It can be seen as manipulative, as research enables political elites to get inside the head of voters. Scammell (2008, 111) noted 'the danger of misleading the public through an increasingly sophisticated understanding of consumer psychology' in branding. Dermody and Hamner-Lloyd (2006, 128) suggested that 'the way in which promotional marketing tools and concepts are being used in election campaigns, with the emphasis on creating distrust and suspicion of the competing parties, does not bode well for the future of democracy in Britain.' Branding can also simplify discourse, so the public relies on the brand without giving detailed scrutiny to elites' behaviour and play on emotion, thus reducing debate (see Needham 2005, Barberio 2006 and Scammell 2008).

Marketing techniques such as segmentation and targeting enable parties to concentrate their efforts and can help smaller parties and new candidates gain support and power. This may help reduce the effect of incumbency. The negative side is that extremist parties might also use such techniques. McGough (2009) revealed that Sinn Fein used research, segmentation, profiling and sales-oriented communication. He suggested from this that 'there is clearly an opportunity here for extremists to achieve a "fair" advantage but use it in an undemocratic manner...the same tactics have the potential to allow groups like Al Qaeda to gain a democratic position...the extremists may gain far more advantages through democracy than they ever did through the bomb and the bullet.'

Realising the democratic benefits

Market analysis helps to jolt the political elite out of planet politics and give them a reality check. Sparrow (2007) explained how politicians live in 'a very different place to the place where most people live....' Focus groups help politicians and their advisors understand the perspective of ordinary people. Braun (2009) said that 'the advantage of focus-groups is that it helps the campaign employees or the people working on the campaign get out of their bubble.' Campaigners are often 'freaking out about a certain issue, and you would take them to some focus-groups where you would ask regular, normal, randomly-chosen voters about the issue, and they'll say like "I hadn't even noticed the issue".' Ansell (2007) explained how 'there's a good way to cure smugness if you're feeling too much in love with your latest idea. It's called sitting in on a focus group. That's the creative person's equivalent of a polar plunge. You sit behind this two-way mirror and watch all these miserable floating voters ripping your cherished ideas limb from limb.'

Practitioners were strongly of the view that, despite the problems that can occur with public opinion formation and expression, market analysis is good for democracy. Of polling Rogers (2009) said, 'it is democracy. Polling is a democratic act. It's saying "I want to make sure I'm in line with the people that put me here".' Gould (2007) argued that market analysis 'has a kind of intrinsic moral good or worth... it is important at all times to allow people to have a voice and to have their opinions heard and to listen to the public.' Gill (2007) asserted that research helped democracy: 'one of the best things that I think has happened for democracy in the last 70 years is the proliferation of opinion polls, because without the public having their opinion it's left to the politicians and the journalists to decipher what the public think.' As Rennard (2006) said, 'on the whole political marketing is positive because it means voters expressing their opinions and parties having to address the concerns that voters have and listen to people, which is a fundamental part of democracy'. Scammell (2008, 111) agreed, saying, 'branding exposes opportunities as well as threats. The reconnection strategy reveals a determined effort to understand voters, take seriously and not dismiss as irrational, their emotional (dis)connections with politics. Theoretically it can assist connection between citizens and leaders.'

Academics have argued that market analysis causes declining voter turnout. Lees-Marshment and Lilleker (2005) argued that the sudden fall in turnout in the UK 2001 election suggested that the greater the use of targeted marketing techniques, such as voter segmentation, the more likely it is that non-target groups are demobilised. Washbourne (2005) asserted that political marketing could reduce debate within the public sphere: 'what is missed out is the idea of public discussion and debate being central to, even representative of, politics... [the] replacement of (some part of) public discussion by polls and focus groups bypasses democratic politics rather than engages it.' The use of more varied market analysis methods acknowledges this, and research can also engage the public. Hyder (2009) said that 'it has the advantage of offering people an opportunity to engage, alright? Because, it creates, but it creates noise, it creates talk', while Glover (2007) notes that 'it's really important... in a mature democracy where people don't participate that strongly... Any kind of participation, as long as it's done well, is good.'

The emphasis on professionalism which seems to accompany the use of marketing in communication can also reduce the importance of internal members while increasing that of unelected advisors (see Sackman 1996). Lilleker (2005b, 573) argues that political marketing can change internal power, as strategists together with the leadership determine policy direction in relation to market intelligence. This 'can leave ordinary members feeling alienated' if they see no response to their demands within that product development process. However, practitioners themselves argued that most advisors hold party values and sentiments. Fenn (2007) noted how consultants are often criticised for 'crash and burn, negative campaigning, the ends justifies the means, however you get elected is fine' type of approaches, but 'there are very few of us who believe in that kind of politics'. Ridder (2007) stated that 'many of us got into this because of ideological beliefs' and 'the ones I'm most proud of are the ones I lose – it isn't all about winning – sometimes the greatest amount of grief I've caused my opponents is when I've lost.' Duffy (2009) said, 'you're doing the lord's work.' Similarly, Mehta (2007) commented that:

> There's always room to stand up for what you believe in... I would much rather go down in flames of defeat and know that we've constantly stood up for what we believe because it was the right thing to do... You get to run again. This is not over... we keep continuing our work because we stand up for what we believe in, we say what we think and we live our values. If we keep doing that, doesn't matter if we win or lose next election, we're going to win in the long run. We're going to win the bigger game.

Pragmatically as well as normatively, elites should consider their internal market. Positioning and branding require differentiation and therefore enhance public choice (see Lilleker 2005a, Needham 2005, Barberio 2006 and Scammell 2008). Although some academics were concerned that party branding removed the freedom of candidates to respond to local voter needs – with Needham (2005, 356) recalling how Freedland (1999) noted that 'Number 10 officials insist that Labour is a "brand" and they cannot let just anybody go into the marketplace with that precious label' – more recently parties have learnt the importance of allowing diversification at local level.

Practitioners conceded that polling can be used in a problematic way: Gould (2007) said, 'in a way it does compromise principle, conviction and [a] kind of integrity' and Braun (2009) observed that 'if politicians only do what voters say, and change their mind based on the public mood changes, I think that's very dangerous. Not only is it bad politics and bad leadership, but it can have dangerous implications.' However, political marketing can also be used by elites to understand and move opinion to overcome the problem. Goot (1999, 237) argued that market intelligence 'may be just as effective as a means of working out how to galvanise support, neutralise opposition or convert those who might otherwise be reluctant to see things the party's way...it is not true that on every issue, or even on all the important ones, polling necessarily commits politicians to the position of the median voter.' Murray's (2006, 495) study of the Reagan presidency concluded that while some party-driven issues were sidelined, and changes were made if too much opposition was encountered, survey data were also used to find potential 'overlap' between the leadership goals and public opinion, 'to thereby identify political opportunities where it could accomplish some of its ideological goals and satisfy some of its partisan constituents, while staying within broad constraints established by majority opinion'. The Promise's work on reconnecting Tony Blair for the 2005 election suggested that there should be a 'Mature Tony', who expressed both conviction and reflection. Therefore, as Mortimore and Gill (2010, 255) argue, 'leadership judgement is also indispensable' to a party using marketing: 'even a party with no ideological principles would need sometimes to defy public opinion', and marketing can help 'create appropriate communication to make them more tolerated'.

Furthermore, abandoning all belief can lose an election. Morris (2002) argues that Al Gore lost the 2000 presidential election against George W. Bush precisely because he did not stand up for the environmental ideals he really believed in. Morris noted how Gore's 1988 bid to win the Democratic presidential nomination, which focused on the environment, was received negatively, and quotes Gore as saying, 'I began to doubt my own political judgement, so I began to ask the pollsters and professional politicians what they thought I ought to talk about' (p. 79). However, when Gore continued to take a more market-driven approach in 2000, he lost what had then become a key strength – Morris (2002, 83) quotes *Time* magazine at the time as saying: 'his strategists figure, quite right, that he can't be elected President solely as Mr. Environment and Technology... If all this means that Gore will soft pedal his signature cause, climate change... that's bad for the earth and unworthy of a politician who has a record for being principled and decisive.' Morris (2002, 86–87) argues that had Gore stuck to his environmental principles he could have gained secure support.

The difficulty for political marketing, however, is identifying precisely how and when leaders should maintain or change their position, and more research will need to be done on this. It could be that alternative market analysis would have identified the changing value of Gore's environmental position between 1988 and 2000. Or it could be impossible to produce a tool which ascertains what makes up a perfect leadership balance. It will be complicated by the difficulty of creating a definition of what makes an initially unpopular leadership drive policy 'good'. Goot (1999, 237) makes the pertinent point that 'typically, though not invariably, those who attack poll-driven policies are less concerned with how the policies are derived than the substance of the policies; the poll-driven decisions they dislike are derided, not the poll-driven decisions they like.' Gore's environmentalism may now be seen as 'good', but Blair's Iraq War is still 'bad'. What elites can do is be aware of the need to aim for such a balance and use marketing to identify a range of options and positions, and different responses to market analysis.

However, voter-driven communication can suit the public interest just as much as that of the elites. Rogers (2009) recalled how civil servants in Canada criticised the government for using research-led communications and thus moving into 'a gimmicky, manipulative, cheap and superficial place'. Notwithstanding, the government's goals were more positive: 'what we were doing was moving to a much more democratic place. It's just that our voters are increasingly busy, they're hearing all kinds of distracting information that's not about what we're trying to do with their money, we have to make a much greater effort to be present in their living room. When the two screaming kids and the parents, just home from work, have five minutes to watch the evening news, it better be apparent what we're talking about pretty quickly. We've got to acknowledge that we have a very narrow slice of their attention, and we are spending their money. So, we had better be spending it on the things that they have asked for.' Similarly, explaining elected leaders' position could be seen as helpful to citizens. Stanzel (2007) said, in relation to the California wildfires, 'it's important for the person who has been displaced from their home to know that the President gathered his cabinet together and had a meeting with them and directed them to do everything that they could to support state and local authorities in responding to the fires.' The advance of the internet could improve the information available to the public. Krohn (2007) observed:

> The media of yesteryear glossed over the complexity of topics, because it was a 30 second spot or sound-bite driven or facts-based or, you know, whatever. But we're now in a period of time – and it's only going to increase – where people have direct access to government information on topics... I believe we're moving into a period where the candidate's success is based on the merits of their issues, not how well they can attack each other. There will always be that degree of debate but hopefully a more educated electorate through ease of access to quality information on the internet. Technology is enabling individuals to base their decisions on issues.

Creating new ways to use political market democratically

In addition to the overall sense that each aspect of political marketing has positives and negatives, there was also a more profound perspective that came from the research: that there is an emergent form of democracy which connects vision and values with the practicalities of electioneering. This is not to deny potential weaknesses with the way political marketing has been used in the past, but to try to overcome them both in practice and theory – with that theory grounded in reality. Savigny (2008a, 3–5) conceded that problems have to be reconciled 'more practically, within contemporary politics', and Henneberg, et al. (2009, 166) caution that 'political marketing should not be judged against ideal and impossible standards of a perfectly informed, knowledgeable and participating electorate, but rather against the real world of relatively low interest and knowledge in politics.'

To explore this, we need to move to a more nuanced understanding that builds on, but is distinct to, earlier arguments, such as those by

Lees-Marshment (2001, 1) that parties 'no longer pursue grand ideologies, fervently arguing for what they believe in and trying to persuade the masses to follow them. They increasingly follow the people.' *Follow* needs to become *responds to*, and responds to needs to include multiple divergent positions in relation to the public. While this does not mean returning to outdated views of marketing as selling, it does mean avoiding the appealing but overly simplistic idea that politicians just follow the public. On a practical level, Ulm (2007) put the dilemma like this: 'in the end, we live in a democracy, people expect to be represented, but they expect their leaders to sort of divinely gather us.' Our understanding needs to mature to a more complex perception of political marketing behaviour. Only then can we engage in a constructive and productive debate about its impact on democracy.

Practitioners, who are living with the complexity of using marketing in politics, suggested that instead of being a problem, political marketing is *part* of the process of moving us to a new form of democracy. Hyder (2009) said, 'whatever I think about political marketing, it works, and it's here to stay. There's no changing that...it's here to stay. If anything I think you'll see more and more of it. Having said that, it will continue to change. It will continue to evolve.' Gould (2007) said, 'I don't believe that opinion polling is the end of that, it's the beginning. It's a kind of provisional condition before we move to a more participatory kind of politics where people become more fully involved.' Utting (2008) contended that:

> We're on the verge...of a major transformation in terms of the democratic process in our society. Our democratic system basically works on a sort of 18th or 19th century...you know, we're all on farms and small villages and it's all paper balloted...all the technology exists to really introduce sort of democratic systems, almost like it was in ancient Greece...there's a [change] in our society for people to have much more interest or much more involvement in decision making than they currently do. I think that polling is kind of the leading edge of that...We've just got to develop the political structures to go that way...I think that probably in 15–20 years' time our kind of democratic system and how it works will be much more engaged, and will be a much more interactive process.

Part of the background to this is that the way we communicate is changing, and the speed of that change is fast and increasing. Public control over political communication has increased. Social networking sites only really emerged at the turn of the twenty-first century, with the creation of YouTube in February 2005, which allowed the public to post their own submissions and whose audio-visual nature can connect politicians to the public more effectively. Hyder (2009) suggested that 'the more information that people have access to, the more they're able to talk to each other, is balancing off what is slowly becoming a deep-rooted cynicism and distrust, and lack of confidence in our public institutions...they are together forming their own cliques, groups, entities, and mobilising...to create more opportunities for engagement, dialogue, discussion, debate.' While the traditional communication sources of the public sphere may be in decline, they are developing elsewhere and are run by the consumers themselves. Dan Jackson (2008, 154–157) explored how a more consumerised media, combined with technological tools such as texting and RSS feeds, enables the public to have 'a more personalised experience of news and current affairs'. Rosenberg (2007) commented that 'Americans are now learning that media is not something to be consumed, it's something they can interact with.' E-marketing supports interactive and two-way communication, consultation and citizen involvement.

This may lift the citizen from passive consumer to active participant, not just in political communication, but in political decision-making. Geiselhart, Griffiths and FitzGerald (2003, 216–217) argue that communication technology could be developed to create a 'truly user-driven interactive democratic model that offers multiple modes for feedback, civic dialogue and participation'. Similarly, Morison and Newman (2001, 177) argued that 'the possibilities that a more thoughtful engagement with the new technologies offer accord very well with a range of approaches within recent political theory which suggest ways in which traditional democracy can be renewed' (p. 177). While this area has to be developed further in political practice, it has potential for growth. Henneberg, Scammell and O'Shaughnessy (2009, 170) note the use of such tools in the London mayoral campaign that Boris Johnson won, and argue that 'while none of this really amounts to political relationship marketing in any finished sense, and it may be seen as fostering the illusion of participation, it nevertheless establishes trajectory along which we are being driven towards relational interactions in politics.'

Indeed, more recent academic literature has argued that politics needs relationship marketing. Hughes and Dann (2009, 92) noted how the Australian Labor Party was using a relationship marketing paradigm in government of 'trust, reciprocity and commitment through the rapid implementation of election promise and the delivery of high profile trust building policy initiatives', such as the indigenous apology at the opening of the first parliamentary session (although further study of the apparent decline in relationship before Rudd was ousted as prime minister will obviously be advantageous). Henneberg and O'Shaughnessy (2009, 13) argue that a political relationship marketing approach would lead to positive implications for democracy, whereby 'voters would be consulted more often (and not only for election purposes), party members turned into stakeholders'. To solve the leadership dilemma, 'a relationship-building approach of political marketing management would provide a framework for elements of leadership which are supposedly destroyed by a more traditional, i.e. customer-(voter) led approach.'

The idea of some kind of relationship also came out of the practitioner data. Speaking after working on the Obama transition, Mehta (2009) said, 'government is not something out there, not something other, it is us... Barack Obama reminded us that the government is you and me. We pick the government that we deserve, and at the end of the day we fund the government, and the government is made up of all of our representatives. If you don't like the government, then you've got no one but yourself to blame because it's your government... Barack said "Get involved. Roll up your sleeves. Be a part of this and take ownership of it. If you don't like the government, fix it!"' Pattillo (2009) said that part of the process of government can be redeveloping the processes of policy development to ensure that they 'have people that are close to the problem and close to the solution intimately involved in developing the best way forward'; instead of just complaining, they 'then are part of creating their element of the solution'. Of course this means, as Mehta suggested Obama himself argued, that the consumer has to fulfil their side of the partnership. As Pattillo (2009) said:

> It's a work-too-hard solution to ask our leaders to take on all of that responsibility without recognising that some of that responsibility actually sits with me as a citizen... what I'd like us to do, and what our clients are often encouraged to do, is not to be the brave decision-maker in the sense of not allowing anybody else to see the complexity and the hardness of the decision that they have to make, but rather to engage people with an experience of the responsibility or the complexity of the problem or the decision that is before them. When government doesn't only ask people to tell us what they think or give us feedback, as opposed to engaging in the complexity of the

decision, everything seems too simple. If all I have to give you is what I think, as opposed to step into the decision-maker's shoes, governments lose the opportunity for people to be empathetic about the complexity of the choices they have to make.

Scullion (2008) suggested that political consumers will also expect 'a share of responsibility and blame when things go wrong, if they appreciate a link between their own choice and the resultant conclusion'.

This would involve a change in the way democracy works, both conceptually and in practice. There is some sense of this to be found in the academic literature, even if it is more of a potential that is not yet realised than something that has already happened and been empirically observed. When discussing online government, Geiselhart, Griffiths and FitzGerald (2003, 229–230) suggest that it has a positive potential for democracy:

> From a theoretical perspective, there is growing awareness that political models developed in the eighteenth century are giving way to a new paradigm. The old models are based on Newtonian mechanics and linear, hierarchical structures, along with assumptions of stability as not just desirable, but possible. The new models recognise and harness diversity and pluralism as micro-drivers of democracy... [over time we will be] modelling governance and developing protocols for participation, using generic democracy indicators and values to generate the rules of interaction.

Lees-Marshment and Winter (2009) suggest synthesising recent theories of political marketing and market-orientation parties from electoral-party behaviour, and deliberative democracy from political theory 'to offer both a more effective framework for consulting the public in both theoretical and practical terms'. Deliberative political theory can help provide a more effective consultation process because it 'is focused on deliberation rather than voting and emphasizes citizen involvement in a political process. It considers opinion and will-formation before voting; and can be an expansion of representative democracy, indeed the res publica itself beyond just interest aggregation.' Furthermore, deliberative mechanisms can provide training or information to the citizen and 'mitigate some of the weaknesses in mass public knowledge and understanding compared to elites'. Henneberg, Scammell and O'Shaughnessy (2009, 176–179) discussed political marketing in relation to competitive elitism (Schumpeter) as well as deliberative democracy (Habermas).

They also noted how Habermas's idea of a public sphere and concept of deliberate democracy encourages participation from citizens between formal elections, unlike Schumpeter's. They conclude that 'a polity constructed as part of on-going relationship building, e.g. using regular referenda, citizens' juries, or electronically-enabled interactions, could bring forth a genre of political marketing which focuses on the goals of information, persuasion and reciprocity, rather than attack and defence.'

Practitioners also discussed a change in approach. Pattillo (2009) said that 'if you give people more time, and you change the nature of the questions you're asking, then you get a different dynamic of people that are interested in the conversation, so then it moves from the debate to dialogue.' Government decision-making often occurs in 'a conspiracy of silence' or 'that seemingly silent vacuum [of] government'. If processes allowed people's participation to have influence this would change behaviour, 'but I don't think we're quite there yet, because I think our fundamental premise about what we're asking government to do and how they might do it – we haven't yet had that conversation'. Hyder (2009) said that 'you need to communicate with them, and they need to communicate with you, and it can't be the orchestrated stuff. It can't be the "30 of my constituency people are coming to tell me that this is what they want, and they happen to all have memberships of my political party, and I'm going to listen to what they say".' When launching a programme of Citizen Juries in September 2007, UK Prime Minister Gordon Brown said, 'the old models of consultation need radical renewal... so we will expand opportunities for deliberation, we will extend democratic participation in our local communities' (http://www.pm.gov.uk/output/Page13008.asp, accessed 5 March 2008).

However, there needs to be a link between such dialogue and the final elite decision-making. Pattillo (2009) recalled how she had sometimes re-engaged with the same people, and they said 'the reason that they had come back is that one, they said that we'd got good information, two, it felt worthwhile and it was easy to be part of, and three, they told us how what we said and did impacted your decision.' Thus their participation was clearly worthwhile. It built a relationship: 'that's a pretty simple relationship building recipe. It's not saying "We came back because you did everything we told you to do." It's people coming back saying "You were up front with us, and reasonable, and you honoured our contribution." That's not hard, and that practice would fit all across the government, I would think. I can't promise you, but that's my guess.' There will always, of course, be times that government has to act more quickly and not consult, but they can always explain why: 'it allows the leaders of our government to say "This isn't how we normally act. We had to act in this way because of X, Y, and Z. This is this instance, but let us be clear about giving you information explaining what we did, and give you the chance to give us that feedback".' As Gould (2007) pointed out:

> My problem with those kinds of participatory activities is that, unless they're done in kind of the right way, you're going to get a situation where the public in those kinds of exercises want to do one thing and the government will want to do something else. And that's a problem. That's a listening-leadership clash again. And that's not been resolved. I think it makes difficulties for democracy. How would you... How do you involve people in the political process? Say, for example, the public come out and say we don't want to have nuclear power. And the government thinks we absolutely have to have nuclear power. What do you do there? And on and on and on. It's difficult. You need a kind of a methodology, a theory of democracy that can deal with it, which is quite hard. David Held has done a lot of work on this, but I think it's quite a hard thing to do. You can't just set them up and hope they're going to work because you know, people want the government to lead, and the government has to lead, and how you involve people in that process, it's difficult. But it's got to be doable, because people do want to be involved and so they should be.

Summary

There are clearly a range of issues and concerns with regard to the democratic implications of political marketing. However, it is less clear that such negatives are inevitable, while there are also several positive consequences from the use of marketing in politics. Table 7.1 provides a summary of the rules for marketing democratically, and this shows that practitioners are developing solutions to problems. Elites are therefore free to choose to what extent to practise political marketing democratically; the tool itself does not dictate its democratic effect. Additionally, practitioners are exploring ways to develop the marketing's potential so that it becomes less of a threat and more of a support in helping democracy evolve in the twenty-first century. This will be developed and discussed further in the Conclusion to this book.

Table 7.1 Rules of the game for marketing democratically

Overcoming potential problems
1. Understand, accept and respect the nature of public interest and knowledge
2. Listen to the public despite potential weaknesses in public opinion
3. Use methods that will increase the value of the opinion collected
4. Consult those who can offer more informed opinions, such as professionals, service users, people living with the problem
5. Provide the public with information and a sense of the constraints of government
6. Encourage consideration of others during research and consultation
7. Avoid letting segmentation lead to responding to some voters more than others; use it to find under-represented interests instead
8. Be aware of the need to view the public as citizens as well as consumers
9. Use research to help address some difficult issues even when they are unpopular
10. Avoid manipulating or misleading the public through research-informed communication
11. Use marketing techniques to combat major party incumbency but without over-inflating minor party support unfairly

Realising the democratic benefits
12. Conduct market analysis to prevent being marooned on planet politics
13. Use market analysis because it is democratic in itself
14. Use market analysis to increase participation and engagement
15. Consider internal and ideological constraints as well as public ones for democratic but also pragmatic reasons
16. Use market research to understand public opinion to inform a balanced leadership strategy
17. Use voter-driven communication to reach and inform the public

Creating new ways to use political market democratically
18. Understand political marketing is more complex and does not fit into distinct categories, such as selling to or following the public
19. Consider more balanced political marketing as part of a multi-faceted evolution towards a new form of democracy
20. Understand the citizen is developing from a passive consumer to active participant
21. Explore how the citizen–government relationship in political marketing is changing
22. Citizens need to work with elites to find the solution to problems
23. Democracy itself is changing
24. The link between market research or public consultation and decision-making needs further development and reconciliation

Conclusion: Political Marketing, Democracy and Partnership

What you saw in 2003 with the Howard Dean campaign was the beginning of a very different model...where you view people out there not as couch potatoes as we called them in the US, but as partner in your fight...it's not a broad based model it's a partnership model.

—Rosenberg (2007)

It was moving from transactional politics to transformational politics: transactional politics is – somebody comes to you and says 'If you vote for us, we'll give you this.' Transformational politics is community building. It's the idea of saying 'We're all in this together. Don't you want to see our community get better? If we elect Barack Obama we will see our lives improve in the following ways. Come do it with me.'

—Mehta (2009)

It needs a much clearer sense about what government's role is.... where are the bits that need an act of partnership between government and community?...while there are instances of really good practice coming out of government in terms of how it works with community, because there isn't a brand...and an expectation built around it, that good practice falls into a void of 'You were lucky, or, I didn't notice.' So, we need to change our market expectations.

—Pattillo (2009)

However pleasant popularity is, 'all things to all people' never lasts for long. Then as I struggled with the levers of power...I was determined to do the right thing. But...if you're not careful, 'doing the right thing' becomes 'I know best'. So, starting with the Big Conversation, I went back out, and...I learnt...the best policy comes from a true partnership between Government and people. Governments can spend. We can exhort. We can legislate. But we cannot cure the sick. We cannot be inside every classroom. We cannot police the streets...So this journey has gone from 'all things to all people' to 'I know best' to 'we can only do it together'. And we all know which is best of those three. A partnership.

—Speech by Tony Blair to Labour's spring conference at the Sage Centre in Gateshead (13 February 2005)

Politics in the twenty-first century will be radically different to what has come before. Political practitioners – whether politician, market researcher, advertiser, strategist, policy advisor, press secretary, campaign manager or party secretary – have at their disposal clear rules on how to use marketing to navigate the complex electoral game. However, to win the political marketing game elites need to make careful choices. Politicians need to adopt principled pragmatism. They need to offer responsive leadership that responds to but does not just follow public opinion; authentic reflectiveness that shows genuine consideration of different demands but does not change position without justification; research informed decisions that are not just led by market analysis; and still have a sense of strategic vision that takes multiple markets into account but also incorporates attempts to achieve belief-stimulated change. Furthermore, politicians need to move towards a partnership relationship with the public whereby both citizens and government work together to find solutions. This chapter will summarise the results of the research, before suggesting a theory of a partnership democracy which will be discussed within the overall context of a changing relationship between the public and politicians.

Winning the political marketing game

The main findings are portrayed in Diagram 1. In terms of the political market, elites need to consider not just voters, but all stakeholders, particularly once they have been elected. Old cleavages and groupings are less relevant, while new segments and groupings are emerging, but elites should still market to partisan voters to get them to actually vote and to participate. Voters are more consumerist and critical in attitude; therefore elites need to respect voters, but also take into account the fact that the quality of their opinion may be qualified by lack of information.

214

Strategy
Develop the strategy first; make clear but flexible; devote time; review and adapt; vary responsiveness to public opinion; consider range interests; integrate vision; start ambitious strategies early; stick with it

Party
Appreciate supporters; offer tailored services; make involvement easy; give support, training and promotion on ability; give volunteers' leadership; build strong organisation and resources over long term; create unity by enabling discussion, explaining wider public demands, explain decisions, relating to vision; give strategy time, build supportive relationships between centre and local; allow local freedom within overall brand

Market analysis
Multi methods & sources on multi-stakeholders. Open to results, consider quality of input, don't misuse, gain skills to interpret. Get advisors who challenge but don't micromanage

Leadership
Choose from range of options; consider multi-markets and sources; balance leading and following public; manage overriding the market by demonstrating awareness and explaining difficult decisions; don't abandon vision at first criticism try to change some opinions; ensure changes are justifiable and credible

Branding
View politician/party as brand; use party brand to build long-term support; make brand simple, distinctive, reassuring, aspirational, symbol of values, credible, competent, trustworthy, create strong perception on honesty, spirit, image, leadership, toughness; manage lifecycle, decontaminate negative then re-brand; successive leaders re-brand to mark new departure

Delivery management
Work with and support civil service; facilitate networks and relationships; build will around vision; expect slow pace for ongoing services; compromise in coalition but keep something for credit; acknowledge failures & find solutions; achieve great not just good success

Competition management
Different distinctive positions; use credible direct/indirect attack on strengths not just weaknesses; open to beneficial competition

Communication
Simplify; credible negative; humour, emotion, positive and unconventional; authentic; manage unpopularity; communicate change early; target but avoid conflicting messages; create unique campaign; respond to receiver's knowledge, interest and concerns; demonstrative responsiveness; two way; individualised; GOTV for all; online version; local politician reputation building; trustworthy media management

Diagram 1 Winning the political marketing game

Some voters are more likely to judge politicians by an emotional reaction to their personality, rather than by their policy. It takes a long time for the public to change their perception of a party; politicians and existing opinions can be reinforced but changing them is much more difficult. Political consumers often want more instant delivery than is possible, and demand will always be insatiable. Public evaluation of delivery is not always accurate, and even where individual experience is positive the consumer will not always generalise such positivity to their overall perception of government performance on the area nationwide.

Therefore, to win the political marketing game, elites need to use a wide range of market research sources, consultants and methods (including polls, focus groups, role play, in-depth interviews, post-election analysis, opposition and candidate research, ideas from other countries, market-back analysis/feedback from those affected by a policy, think tanks, public sector staff, policy advisors, communication staff, online discussion, public consultation, on-the-ground feedback, internal supporters and gut instinct). Analysis needs to be conducted on all stakeholders (volunteers/members, donors, experts, think tanks, candidates, public sector staff, competitors, the media, unions, party staff), not just voters. Analysis that encourages more informed and solution-oriented feedback will be most valuable, but when using consultation to make it effective elites need to ensure it is run scientifically and that participants reflect society or the segment being consulted rather than their own special interests. Candidates can conduct their own market analysis and demonstrate this. Segmentation can be used to create new groups in the market using a range of factors (geography, demography, family, lifestyle, political views, internet usage and voter profiling), while political elites should also build long-term databases on voters. When taking ideas from another country, elites should look for examples where there were similar circumstances, or particular features, albeit ensure that the idea suits their unique campaign/election each time. When working in a different country advisors have to get to know the local market and adapt their ideas.

Overall, elites need to understand that all analysis is limited by data and assumptions, and that market analysis is more of an art than a science. Parties and politicians need to use skilled and experienced advisors to interpret the results, and there needs to be a positive relationship between consultants/advisors and politicians. Politicians need to actually want market analysis, know what they want from it, commission it and bring advisors into the process early enough for the research to be useful and for advisors to do their job effectively. Advisors should also be given room to do their job properly without politicians trying to bias the results by not letting them act independently. Therefore, politicians need to ensure their advisors can get access to decision-makers to be effective. They need to listen to objective results, accept negative results gracefully and avoid using the results selectively to justify a particular position. They should also ensure that they understand or get training to understand the results.

Advisors need to present a range of different options from the results, and should present recommendations, especially negative ones, with care. Generally, they need to challenge politicians without micromanaging them, work with their abilities and character, and keep politicians focused on their strategic goals and vision.

The different areas of marketing, while distinct, overlap with each other and market analysis informs all other aspects of marketing in a range of ways to suit different purposes and timing. Thus, elites can use marketing analysis for a range of purposes in product development: confirm the existing position; check a new direction is gaining support; suggest adjustment, specific changes, whole-scale change; identify where it is not possible to change opinion. In communication, it can be used to understand the general picture, identify the most popular product aspects and the issues people care most about, communicate issues politicians care about, sell policy, check assumptions, test negative communication, inform the changing perception of the leader, make communication more effective and increase the chances of changing opinion over time. Together with strategy, segmentation can help identify new groupings politicians can represent: it can identify the next tier of existing supporters, a part of the market that has been ignored and new areas the party has not done well in before. The party can then segment volunteers to create tailored services and requests for funds to donors, offering different levels of contact. Leaders can use marketing to find, or re-find, a balance between leading and following and achieve change and gain public acceptance for their decisions, rather than changing themselves to suit the market all the time. They should use market analysis proactively to achieve their vision and broader goals; to identify when a new policy can be sold, or opinion changes, or when something cannot be made to work and must be given up. With regard to competition management, political staff can use candidate research to predict competition attacks and uncover any inconsistency or change in position, and formulate a rationale to combat these; use market analysis and opposition research to assess the competition and suggest ways in which the party or candidate can position themselves in relationship to them and make their competition strategy most effective. And, in government, politicians can get feedback via market-back analysis to ensure that what they deliver has the desired impact. They can also use consultation to help create a willingness to change amongst different markets and ease the implementation of decisions made.

Political practitioners need to develop the strategy first, and, in doing so, consider different interests, options and visions as well as pragmatic goals. They need to set clear goals and dedicate time to strategy creation and review of process. They should ensure, however, that the strategy is flexible and can evolve as circumstances change. Politicians can choose a variety of strategies and responsiveness to public opinion, depending on their goals. Pure market- or leader-led campaigns do not work – responsiveness works, but only while maintaining vision and integrity. Therefore, politicians need to start more ambitious strategies earlier, be open to strategising even when support is high and keep focused on the strategy in spite of criticism. As for using strategy, it should inform all communication; a communications strategy needs to be thought out in advance and adhered to, despite media criticism or unforeseeable events. In government, elites need to put aside time to review the strategy in order to keep it on course and adopt a learning orientation, so that they can reflect on the progress of goals and new ideas.

In competition management, politicians need to differentiate, be distinctive and have clear consistent advantages in comparison to the competition. Re-positioning needs significant action and communication to change public perception. Politicans can develop credible direct and indirect ways to attack opponents, including weakening their strengths not just focusing on their weaknesses. Negative attacks need, however, to be credible and parties should be open to co-operation where it is beneficial and wary of attacking coalition partners. They should also make sure that their product offers solutions, not just criticisms of the competition, and ensure that these more tactical considerations fit the overall strategy.

Elites should see the candidate/leader/party as a brand: a longer-term, more psychological concept. They need to put resources into the party brand, even in candidate-based systems, and use the brand to build up long-term support, which impacts on support for individual candidates. They should make the brand simple, distinctive, reassuring, aspirational, a symbol of internal values, credible, competent, trustworthy and able to deliver, and ensure it rates highly on honesty, spirit, image, leadership, toughness and uniqueness. It is hard to change a brand. Leadership brands will go through a product life cycle bell curve, which needs to be managed with re-branding when they become unpopular. If a brand becomes contaminated, the public's perception of its negativity needs to be removed before re-branding can attract new support. Politicians who succeed a strong brand leader in the same party need to use their own branding to make them distinct from their predecessor, and internal members need to support such re-branding.

Political decision-makers and leaders have options and can choose a range of ways in which to use marketing. They should consider a range of markets and opinions and sources when making decisions, and ensure the candidate is representative of society. They need to balance leading and following the public: overriding the market causes a loss in popularity, but this can be managed by showing an understanding of the market and explaining difficult decisions. Leaders should not abandon their vision when criticism first arises; opinions can change, but changes made to the vision need to be backed by a good reason to be seen as credible.

Elites need to value and show appreciation of members, supporters or volunteers and donors, developing services that meet their needs in order to increase their activity, attachment, commitment and understanding of elite decisions. Elites should make it as easy as possible for the public to get involved, offering support and training to volunteers, promoting them on the basis of skills not connections or time served, and letting them become part of the campaign and take leadership positions. It is prudent to maintain a strong organisation and staff in all areas over the long term, not just for the campaign, even in candidate-based systems. Internal unity in the party and campaign needs to be maintained, and ways to do this are to ensure that there is internal debate and discussion about politics and policy, explain how public demands differ from supporters' demands, explain the reasons for elite decisions which do not follow internal views and connect change to the overall vision. It will take time for new strategies to be accepted. Party headquarters need to build positive, supportive relationships with local branches and allow local candidates freedom to offer distinctive, locally relevant strategies while maintaining the same overall sense of the party brand.

The party will influence product development, as elites need to consider all stakeholders when developing the product, adjust some decisions to suit the party but also challenge internal views – given that activists' views tend to be more extreme and parliamentary parties can be out of touch. In relation to communication, the party should back the new direction so that the public comes to accept changes in the product. Campaign managers need to develop a positive team spirit and manage any tensions if they are going to be successful in campaign communication.

Advertising enables elites to convey a controlled message and can simplify messages for those less interested in detail. It needs to reflect the party/politician and be authentic. Caution should be taken with regard to negative communication; it must stand up to questioning, be credible and be accepted by the public. To help get attention, communication should use humour, emotion, positive proposals for the future and unconventional methods. Media advisors help present politicians to the public, and can overcome weaknesses, including physical appearance. Furthermore, leaders can be re-launched if they become unpopular. Communicating change is something that should be started as early as possible, and politicians need to be prepared to explain any changes to the media. Communication should be targeted in terms of what is said, not just who it is said to, and conflicting messages to different target groups must be avoided. In terms of detail, while most communication should focus on two to three areas, the information level can be varied to suit different audiences, with detail kept for experts or those of the public who seek it online. A unique campaign should be created for each individual election, and generally practitioners should be prepared for uncontrollable elements. Communication is more effective if it is responsive to the receiver. It should connect with ordinary people and reflect their levels of knowledge and interest, focus on what they care about, reflect what they already think and demonstrate responsiveness. Two-way communication enables the public to become an active partner rather than just a receiver of elite information. Communication can become individualised through direct marketing or online communication, and parties should support on-the-ground word of mouth. Get out the vote (GOTV) should be used on all types of supporters. Online communication staff need to be supported to explore the potential of the medium: micro-targeting, GOTV and face-to-face campaigning can be done virtually and be more precise, less presumptive, less costly and delivered to mobile communication vehicles. Parties need to encourage local level communication, using face-to-face communication and the local media to reach voters, while local MPs/representatives should use long-term local communication to help build a positive reputation for a candidate and mitigate problems with the party. Media management must be based on fact, work with the nature of the medium and be based on a trusting relationship with journalists. Elites should remember that they have limited ability to directly influence reporting. Politicians have to overcome the barriers the media present to political marketing, such as being reluctant to convey positive product change and positive delivery progress. The media do explore non-mainstream issues and offer a variety of commentary, even if this is not always noticed. They also try to explain why an issue is important to ordinary members of the public, and communicate complex issues comprehensibly.

Communication in relation to the product and leadership includes using communication to help gain support for policy that might be beneficial but not popular at first, and using a fresh style, a new label and new leadership to convey change in the product, position or brand. In relation to competition management, communication needs to be used to define the politician before the opposition does. In relation to the party, internal communication can be used to ease the potential tension that occurs between internal demands and those of voters, as well as to communicate and explain changes in the product and strategy or the inability to make progress on new policy that supporters would like.

Once in power, elites need to manage competing demands and overcome obstacles from stakeholders to deliver their election promises. To get delivery to succeed they need to work with the civil service, avoid blaming them for problems, offer support and help where deficiencies or underperformance is identified, and more widely facilitate networks and relationships among all stakeholders to achieve progress. Making the overall vision clear helps maintain a will for and a focus on delivery. Delivery is slow on ongoing services and in coalition parties have to compromise on promises. However, they also need to ensure that there is something distinct that all can claim credit for. Politicians need to acknowledge any failures in delivery and find solutions to them. To get attention from the public, they must achieve great, not just good, success in delivery, and avoid focusing on what can be communicated instead of what needs to be delivered; not all good delivery makes a good story.

Government and delivery influence the product as politicians need to ensure the product is achievable and scale promises down, if necessary, before the election. In leadership terms, they need to take extra care to avoid becoming too marooned on 'planet politics'. The longer politicians are in power the more elitist images are shown of them, such as attending overseas meetings with other world leaders, and thus the harder they need to work to maintain responsiveness and ensure advisors can get access to leaders. In relation to strategy, they should try to manage expectations of delivery before election. On communication, before the election they need to build credibility using pledge- or contract-type tools and communicate delivery capability. Once in power, they should use delivery reports at national and individual MP/representative level; demonstrate that they do not just allege delivery; convey progress relevant to the individual, using real-world significant cases at a local level; provide local versions, facts and figures of federal-level policies or stories for local MPs to communicate; and convey the progress if not the wholesale completion of delivery.

Overall, leaders and their advisors are finding ways to use political marketing to merge pragmatism with principle to achieve broader goals, including advancing change. They have many options and choices in this field; nevertheless, marketing does not dictate decisions, it merely informs them. That politicians have options to choose from when using political marketing changes its democratic implications. Diagram 2 explores the potential that might be realised if elites used political marketing more positively. All stakeholders are considered as market analysis comes from a variety of sources and utilises a range of methods. Market analysis (including consultation) uses methods that seek unity of opinion, open possibilities for change and identify solutions. Leaders offer a range of responsiveness to market analysis and stakeholders (maintain the status quo, make small changes, explain the position, change opinion, defend unpopular decisions or change the product significantly). Marketing is used to achieve change; non-consultative decisions are rare but are subsequently explained and further feedback is sought. Branding and competition management are used to create distinctive, visionary products, thus providing choice for voters. The product, brand, position and communication must be authentic and any changes to these must be thought out and justified. Advisors present different options for politicians to help them achieve their particular goals, rather than dictate the strategy. Minor parties can use marketing to maximise the effectiveness of their limited resources to combat their incumbency and other barriers. Marketing tools are applied to all voters and volunteers, not just target segments, and previously under-represented groups, which increase participation.

Opposition research is verifiable and factual and focuses on matters relevant to the sought position only. It identifies and questions changes in the government's position to encourage greater integrity and authenticity. The public keeps itself informed, government-aware and community-oriented, and can thus accept responsibilities as well as rights and become a partner in government not just a user. Parties develop engagement to suit the user, view volunteers as partners in the

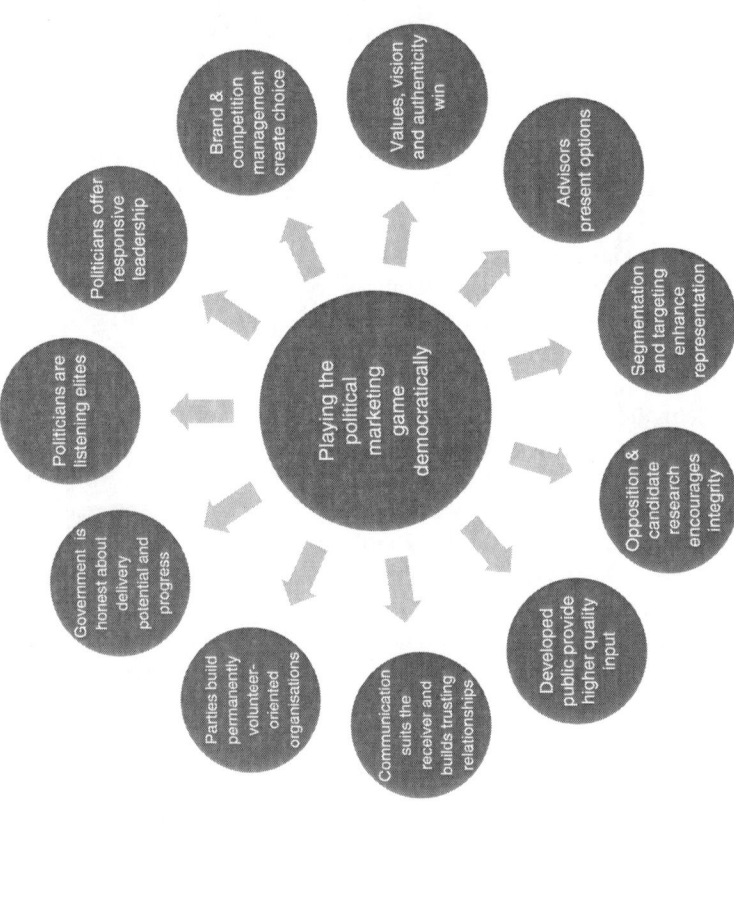

Diagram 2 Playing the political marketing game democratically

campaign, maintain organisation and contact in all areas so no one is neglected, and maintain vision, belief and value. Communication responds to varied needs and behaviours; it includes voter-driven, two-way and citizen-led communication, and, by allowing debate, it develops conversation and debate within the public sphere. Relationships internally and with the media are based on truth and trust. There is room for freedom and diversification by individual candidates within the overall brand. Politicians should avoid over-promising and adjust their product to make it realistic; in government they need to admit failures in delivery and communicate progress on delivery in a way which is relevant to individuals and is not just about national statistics.

Towards a partnership democracy

Given the positive potential of how elites could use political marketing democratically, and the impact this could have on the relationship between citizens and government, it is possible to argue that democracy itself will evolve. Therefore, this section presents a new theory of partnership democracy. Theory creation is an important process in academia because it opens up new ways of thinking. It visualises how things could be or may be, not just how (we think) they are right now. The task is, of course, fraught with difficulty and no theory is ever 100 per cent successful in its aims. Thus, this theory is presented here without any grandiose claims to perfection or final words. Discussion is focused in three key areas – market analysis, the public and leaders – within the overall relationship between politician and the public. A summary can be found in Diagram 3, while the basic principles are explained in further detail later.

The public

The public need to become more effective at providing valuable input into the political system, not just at election time but all times, and ensure that their input is as valuable as possible. They need to become more informed, more community-minded, and constructive in what they say and do. While the most obvious role of the political consumer is about asserting rights and demands, this needs re-balancing to include responsibilities. Instead of just criticising elites, the public need to offer constructive feedback and develop a better understanding of the perspective of those making decisions. They also need to listen to elites as much as they expect elites to listen to them, especially regarding the complexity of government, but must, nevertheless, maintain the right

224

A partnership democracy

People part of government; 'yes WE can' not 'yes YOU can'; take more responsibility and participate; room for politicians to say no and be leaders but explain why; a partnership whereby elites and masses work together to create solutions

The public	Deliberative market analysis	Politicians
Informed and community minded	A nationwide system of dialogue	Consider a range of stakeholders, even if the public quality input is most influential
Demands balanced with responsibility	All forms of publicly funded analysis	
Not just critical but constructive	Activity transparent	Consider history and beliefs, the party, achievability, credibility, the vision
Understand decision-makers perspective	Results available to all	
	Administered by independent body	Take varying responses in relation to market analysis: following public opinion, changing the product significantly, making small changes, or maintaining the status quo, explaining the position further, trying to change opinion, defending unpopular decisions, overruling the public
Listen to elites as much as they expect elites to listen to them	Collected from variety of sources	
Respect elites and the work they do	Deliberative solution-oriented methods	
Give credit where credit is due	Participants selected to suit scientific and democratic guidelines	
Continue to demand further progress	Participants informed & aware	
Become a partner in government not just a critical consumer	Continual; before and after policy decisions & implementation	When necessary make quick decisions without consultation; but should later explain why and get feedback
	Linked to government decision-making	
	Funded by collating resources already spent	Be honest about delivery potential, problems and progress
	A new form of public sphere and participation	

Diagram 3 A partnership democracy

to question and form their own opinion thereafter. The public need to respect elites and should give credit for delivery and other successes, as well as continuing to demand further progress. Being overtly critical may not bring out the best in politicians, and the public need to be willing to give new politicians, leaders and re-branded parties more of a chance. The public needs to become a partner in government, not just a critical consumer.

Leaders

While politicians need to be responsive, responsiveness can come in many different forms. Awareness of and respect for the public at all times is essential, but this does not mean that leaders should follow every change in public opinion or completely neglect other actors in the political system, such as the party. Instead, they need to consider a range of stakeholders, even if quality input from the public is the most influential, such as history and beliefs, the party, achievability, credibility and the vision. Leaders need to hold varying responses in relation to market analysis: following public opinion, changing the product significantly, making small changes, or maintaining the status quo, explaining the position further, trying to change opinion, defending unpopular decisions, overruling the public. When necessary they should make quick decisions without consultation, but should later explain their reasoning and get feedback on their decision. They must be honest about delivery potential, problems and progress.

Deliberative market analysis

Market analysis is the activity that holds the potential to connect the political and public arenas. That is not to dismiss the importance of the party, participation, parliament or other bodies we have traditionally seen as playing a mediation role between elites and the masses. But when reflecting the change in the way discussion and debate links with elite decision-making in the twenty-first century, as well as the potential integration of innovative consultation methods, it is clear that deliberative market analysis is the new system of voter input in politics. The old system whereby voters simply voted on politicians' promises and rhetoric at election time and then waited to see how they performed (possibly voting against them at the next election if they did not like what they did) is now over. It may not be official, but elections are less important than they once were – at least in terms of providing voter input and influence. Instead, candidates, parties and governments at all levels conduct a range of market analysis in different forms (focus groups, polls, role plays, big talks or public consultations) to understand the public outwith elections. As Cain et al. (2003, 266) observed, 'widespread use of polling by governments to monitor public opinion' has increased 'the public opinion signal between electoral cycles'. This means that 'citizens can influence policy-making through the party system and electoral process as before, but they can also intercede to influence elected officials before they make their decisions; and even after the decisions are made they can attempt to influence administrators as they implement the policies' (p. 268). Market analysis is not an acknowledged part of the political system or governance, but it needs to be.

At present, market analysis varies in time, method, quality and influence. It is conducted in government at all levels. Around the world there are countries doing public consultation, private public opinion research, and departmental and policy research. Although there is actually a lot already occurring – sometimes even too much, creating consultation fatigue – it is being done in a disjointed way, which is kept slightly hidden from the public. While what is being done will have already been using substantial funds, their cumulative and summative extent will not be known. If an audit was conducted identifying the cost of all forms of research, analysis and consultation with the public, the overall sum could be reused for a new system that could be centralised and organised to meet certain principles.

It would be a nationwide system of dialogue/consultation/analysis, integrating all forms of publicly funded market analysis, including polls and surveys and also consultation linked to government decision-making to demonstrate impact. Activity and results would be transparent and available to all interested parties/public/think tanks, not just the governing party. The results could be built into a long-term archival resource. This would be administered by an independent body – out of parliament – so that the results would be non-partisan and collected using variety of sources and consultants. As well as traditional polling work, this system should use deliberative methods so that participants are informed in the way that suits them, they are aware of the complexity of decision-making, they see different views and they therefore provide less selfish and more solution-oriented feedback. Participants need to be selected to suit scientific and democratic guidelines and to avoid the influence of select interests. Analysis should be conducted before and after policy decisions are made, and implemented, leading to a system of permanent evaluation. The public would then know that they are going to be consulted at the beginning of policy decisions as well as through their implementation, and also that such consultations will be evaluated and improved, so they become a continual development process rather than an ad hoc or only at election time formal system of feedback. It could both improve policy and ensure that any bad implementation of good policy was prevented in time to save the policy. At first, this system may have to operate for only certain policies – perhaps those more amenable to cross-party decision-making or conscience voting – before the link between market analysis and decision-making is worked out. It would be funded by collating resources now spent in different government departments at federal, national government, state and local level. Over time it would be developed to involve local parliaments, citizen representatives, expert citizens and specialist professional experts – thus deliberative consultative market analysis then becomes a new form of public sphere and participation.

Overall relationship: a partnership between politician and the public

Overall, governments need to move to more of a partnership orientation and build relationships with the public. Academics argued that elites need to use relationship marketing; and practitioners that they need to view the people as part of the government and develop a system to involve those closest to the problem in finding a solution, which could mean more expert citizens with direct experience of the problem. Equally, the public need to feel and act as though they are the government too: Obama said 'yes WE can' not 'yes I can'. They need to take more responsibility and participate in appropriate deliberative market analysis and give feedback that is solution-oriented. The movement towards greater engagement, involvement, citizen-led communication and deliberative democracy fits this direction. Elites can work in partnership with the people. In developing the nationwide system of dialogue/consultation/analysis that links to government decision-making there also needs to be room for politicians to say no and be leaders but explain why; building a partnership whereby elites and masses work together to create solutions. This will, of course, only be achieved over several decades, and both cultural and institutional obstacles will need to be overcome. However, this provides possibilities as to the future of political marketing, or even politics itself.

A partnership democracy in context

The Political Marketing Game shows that elites have to use marketing with authenticity, values and vision; they are as much a part of a winning strategy as market-savvy pragmatism. If a politician asks, do I need to use marketing? the answer would be yes, ignore it at your peril. But using political marketing does not mean abandoning all goals and principle. Rather it means being informed so one is able to make the most appropriate choice and balance competing goals and interests. Politics is a complex game with multiple inter-influential actors and interests and politicians have to navigate this territory carefully, but marketing can act as an important tool when developing the game plan to ensure not just votes but progress is won. Principle can be reconciled with pragmatism and a new system is emerging that could develop to overcome current limitations towards a partnership democracy, where people are part of government and look for elites who say 'yes WE can' not 'yes I can'. This fits with the same conclusions about the changing relationship between elites and the public discussed in a broad range of traditional and new fields and specialisms in political science, in which research can be found that talks of an increased role by the citizen in elite decision. In this section, a few examples in each area are highlighted to help us understand partnership democracy as part of a series of emerging trends in political behaviour.

The changing role of citizens

Citizen journalism notes how the public, once a passive audience, is increasingly producing the media rather than just watching it; one example is Gilmour (2006, xxiv) who observes how 'the lines will blur between producers and consumers, changing the role of both.' Public journalism is, as Dzur (2002) explains, about the media promoting public deliberation and listening to the public's opinion as to what important issues should be covered. Regarding public opinion, Jacobs and Shapiro (2000a and b) argue that the idea that politicians pander to public opinion is a myth; responsiveness varies over time and can vary according to political and institutional conditions. Polsby and Wildavsky (2008, 257) also observed that, since the 1960s in the US, there has been a significant increase in public participation in processes that were formerly elite and party dominant, even if 'complex deliberative decision making' remained difficult in practice and 'the need for organisations to do the job of parties continues.' In e-government, Chadwick and May (2003, 280) cite Masuda (1980), a Japanese scholar who created six basic principles of political participation in an information society, such as: all citizens participate, there is a spirit of mutual assistance for the overall common good and people are well informed. Blumler and Coleman (2001, 16) argued that there is the need for a publicly funded civic commons in cyberspace: 'an entirely new kind of public agency' to bring current efforts 'under a more capacious electronic roof, backing them up with substantial production resources and expertise, and enhancing their visibility, status and clout'. Participation studies talk of changing public engagement, with Barnes et al. (2007, 53) encouraging us to 'understand the extent to which, and in what ways, the plethora of new initiatives might be able to produce fundamental shifts in relationships between state and citizens'. Ackerman (2004) argues for co-governance, whereby ordinary citizens can be actively involved in the state apparatus.

With regard to public administration, Vigoda (2008, 473) discusses collaboration and partnership and explains that 'while responsiveness is mostly seen as a passive, unidirectional reaction to the people's needs and demands, collaboration represents a more active, bidirectional act of participation, involvement and unification of forces between the two (or more) parties.' Bourgon (2007, 11) argues that 'the public policy issues of the twenty-first century are increasingly complex and will require even more interaction including... interaction between elected officials and citizens who are claiming a larger voice in the policy decisions that will most affect them in the future.' She puts forward a new public administration theory that argues that elites do not simply respond to demands from the public but that, instead, activity involves building collaborative relationships between citizens and governments and encouraging shared responsibility (p. 22). Bevir (2006, 433) suggests that there is the need for 'a dialogic public policy' within a 'radical democracy', whereby politicians and civil servants would engage, not just consult, with public groups. Adams and Hess (2001, 13) discuss how partnership, mutuality, trust, reciprocity and community building 'represents a potential shift in relations between the state, the market, and community, as the key systems underpinning liberal democracies'. The concepts of co-operative inquiry, mutual responsibility and citizen participation are being used in public policy. Mutual responsibility argues that members of a society need to feel a responsibility towards each other, based on values such as love, justice and wisdom and trust (Adams and Hess 2001, 19).

In political theory public input into elite decision-making is generally seen as a fundamental basis of democracy (see Weale 2007, 18 and Held 2006, 230), though, of course, there has always been a lively debate about the value, nature and extent of public input. As Rehfeld (2009, 214) observed, 'no one expects there to be an exact correspondence between...how closely the laws of a nation should correspond to the preferences of the citizens government by them.' Political marketing as portrayed in this research is an operationalisation of democracy: market analysis and varying leadership responsiveness offers the mechanisms to achieve linkage between elites and public preferences – but avoids the problems associated with the caricature of political marketing as elites always following an ignorant public at all times without thinking. Regarding elite theory, new studies challenge accepting the authority of politicians to act alone without consulting the public. Tetlock's (2005) study found that experts do not necessarily make better decisions than the ordinary public, because they lack the ability to assimilate new information that is contrary to their previous beliefs.

In particular, the idea of a partnership democracy can closely aligned with deliberative democracy, which is one of the most recent theories and emerged in the 1980s (Held 2006, 232), about the same time as political marketing. Few pieces of research connect political marketing to deliberative democracy (for an exception see Henneberg et al. 2009), but it follows political marketing's emphasis on voter input into the political product, and the need for leaders to listen to public demands. The difference is that it argues that citizens need to discuss and debate before offering their opinions, and that it offers further suggestions on how to maximise the value of this input with concrete, practical operationalisation (Fishkin et al. 2000, Ackerman and Fishkin 2004, Gutman and Thompson 2004 and Fishkin 2006). The methods it suggests include citizen juries, national deliberation days, local parliaments, neighbourhood initiatives, citizen panels, planning cells, consensus conferences, town meetings, national issue forums and deliberative polls (see Rowe and Frewer 2005, 257 for a comprehensive list). As Carson (2002, 12) argued, 'Australia is grappling with many complex issues: stem cell research, reconciliation, asylum seeking and more. Citizens continue to demonstrate that they are capable of tackling such difficult, seemingly unresolvable matters within deliberative spaces.' Some political theorists have made a link between deliberation and marketing. For example, Goodin (2009, 4) notes how 'market testing' can be included in deliberation:

Market-testing might sound like a derisive description. But in truth it is an important contribution, not just from the crassly careerist perspective of politicians seeking election but also from the perspective of the loftiest democratic theory. Good decisions, democratic or otherwise, require that we scope the range of the possible – what the possible problems and options are, what the possible positions and solutions might be.

Ackerman and Fishkin (2004, 210–218) also make that link, critiquing focus groups in comparison with the concept of a deliberation day, and suggesting agreement with the idea that market analysis, in a deliberative form, would be advantageous in a partnership democracy.

Deliberative theory also makes suggestions for overcoming weaknesses in public opinion: as Fishkin (2006, 165) argues, 'different institutional designs...can have the effect of bringing the potential civic competence of the public to life.' Deliberation offers methods that provide training or information to overcome a lack of knowledge within one individual; emphasise reason over self-interest; require a justification of perspectives rather than just a statement of demands; and show the complexities involved in political decision-making. As Held (2006, 237) explained, 'through sharing information and pooling knowledge, public deliberation can transform individuals' understanding and enhance their grasp of complex problems. People may come to understand elements of their situation which they had not appreciated before.' Such principles align with a partnership democracy which argues that more deliberative market research will help citizens contribute higher quality input. This is not to deny the weaknesses in many consultation events: as Goodin and Dryzek (2009, 36) noted, there is 'a long tradition in policy studies that delights in exposing failure' in empirical assessments of actual practice. But just as Diagram 2 suggested, the value of marketing activities in politics depends on how elites choose to use them. Market analysis and consultation have potential value that is only realised if guidelines for best practice are followed; we need to explore the potentially positive uses of the same tool rather than just add to the 'failed' list.

The emergence of partnership

The term 'partner' can be found in a range of literature. Weale (2007, 79) quotes Sir Ernest Barker (1951, 67–68) who discussed the need for people to work together so that they 'pooled their minds', which when connected to notions of democracy meant that:

> Any society, to be worthy of the name, must consist of partners, who enjoy a say in the affairs of the society. When a society ceases to be that, it ceases to be a society. It becomes a mere heap of the leader and his followers – followers strung together, like so many dead birds on a string, by the compulsion of leadership.

Munro et al. (2008) discuss partnership and how it can involve inclusion and citizen participation within the collaborative space. Innes and Booher (2004, 422) argue for collaborative participation, where consultation is more than 'one-way communication from citizens to government or government to citizens' and instead moves towards a 'multi-dimensional model where communication, learning and action are joined together and where the polity, interests and citizenry co-evolve'. Callahan (2007a, 1187) discusses a range of relationships between elites and the public, one of which is the co-producer relationship, whereby 'citizens and administrators collaborate with one another to solve problems and get things done. The relationship reflects an active partnership with shared responsibility.' Callahan (2007b, 163) also debates the idea of collaborative governance and collaborative participation, 'where all the stakeholders communicate and work in both formal and informal ways to influence action and bring about positive results'. Arnstein (1969) suggests a ladder of participation, one rung of which is partnership, Shand and Arnberg's (1996) participation continuum talks of partnership, while Bishop and Davies (2001b, 20) suggest that partnership – 'government and community working together to solve local problems' – hands more control to the public than consultation, but without fully delegating power. They observed how elites and the public 'work together to develop and deliver a product', something which can already be seen in parent teacher associations or neighbourhood watches, where educational and police elites work with the community to achieve progress. It is not just about the public having more say, but about a shift in responsibility as well as rights from elites to the public, so citizens feel responsible for making the political process work (p. 23).

A partnership democracy would, of course, require not just the system and elites to evolve, but the public also. As Goodin (2009, 1–2) argued, the existing 'minimalist democracy does not ask that citizens inform themselves before they vote. It does not ask them to pay attention to public debates on the issue of the day. It does not ask them to get together with others to discuss the issues...a wide range of critics have long insisted that this is simply not good enough.' Chia and Patmore (2004) discuss the activists' model of citizenship, which 'suggests that citizens are not only the fundamental units of a democratic polity, but also its agents' (p. 4), and that this 'puts the citizen back at the heart of the democratic story, making politics not a fight to capture the largest share of voters by out-managing the other party, but a way of realising our human potential' (p. 18). Boyte (2004, xvii) also notes how the idea of public work, related to citizenship in the US, 'conveys the idea of the citizen as a co-creator of democracy, understood as a way of life not simply periodic elections'. To support this, elites need to change their conception of citizens as a source of needs and demands they need to respond to, to perceiving citizens as a potential source of the solution, while citizens need to understand that 'problems besetting poor or working-class communities are not a result of callous leaders or bad values' (p. 740). Public work 'illustrates citizen-government partnerships' (Boyte 2003, 703). Cornwall (2008, 77) observes that there is a need to provide an infrastructure for participatory institutions to train politicians and citizens, so as 'to equip them with the skills and knowledge to participate' in partnership-type politics effectively.

Institutionalising deliberative market analysis

Academic literature that discusses public involvement in elite decision-making has also suggested that there is a need for a change in our institutional structures to enable it to function appropriately. Cornwall (2008, 39) talks of invited spaces for participation, arguing that 'governments can create, institutionalize and resource invited spaces.' Bishop and Davies (2001a, 194) argue that 'the need to re-establish consent through new structures is becoming more urgent.' Ackerman and Fishkin's (2004, 25) core concept, that of a deliberation day, is proposed as a national holiday held 2 weeks before national elections, which systemises deliberation to some degree. Held's (2006, 253) model of deliberative democracy calls for public funding of deliberative bodies and practices and the secondary associations which support them, and public institutions that support reflective preferences. Ackerman (2004, 459) explains that 'once initiated, the best way to assure the sustainability of a participatory framework is through its 'full institutionalization.'

Deliberative market analysis could become an institution of its own kind: a public parliament, so that there is one parliament for politicians, and one for the public. The limitations of the one-off, disconnected consultations that take place currently is that they fall into what Goodin and Dryzek (2009, 11–12) call 'mini-publics': being small scale, they are unable to be statistically representative and, therefore, unable to influence national scale decision-making. This may be why decision-makers rarely let consultation impact on decision-making. Arguably, using Goodin's terminology, if not his argument, it is only by making *mini*-publics *macro*-publics that they could have a connection to the larger political system. There needs to be a national deliberative market analysis system, whether it is called a public parliament or not, that is formally connected to the government decision-making process. If replicated, systemised, checked and centralised, it would become more useful than ad hoc events, by providing an institutional mechanism to improve the quality of public input and its utility for elites working within the existing representative system. Public parliaments may be more effective if they are local parliaments. Creating completely new institutions would be a very public exercise and generate the potential for opposition; a softer option would be a simple organisational unit that syntheses existing market research and consultation, is reported online in one website and is managed by following the guidelines of a partnership democracy, including transparency of results. While the suggested institutional components of the partnership democracy may seem ambitious, others have, at least partly, made similar suggestions. Goodin and Niemeyer (2009, 62–63) suggest that independent organisations such as the League of Women Voters could provide briefing books. Fishkin et al. (2000, 665) note the cost of deliberative measures, but also caution that 'the mistakes of government cost even more.'

A partnership democracy and elite decision-making

There is one gap in the literature, and that is how consultation could or should lead to actual influence and affect decision-making. Theories and isolated deliberative or consultative events have value in themselves, but for a partnership democracy to evolve they need to become practically integrated and reconciled to the reality of electioneering. Deliberative democracy tends to neglect considering the role of elites and their connection to government decision-making (Johnson 2006, 48). In part this is due to a foundationary belief that deliberation should produce the decision itself. But this is, at present, unrealistic for national governments. Fishkin et al. (2000, 665) concede that 'the method is not suitable for every problem facing government. Crisis measures require instant decisions', but a partnership democracy suggests that in such cases leaders need to explain their decisions and get feedback on their implementation.

However, the detail of how a public parliament would work and feed into decision-making would need to be developed, tried, tested and reformed. A partnership democracy departs from classic deliberative democratic theory by suggesting elites need to retain the room to make decisions and that leaders have a range of influences upon their decision-making and should hold varying responses to public opinion when they make decisions. A partnership democracy does not fit pure concepts of deliberative democracy. A partnership democracy fits the advising aspect of influence of decision-making described by Bekkers et al. (2007, 168) better, where 'the decisions-makers are willing to share some agenda-setting power. Citizens are given the opportunity to comment on the problem-definitions in the proposals, and to bring forward their own problems and proposals. The decision-makers commit themselves to consider these recommendations and to give feedback on how they have used them in their final decision-making.' A partnership democracy would include the best elements of deliberative democracy theory – deliberative market analysis and a public that provides higher quality input – but without the less practical suggestion of the public collectively making decisions. A partnership democracy may rather represent a practical integration of representative democracy and deliberative democracy. McDonald and Samples (2006, 10) noted that 'deliberative democracy thus seems to be more about arguments among citizens than about competition among candidates for voters.' A partnership democracy aims to change this and link the two. In a similar way to Fiskin's (1991) idea of deliberative polls, a partnership democracy represents a synergy between political marketing, an empirically oriented, pragmatic electioneering activity and deliberative democracy; it is thus an ideal theoretical concept.

A partnership democracy also suggests that political representation theories need to develop an understanding that there can be varied leadership responsiveness to public opinion. The range of leadership positions included in the theory fits the recent notion of reflection put forward by Goodin (2003), and discussed further by Goodin and Niemeyer (2003; see also Olson (2006) on reflexive democracy), although this internal process also needs to be demonstrated in some way to the public to show that they have been listened to. A partnership democracy also aligns with recent work to blur the boundaries between traditional notions of trustee and delegate representation. Mansbridge (2003) argued that there is the need to move on from the dichotomy of trustees and delegates to a broader set of classifications: promissory (unfulfilled promises, for which they can be unelected), anticipatory, gyroscopic (less responsive to the public) and surrogate. Rehfield (2009, 220) suggests that politicians need to be measured along different, crossover terms on three levels: self-reliant or dependent judgement; republican or pluralist aims; and less or more responsive to sanction, thus creating eight new 'cells'. Catt and Murphy (2003, 417) offer a matrix from consultation, where there are varying roles played by participants including synthesis, contestation and provision of information. This suggests that the involvement of the public can also vary and change in response to different leadership positions. A partnership democracy suggests that politicians would in fact fit into several classifications at different times, but in relation to deliberative market analysis and considerations of party, government and the individual politician, rather than having any fixed professional position.

Democracy in evolution

Across a range of subfields there is a sense of a change in elite–public relationships; an evolution in democratic practice, but one that is not yet complete. While we may have thought that achieving one person one vote was enough to advance democracy, research on dissatisfied citizens (Norris 2005, Pharr and Putnam 2000 and Dalton 2006) suggests that further development is necessary. However, such problems can generate solutions, as Dalton (2008, 93) commented, 'instead of just lamenting the decline of duty-based citizenship, we should also consider the positive implications of new patterns of political participation... non-electoral methods of political action expand the potential influence of the citizenry... [and] political institutions are also adapting to accept and encourage these new forms of citizen access.' Leighninger (2005, 27) argued that:

> In twenty years, the political landscape will certainly differ from what it is today... governments will adapt to twenty-first conditions by becoming more interactive and citizen-centred... we seem to be headed toward a new definition of democracy, in which public officials bring politics to the people, politics take place in small groups, and people take an active role in problem solving.

In the last century new political institutions were created which were once unthinkable, such as the United Nations and European Union. Weale (2007, 99–100) argued that 'a system that may seem to institutionalise deliberation adequate for a politics of economic management, of the sort that has dominated democratic politics since the first part of the twentieth century, may not be the right sort of system of a politics of identity of bioethical controversy, of the sort that may come to dominate in the twenty-first century.' Cain et al. (2003, 2) argue that 'a chorus of voices is calling for democracies to reform' and conclude that 'a new model of democracy is evolving. The contemporary democratic process requires more of its citizens. It also challenges politicians and bureaucrats to figure out what it means to move past a trustee model of politics without abdicating political leadership' (p. 274). Similarly, Cornwall (2008, 74) observed how 'around the world, in the most unlikely places, pockets of innovation in governance are starting to expand. New ideas are catching on. Governments are learning that there is actually something very valuable to be gained from investing in creating the conditions for and fostering citizen engagement in governance.' The theory of a partnership democracy concurs with these observations even if it is just a theory of possibility than a practice of actuality. As Bourgon (2007, 24) said, 'everything that has taken place to date has been part of a learning process. Everything that lies ahead of us will be part of a journey of discovery for there is no end to our quest for better governance.' However, consideration of positive possibility is important to see what could come in the future. Ackerman and Fishkin (2004, 16) argue that 'without continuing experiments, it is hard to see how democracy will remain a flourishing enterprise in the twenty-first century.' Their opening chapter in *Deliberation Day* is entitled 'Imagine'. Just imagine if politicians and the public could work in partnership? And if market research – once criticised for being just another tool of elite manipulation – became the connecting voice between the two, enabling a more positive, trusting relationship to develop between elites and the masses? The twenty-first century may see as much dramatic change as its predecessor, as elites and the public fight, debate, criticise and work together to understand not just what works in political marketing but how to use it to make democracy itself work better.

Academic References

Aberbach, J. D. and Tom Christensen (2005). 'Citizens and Consumers.' *Public Management Review*, 7(2): 226–245.
Aberbach, J. D. and B. A. Rockman (2002). 'Conducting and Coding Elite Interviews.' *PS: Political Science and Politics*, 35(4): 673–676.
Ackerman, J. (2004). 'Co-governance for Accountability: Beyond "Exit" and "Voice".' *World Development*, 32(3): 447–463.
Ackerman, B. A. and J. S. Fishkin (2004). *Deliberation Day*. New Haven, CT: Yale University Press.
Adams, D. and M. Hess (2001). 'Community in Public Policy: Fad or Foundation?.' *Australian Journal of Public Administration*, 60(2): 13–23.
Allington, N., Philip Morgan and Nicholas O'Shaughnessy (1999). 'How Marketing Changed the World. The Political Marketing of an Idea: A Case Study of Privatization,' Chapter 34, in Bruce Newman (ed.), *Handbook of Political Marketing*, Thousand Oaks, CA: Sage Publications, pp. 627–642.
Arnstein, S. R. (1969). 'A Ladder of Citizen Participation.' *Journal of the American Institute of Planners*, 35(4): 216–224.
Arterton, F. Christopher (2007). 'Strategy and Politics: The Example of the United States of America,' in T. Fischer, G. Peter Scmitz and M. Seberich (eds), *The Strategy of Politics: Results of a Comparative Study*, Butersloh: Verlag Bertelsmann Stiftung, pp. 133–172.
Aspinwall, M. (2006). 'Studying the British.' *Politics*, 26(1): 3–10.
Atkinson, R. D. and Andrew Leigh (2003). 'Serving the Stakeholders. Customer-Oriented E-Government: Can We Ever Get There?.' *Journal of Political Marketing*, 2(3/4): 159–181.
Baines, P. R. (1999). 'Voter Segmentation and Candidate Positioning,' in B. Newman (ed.), *Handbook of Political Marketing*, Thousand Oaks, CA: Sage Publications, pp. 403–420.
Baines, P. R. and Richard Lynch (2005). 'Guest Editorial: The Context, Content and Process of Political Marketing Strategy.' *Journal of Political Marketing*, 4(2/3): 1–18.
Baines, P. R. and Robert M. Worcester (2004). 'Two Triangulation Models in Political Marketing: The Market Positioning Analogy.' *Elections on the Horizon Conference*, 15 March 2004.
Baines, P. R., Phil Harris and Barbara R. Lewis (2002). 'The Political Marketing Planning Process: Improving Image and Message in Strategic Target Areas.' *Market Intelligence and Planning*, 20(1): 6–14.
Baines, P. R., Robert M. Worcester, David Jarrett and Roger Mortimore (2003). 'Market Segmentation and Product Differentiation in Political Campaigns: A Technical Feature Perspective.' *Journal of Marketing Management*, 19(1/2): 225–249.
Bannon, D. (2004). 'Marketing Segmentation and Political Marketing.' Paper presented to the UK Political Studies Association.

Bannon, D. (2005). 'Internal Marketing and Political Marketing.' Paper presented at the PSA Annual Conference, University of Leeds, 4–7 April.
Barber, M. (2007). *Instruction to Deliver*. London: Politicos.
Barber, S. (2005). *Political Strategy: Modern Politics in Contemporary Britain*. Liverpool: Liverpool Academic Press.
Barberio, R. P. (2006). 'Branding: Presidential Politics and Crafted Political Communications.' Paper presented at the 2006 Annual Meeting of the American Political Science Association, 30 August to 3 September.
Barker, E. (1951). *Essays on Government*. Clarendon: Oxford.
Barnes, M., J. Newman and H. Sullivan (2007). *Power, Participation and Political Renewal: Case Studies in Public Participation*. Bristol: The Policy Press.
Bartle, J. (2001). 'Changing Voters or Changing Models of Voting,' in J. Bartle, S. Atkinson and R. Mortimore (eds), *Political Communications: The General Election Campaign of 2001*, London: Frank Cass, pp. 16–34.
Bartle, J. and Dylan Griffiths (2002). 'Social-Psychological, Economic and Marketing Models of Voting Behaviour Compared,' Chapter 2, in N. O'Shaughnessy and S. Henneberg (eds), *The Idea of Political Marketing*, London: Praeger, pp. 19–38.
Bauer, H. H., Frank Huber and Andreas Herrman (1996). 'Political Marketing: An Information-Economic Analysis.' *European Journal of Marketing*, 30: 159–172.
Bekkers, V., G. Dijkstra, A. Edwards and M. Fenger (eds) (2007). *Governance and the Democratic Deficit: Assessing the Democratic Legitimacy of Governance Practices*, Aldershot, England; Burlington, VT: Ashgate.
Berry, M. J. (2002). 'Validity and Reliability Issues in Elite Interviews.' *PS: Political Science and Politics*, 35(4): 679–682.
Bevir, M. (2006). 'Democratic Governance: Systems and Radical Perspectives.' *Public Administration Review*, 66(3): 426–436.
Bishop, P. and G. Davies (2001a). 'Developing Consent: Consultation, Participation and Governance,' in G. Davies and P. Weller (eds), *Are you Being Served?: State, Citizens and Governance*, Crows Nest, NSW: Allen & Unwin, pp. 175–195.
Bishop, P. and G. Davies (2001b). 'Mapping Public Participation in Policy Choices.' *Australian Journal of Public Administration*, 61(1): 14–29.
Blumler, J. G. and Stephen Coleman (2001). *Realising Democracy Online: A Civic Commons in Cyberspace*. London: Institute of Public Policy Research. Research publication no. 2, March.
Bourgon, J. (2007). 'Responsive, Responsible and Respected Government: Towards a New Public Administration Theory.' *International Review of Administrative Sciences*, 73(1): 7–26.
Boyte, H. C. (2003). 'Civic Populism.' *Perspectives on Politics*, 1(4): 737–742.
Boyte, H. C. (2004). *Everyday Politics: Reconnecting Citizens and Public Life*. Philadelphia, PA: University of Pennsylvania Press.
Bryant, I. (2008). 'An Inside Look at Obama's Grassroots Marketing.' *Adweek*, 12 March 2008. Accessed from http://www.adweek.com/aw/content_display/community/columns/other-columns/e3i714b5acb6525107fda1eb890ff94a48a on 1 April 2008.
Burnham, P., K. Gillard and Z. Layton-Henry (2004). *Research Methods in Politics*. Basingstoke: Palgrave Macmillan.
Butler, P. and Neil Collins (1996). 'Strategic Analysis in Political Markets.' *European Journal of Marketing*, 30(10 & 11): 32–44.

Butler, P. and Neil Collins (1998). 'Public Services in Ireland: A Marketing Perspective.' Working Paper, Department of Public Administration, National University of Ireland, Cork, no. VII (August).

Cain, B. E., R. J. Dalton and Susan Scarrow (eds) (2003). *Democracy Transformed? Expanding Political Opportunities in Advanced Industrial Democracies*, Oxford: Oxford University Press.

Callahan, K. (2007a). 'Citizen Participation: Models and Methods.' *International Journal of Public Administration*, 30(11): 1179–1196.

Callahan, K. (ed.) (2007b). *Elements of Effective Governance: Measurement, Accountability and Participation*, Boca Raton: CRC and Taylor & Francis.

Carson, L. (2002). 'Community Consultation in Environmental Policy Making.' *Drawing Board*, 3(1): 215KB.

Catt, H. and M. Murphy (2003). 'What Voice for the People? Categorising Methods of [Australian] Public Consultation.' *Australian Journal of Political Science*, 38(3): 407–421.

Chadwick, A. and C. May (2003). 'Interaction between States and Citizens in the Age of the Internet: "E-Government" in the United States, Britain, and the European Union.' *Governance*, 16(2): 271–300.

Chia, J. and G. Patmore (2004). 'The Vocal Citizen,' in G. Patmore and G. Jungwirth (eds), *The Vocal Citizen: Labor Essays 2004*, Melbourne: Arena Printing and Publishing, pp. 1–21.

Coleman, S. (2007). 'Review of Lilleker and Lees-Marshment (2005): Political Marketing: A Comparative Perspective.' *Parliamentary Affairs*, 60(1): 180–186.

Cornwall, A. (2008). 'Democratising Engagement: What the UK Can Learn From International Experience.' *Demos*, 29(97): 1–102, April.

Cosgrove, K. (2007). 'Midterm Marketing: An Examination of Marketing Strategies in the 2006, 2002, 1998, and 1994 Elections.' Paper presented at the annual meeting of the American Political Science Association. Accessed from http://www.allacademic.com/meta/p209749_index.html on 19 March 2008.

Cosgrove, K. (2009). 'Case Study 5.4: Branded American Politics,' in J. Lees-Marshment (ed.), *Political Marketing: Principles and Applications*, Abingdon, Oxon: Routledge.

Dalton, R. J. (2006). *Citizen Politics: Public Opinion and Political Parties in Advanced Industrial Democracies*. Washington, DC: CQ Press.

Dalton, R. J. (2008). 'Citizenship Norms and the Expansion of Political Participation.' *Political Studies*, 56(1): 76–98.

Davidson, S. (2005). 'Grey Power, School Gate Mums and the Youth Vote: Age as a Key Factor in Voter Segmentation and Engagement in the 2005 UK General Election.' *Journal of Marketing Management*, 21(9/10): 1179–1192.

Dean, D. and Robin Croft (2001). 'Friends and Relations: Long-Term Approaches to Political Campaigning.' *European Journal of Marketing*, 35(11/12): 1197–1216.

Debate Held at the House of Commons on 19th September, 2003. *Journal of Public Affairs*, 4(3) (2004): 299–313.

Dermody, J. and Stuart Hamner-Lloyd (2006). 'A Marketing Analysis of the 2005 General Election Advertising Campaigns,' Chapter 5, in D. G. Lilleker, N. A. Jackson and R. Scullion (eds), *The Marketing of Political Parties*, Manchester: Manchester University Press, pp. 101–131.

Desmond, M. (2004). 'Methodological Challenges Posed in Studying in an Elite Field.' *Area*, 36(3): 262–269.
Dzur, A. W. (2002). 'Public Journalism and Deliberative Democracy.' *Polity*, 34(3): 313–336.
Fischer, T., Gregor Peter Schmitz and Michael Seberich (eds) (2007). *The Strategy of Politics: Results of a Comparative Study*, Butersloh: Verlag Bertelsmann Stiftung.
Fishkin, J. S. (1991). *Democracy and Deliberation: New Directions for Democratic Reform*. New Haven, CT: Yale University Press.
Fishkin, J. S. (2006). 'Beyond Polling Alone: The Quest for an Informed Public.' *Critical Review*, 18(1–3): 157–165.
Fishkin, J. S., R. C. Luskin and Roger Jowell (2000). 'Deliberative Polling and Public Consultation.' *Parliamentary Affairs*, 53(4): 657–666.
Franklin, B. (1994). *Packaging Politics: Political Communications in Britain's Media Democracy*. London, and New York: Edward Arnold.
Freedland, J. (1999). 'The Trashing of Ken.' *Guardian*, London, 17 November 1999.
Geiselhart, K., Mary Griffiths and Bronwen FitzGerald (2003). 'What Lies Beyond Service Delivery – An Australian Perspective.' *Journal of Political Marketing*, 2(3/4): 213–233.
Gelders, D. and Steven Van De Walle (2005). 'Marketing Government Reforms,' in W. Wymer and J. Lees-Marshment (eds), *Current Issues in Political Marketing*, Binghampton, NY: Haworth Press.
Gillmor, D. (2006). *We the Media: Grassroots Journalism by the People, for the People*. Sebastopol, CA: O'Reilly.
Glaab, M. (2007). 'Strategy and Politics: The Example of Germany,' in T. Fischer, G. P. Schmitz and M. Seberich (eds), *The Strategy of Politics: Results of a Comparative Study*, Butersloh: Verlag Bertelsmann Stiftung.
Goodin, R. E. (2003). *Reflective Democracy*. Oxford: Oxford University Press.
Goodin, R. E. (2009). *Innovating Democracy: Democratic Theory & Practice After the Deliberative Turn*. Oxford: Oxford University Press.
Goodin, R. E. and John S. Dryzek (2009). 'Making Use of Minipublics,' Chapter 2, in Goodin, R. E. (ed.), *Innovating Democracy: Democratic Theory & Practice After the Deliberative Turn*, Oxford: Oxford University Press.
Goodin, R. E. and Simon J. Niemeyer (2003). 'When Does Deliberation Begin? Internal Reflection versus Public Discussion in Deliberative Democracy.' *Political Studies*, 51(4): 627–649.
Goodin, R. E. and Simon J. Niemeyer (2009). 'When Does Deliberation Begin?' Chapter 3, in Goodin, Robert E. (ed.), *Innovating Democracy: Democratic Theory & Practice After the Deliberative Turn*, Oxford: Oxford University Press.
Goot, M. (1999). 'Public Opinion, Privatization and the Electoral Politics of Telstra.' *Australian Journal of Politics and History*, 45(2): 214–238.
Gorbounova, D. and J. Lees-Marshment (2009). 'US Presidential Political Marketing Strategy Model,' Figure in J. Lees-Marshment, *Political Marketing: Principles and Applications*, Abingdon, Oxon: Routledge.
Gould, P. (1998). *The Unfinished Revolution: How the Modernisers Saved the Labour Party*. London: Little Brown.
Granik, S. (2005a). 'Internal Consumers – What Makes Your Party Members Join Your Election Effort?.' Paper presented at the Political Marketing Group Conference, London, 24–25 February.

Granik, S. (2005b). 'Membership Benefits, Membership Action: Why Incentives for Activism Are What Members Want,' in W. Wymer and J. Lees-Marshment (eds), *Current Issues in Political Marketing*, Binghampton, NY: Haworth Press.

Grix, J. (2002). 'Introducing Students to the Generic Terminology of Social Research.' *Politics*, 22(3): 175–186.

Gutman, A. and D. Thompson (2004). *Why Deliberative Democracy*. Princeton, NJ: Princeton University Press.

Hamburger, P. (2006). 'The Australian Government Cabinet Implementation Unit,' in *Improving Implementation: Organisational Change and Project Management*. ANZSOG/ANU. Accessed from http://epress.anu.edu.au/anzsog/imp/mobile_devices/ch18.html on 11 April 2008.

Harris, P. (2001). 'Machiavelli, Political Marketing and Reinventing Government.' *European Journal of Marketing*, 35(9.10): 1135–1154.

Held, D. (2006). *Models of Democracy*. Malden, MA: Polity Press.

Henneberg, S. C. (2006). 'Strategic Postures of Political Marketing: An Exploratory Operationalization.' *Journal of Public Affairs*, 6(1): 15–30.

Henneberg, S. C. and N. O'Shaughnessy (2009). 'Political Relationship Marketing: Some Macro/Micro Thoughts.' *Journal of Marketing Management*, 25(1/2): 5–29.

Henneberg, S. C., Margaret Scammell and Nicholas J. O'Shaughnessy (2009). 'Political Marketing Management and Theories of Democracy.' *Marketing Theory*, 9(2): 165–188.

Herod, A. (1999). 'Reflections on Interviewing Foreign Elites: Praxis Positionality, Validity and the Cult of the Insider.' *Geoforum*, 30(4): 313–327.

Hughes, A. and S. Dann (2006). 'Political Marketing and Stakeholders.' Paper presented at the Australian and New Zealand Marketing Academy Conference, QUT, 4–6 December.

Hughes, A. and S. Dann (2009). 'Political Marketing and Stakeholder Engagement.' *Marketing Theory*, 9(2): 243–256.

Hughes, A. and S. Dann (2010). 'Australian Political Marketing: Substance Backed by Style,' in J. Lees-Marshment, J. Strömbäck and C. Rudd (eds), *Global Political Marketing*, Abingdon, Oxon: Routledge, pp. 82–95.

Ietcu-Fairclough, I. (2008). 'Branding and Strategic Maneuvering in the Romanian Presidential Election of 2004: A Critical Discourse-Analytical and Pragma-Dialectical Perspective.' *Journal of Language and Politics*, 7(3): 372–390.

Ingram, P. and J. Lees-Marshment (2002). 'The Anglicisation of Political Marketing: How Blair "Out-Marketed" Clinton.' *Journal of Public Affairs*, 2(2): 44–57.

Innes, J. E. and D. E. Booher (2004). 'Reframing Public Participation: Strategies for the 21st Century.' *Planning Theory & Practice*, 5(4): 419–436, December.

Jackson, D. (2008). 'Citizens, Consumers and the Demands of Market-Driven News,' in D. Lilleker and R. Scullion (eds), *Voters or Consumers: Imagining the Contemporary Electorate*, Newcastle: Cambridge Scholars Publishing.

Jackson, N. (2005). 'Vote Winner or a Nuisance: Email and Elected Politicians' Relationship with Their Constituents,' in W. Wymer and J. Lees-Marshment (eds), *Current Issues in Political Marketing*, Binghampton, NY: Haworth Press, pp. 91–108.

Jackson, N. (2009). 'Case Study 7.3: UK MPs and the Marketing of Their Websites,' in J. Lees-Marshment (ed.), *Political Marketing: Principles and Applications*, Routledge.

Jackson, N. A. and Darren G. Lilleker (2004). 'Just Public Relations or an Attempt at Interaction? British MPs in the Press, on the Web and "In Your Face".' *European Journal of Communication*, 19(4): 507–533.

Jacobs, L. R. and R. Y. Shapiro (2000a). *Politicians Don't Pander: Political Manipulation and the Loss of Democratic Responsiveness*. Chicago, IL: University of Chicago Press.

Jacobs, L. R. and R. Y. Shapiro (2000b). 'Polling and Pandering.' *Society*, 37(6): 11–13.

Johansson, J. (2009). 'Case Study 5.7: To Thine Own Self Be True: Branding, Authenticity & Political Leadership – the Case of Don Brash,' in J. Lees-Marshment, *Political Marketing: Principles and Applications*, Abingdon, Oxon: Routledge.

Johnson, D. W. (2007). *No Place for Amateurs* (2nd edn). New York: Routledge.

Johnson, D. W. (2009). 'Case Study 9.1: Top Down or Bottom Up?,' in J. Lees-Marshment, *Political Marketing: Principles and Applications*, Abingdon, Oxon: Routledge.

Johnson, J. (2006). 'Political Parties and Deliberative Democracy?' in R. S. A. C. Katz and William J. (ed.), *Handbook of Party Politics*, Thousand Oaks, CA: Sage Publications, pp. 47–50.

Kavanagh, D. (1995). *Election Campaigning: The New Marketing of Politics*. Oxford: Blackwell Publishing.

Kavanagh, D. (1996). 'Speaking Truth to Power? Pollsters as Campaign Advisers?.' *European Journal of Marketing*, 30(10/11): 104–113.

Kezar, A. (2003). 'Transformational Elite Interviews: Principles and Problems.' *Qualitative Inquiry*, 9(3): 395–415.

King, N. (2004). 'Using Interviews in Qualitative Research,' in C. Cassell and G. Symon (eds), *Essential Guide to Qualitative Methods in Organizational Research*, London: Sage Publications.

Kiss, B. (2009). 'Case Study 5.2: The Hungarian Socialist Party Winning the Youth,' in J. Lees-Marshment (ed.), *Political Marketing: Principles and Applications*, Routledge.

Knuckey, J. (2010). 'Political Marketing in the United States: From Market-Towards Sales-Orientation,?' in J. Lees-Marshment, J. Strömbäck and C. Rudd (eds), *Global Political Marketing*, London: Routledge, pp. 96–112.

Knuckey, J. and J. Lees-Marshment (2005). 'American Political Marketing: George W. Bush and the Republican Party,' in D. Lilleker and J. Lees-Marshment (eds), *Political Marketing: A Comparative Perspective*, Manchester: Manchester University Press.

Kotzaivazoglou, I. (2009). 'The Market-Oriented Candidate,' Figure in J. Lees-Marshment (ed.), *Political Marketing: Principles and Applications*, Abingdon, Oxon: Routledge.

Kuper, A. and L. Lingard and W. Levinson (2008). 'Critically Appraising Qualitative Research.' *British Medical Journal*, 3(37): 687–689.

Lane, R. E. (1991). *The Market Experience*. Cambridge: Cambridge University Press.

Lane, R. E. (1996). 'Losing Tough in a Democracy: Demands versus Needs,' in J. Hayward (ed.), *Elitism, Populism and European Politics*, Oxford: Clarendon Press.

Lane, R. E. (2000). *The Loss of Happiness in Market Democracies*. New Haven, CT and London: Yale University Press.

Langmaid, R. (2006). 'Leading from the Top,' *Brand Strategy*, 1 April. Accessed from http://www.mad.co.uk/Main/News/Disciplines/Marketing/Articles/e574 52e34386487ab7b4a93019da965c/Leading-from-the-top.html on 19 March 2008.

Langmaid, R., Charles Trevail and B. Hayman (2006). 'Reconnecting the Prime Minister.' Paper presented at the Annual Conference of the Market Research Society, London.

Lebel, G. G. (1999). 'Managing Volunteers: Time Has Changed – Or Have They?' Chapter 8, in B. Newman (ed.), *Handbook of Political Marketing*, Thousand Oaks, CA: Sage Publications, pp. 129–142.

Lederer, A., F. Plasser and Scheucher, C. (2005). 'The Rise and Fall of Populism in Austria – A Political Marketing Perspective,' in D. G. Lilleker and J. Lees-Marshment (eds), *Political Marketing in Comparative Perspective*, Manchester: Manchester University Press.

Leech, B. L. (2002). 'Asking Questions: Techniques for Semistructured Interviews.' *PS: Political Science and Politics*, 35(4): 665–668.

Lees, C. (2005). 'Political Marketing in Germany: The Case of the Social Democratic Party,' in D. G. Lilleker and J. Lees-Marshment (eds), *Political Marketing in Comparative Perspective*, Manchester: Manchester University Press.

Lees-Marshment, J. (2001). *Political Marketing and British Political Parties: The Party's Just Begun*. Manchester and New York: Manchester University Press.

Lees-Marshment, J. (2004). *The Political Marketing Revolution: Transforming the Government of the UK*. Manchester: Manchester University Press.

Lees-Marshment, J. (2005). 'The Marketing Campaign: The British General Election of 2005.' *Journal of Marketing Management*, 21(9/10): 1151–1160.

Lees-Marshment, J. (2008). *Political Marketing and British Political Parties: The Party's Just Begun* (2nd edn). Manchester and New York: Manchester University Press.

Lees-Marshment, J. (2009a). *Political Marketing: Principles and Applications*. Abingdon, Oxon: Routledge.

Lees-Marshment, J. (2009b). 'Marketing After the Election: The Potential and Limitations of Maintaining a Market-Orientation in Government.' *The Canadian Journal of Communication*, Special issue 'Rethinking Public Relations,' 34: 205–227.

Lees-Marshment, J. (2009c). 'Political Marketing and the 2008 New Zealand Election: A Comparative Perspective.' *Australian Journal of Political Science*, 44(3): 457–475.

Lees-Marshment, J. (2009d). 'Global Political Marketing,' Chapter 1, in J. Lees-Marshment, J. Strömbäck and C. Rudd (eds), *Global Political Marketing*, Abingdon, Oxon: Routledge, pp. 1–15.

Lees-Marshment, J. and Darren G. Lilleker (2005). 'Political Marketing in the UK: A Positive Start but an Uncertain Future,' in D. G. Lilleker and J. Lees-Marshment (eds), *Political Marketing: A Comparative Perspective*, Manchester: Manchester University Press.

Lees-Marshment, J. and Robin Pettitt (2010). 'UK Political Marketing: A Question of Leadership?,' in J. Lees-Marshment, J. Strömbäck and C. Rudd (eds), *Global Political Marketing*, Abingdon, Oxon: Routledge.

Lees-Marshment, J. and Stuart Quayle (2001). 'Empowering the Members or Marketing the Party? The Conservative Reforms of 1998.' *The Political Quarterly*, 72(2): 204–212.
Lees-Marshment, J. and Stephen Winter (2009). 'Figure 10.5 Reconciling Political Marketing Market-Oriented Party Theory with Deliberative Democracy: Initial Conceptual Thoughts,' in J. Lees-Marshment (ed.), *Political Marketing: Principles and Applications*, Abingdon, Oxon: Routledge.
Lees-Marshment, J., Jesper Strömbäck and Chris Rudd (eds) (2010). *Global Political Marketing*, Abingdon, Oxon: Routledge.
Leighninger, M. (2005). 'The Recent Evolution of Democracy.' *National Civic Review*, 94(1): 17–28, Spring 2005.
Lilleker, D. G. (2003). 'Interviewing the Political Elite: Navigating a Potential Minefield.' *Politics*, 23(3): 207–214.
Lilleker, D. G. (2005a). 'Political Marketing: The Cause of an Emerging Democratic Deficit in Britain?,' in W. Wymer and J. Lees-Marshment (eds), *Current Issues in Political Marketing*, Binghampton, NY: Haworth Press.
Lilleker, D. G. (2005b). 'Local Campaign Management: Winning Votes or Wasting Resources?.' *Journal of Marketing Management*, 21(9/10): 979–1003.
Lilleker, D. G. (2005c). 'The Impact of Political Marketing on Internal Party Democracy.' *Parliamentary Affairs*, 58(3): 570–584.
Lilleker, D. G. (2006). 'Local Political Marketing: Political Marketing as Public Service,' Chapter 9, in D. G. Lilleker, N. A. Jackson and R. Scullion (eds), *The Marketing of Political Parties*, Manchester: Manchester University Press, pp. 206–230.
Lilleker, D. G. (2009). 'Case Study 7.5: Local Political Marketing: Connecting UK Politicians and Voters,' in J. Lees-Marshment, *Political Marketing: Principles and Applications*, Abingdon, Oxon: Routledge.
Lilleker, D. G. and J. Lees-Marshment (2005). *Political Marketing: A Comparative Perspective*, Manchester: Manchester University Press.
Lilleker, D. G. and Ralph Negrine (2002). 'Marketing Techniques and Political Campaigns: The Limitations for the Marketing of British Political Parties.' Paper presented to the UK PSA association.
Lilleker, D. G. and R. Scullion (eds) (2008). *Voters or Consumers: Imagining the Contemporary Electorate*, Newcastle: Cambridge Scholars Publishing.
Lilleker, D. G., Jackson, Nigel, A. and Richard Scullion (2006). *The Marketing of Political Parties: Political Marketing at the British 2005 General Election*. Manchester: Manchester University Press.
Lindholm, M. R. and Anette Prehn (2007). 'Strategy and Politics: The Example of Denmark,' in T. Fischer, G. Peter Scmitz and M. Seberich (eds), *The Strategy of Politics: Results of a Comparative Study*, Butersloh: Verlag Bertelsmann Stiftung.
Lloyd, J. (2005). 'Square Peg, Round Hole: Can Marketing-Based Concepts Such as the "Product" and the "Marketing Mix" Have a Useful Role in the Political Arena?,' in W. Wymer and J. Lees-Marshment (eds), *Current Issues in Political Marketing*, Binghampton, NY: Haworth Press.
Lloyd, J. (2006). 'The 2005 General Election and the Emergence of the Negative Brand,' in D. Lilleker, N. Jackson and R. Scullion (eds), *The Marketing of Political Parties*, Manchester: Manchester University Press.

Lloyd, J. (2008). 'Marketing Politics...Saving Democracy,' Chapter 18, in A. Sargeant and W. Wymer (eds), *The Routledge Companion to Nonprofit Marketing*, Abingdon, Oxon Routledge, pp. 299–315.

Lloyd, J. (2009). 'Case Study 8.4: After Blair...the Challenge of Communicating Brown's Brand of Labour,' in J. Lees-Marshment (ed.), *Political Marketing: Principles and Applications*, Routledge.

Lynch, R., Paul Baines and John Egan (2006). 'Long-Term Performance of Political Parties: Towards a Competitive Resource-Based Perspective.' *Journal of Political Marketing*, 5(3): 71–92.

McDonald, M. P. and John Samples (eds) (2006). *The Marketplace of Democracy*, Washington, DC: Brookings Press.

McGough, S. (2005). 'Political Marketing in Irish Politics: The Case of Sinn Féin,' in D. Lilleker and J. Lees-Marshment (eds), *Political Marketing: A Comparative Perspective*, Manchester: Manchester University Press.

McGough, S. (2009). 'Case Study 10.3: Political Marketing, Democracy and Terrorism: Ireland Highlights the Dangers,' in J. Lees-Marshment, *Political Marketing: Principles and Applications*, Abingdon, Oxon: Routledge.

Mansbridge, J. (2003). 'Rethinking Representation.' *American Political Science Review*, 97(4): 515–528.

Marland, A. (2003). 'Marketing Political Soap: A Political Marketing View of Selling Candidates Like Soap, of Electioneering as a Ritual, and of Electoral Military Analogies.' *Journal of Public Affairs*, 3(2): 103–115.

Marland, A. (2009). 'Case Study 7.6: Canadian Constituency Campaigns,' in J. Lees-Marshment (ed.), *Political Marketing: Principles and Applications*, Routledge.

Masuda, Y. (1980). *The Information Society as Post-Industrial Society.* Tokyo: Institute for Information Society. Reprinted in 1990 as *Managing in the Information Society: Releasing Synergy Japanese Style*. Oxford: Basil Blackwell.

Medvic, S. K. (2006). 'Understanding Campaign Strategy "Deliberate Priming" and the Role of Professional Political Consultants.' *Journal of Political Marketing*, 5(1/2): 11–32.

Mehlman, S. (2006). 'California's Special Election: Political Miscalculations and Pr Missteps.' *Public Relations Tactics*, 13(2): 12–13.

Middleton, G. (2009). 'Case Study 7.4: ACT New Zealand Party and the Limits of Technological marketing,' in J. Lees-Marshment (ed.), *Political Marketing: Principles and Applications*, Routledge.

Morison, J. and David R. Newman, (2001). 'On-line Citizenship: Consultation and Participation in New Labour's Britain and Beyond.' *International Review of Law Computers and Technology*, 15(2): 171–104.

Morris, D. (2002). *Power Plays: Win or Lose – How History's Great Political Leaders Play the Game*. New York: HarperCollins.

Mortimore, R. (2003). 'Why Politics Needs Marketing.' *International Journal of Non-profit and Voluntary Sector Marketing*, special issue on Broadening the Concept of Political Marketing, 8(2): 107–121.

Mortimore, R. and Mark Gill (2010). 'Implementing and Interpreting Market Orientation in Practice: Lessons from Britain,' in J. Lees-Marshment, J. Strömbäck and C. Rudd (eds), *Global Political Marketing*, Abingdon, Oxon: Routledge, pp. 249–262.

Munro, H. A. D., M. Roberts and C. Skelcher (2008). 'Partnership Governance and Democratic Effectiveness: Community Leaders and Public Managers as Dual Intermediaries.' *Public Policy and Administration*, 23(1): 61–79.

Murray, S.-K. (2006). 'Private Polls and Presidential Policymaking: Reagan as a Facilitator of Change.' *Public Opinion Quarterly*, 70(4): 477–498.

Mylona, I. (2008). 'SMS in Everyday Political Marketing in Greece.' *Journal of Political Marketing*, 7(3): 278–294.

Needham, C. (2003). *Citizen-Consumers: New Labour's Marketplace Democracy*. London: Catalyst Book Press.

Needham, C. (2005). 'Brand Leaders: Clinton, Blair and the Limitations of the Permanent Campaign.' *Political Studies*, 53(2): 343–361.

Needham, C. (2006). 'Brands and Political Loyalty.' *Journal of Brand Management*, 13(3): 178–187.

Newman, B. I. (1994). *The Marketing of the President: Political Marketing as Campaign Strategy*. Thousand Oaks, CA: Sage Publications.

Newman, B. I. (1999). *The Mass Marketing of Politics: Democracy in an Age of Manufactured Images*. Thousand Oaks, CA: Sage Publications.

Newman, B. I. (2001). 'An Assessment of the 2000 US Presidential Election: A Set of Political Marketing Guidelines.' *Journal of Public Affairs*, 1(3): 210.

Norris, P. (ed.) (2005). *Critical Citizens*, Oxford, UK: Oxford University Press.

Oakley, A. (1981). 'Interviewing Women: A Contradiction in Terms,' in H. Roberts (ed.), *Doing Feminist Research*, London: Routledge and Kegan Paul.

O'Cass, A. (2009). 'A Resource-Based View of the Political Party and Value Creation for the Voter-Citizen: An Integrated Framework for Political Marketing.' *Marketing Theory*, 9(2): 189–208.

Olson, K. (2006). *Reflexive Democracy: Political Equality and the Welfare State*. Cambridge, MA: MIT Press.

Ormrod, R. P. and Stephan C. Henneberg (2006). 'Different Facets of Market Orientation: A Comparative Exploratory Analysis of Party Manifestos in Britain and Germany.' Paper presented at the 3rd International Conference on Political Marketing, 5 April 2006.

Ormrod, R. P., Stephan C. Henneberg, Nick Forward, James Miller and Leigh Tymms (2007). 'Political Marketing in Untraditional Campaigns: The Case of David Cameron's Conservative Party Leadership Victory.' *Journal of Public Affairs*, 7(3): 235–248.

O'Shaughnessy, N. J. and Stephan C. Henneberg (2007). 'The Selling of the President 2004: A Marketing Perspective.' *Journal of Public Affairs*, 7(3): 249–268.

Paleologos, D. A. (1997). 'A Pollster on Polling.' *American Behavioral Scientist*, 40(8): 1183–1189.

Paré, D. J. (2009). 'Case Study 10.2: Political Marking in the 2006 Canadian Federal Election: Delivering Citizen or Party Needs and Wants?,' in J. Lees-Marshment (ed.), *Political Marketing: Principles and Applications*, Routledge.

Paré, D. J. and Flavia Berger (2008). 'Political Marketing Canadian Style? The Conservative Party and the 2006 Federal Election.' *Canadian Journal of Communication*, 33(1): 39–63.

Patrón-Galindo, P. (2004). 'Symbolism and the Construction of Political Products: Analysis of the Political Marketing Strategies of Peruvian President Alejandro Toledo.' *Journal of Public Affairs*, 4(2): 115–124.

Penn, M. with E. Kinney Zalesne (2007). *Micro-Trends: The Small Forces Behind Tomorrow's Big Changes*. New York: Twelve, Hatchett Book Group.

Pettitt, R. (2009). 'Case Study 6.3: Resisting Marketing: The Case of the British Labour Party Under Blair,' in J. Lees-Marshment (ed.), *Political Marketing: Principles and Applications*, Routledge.

Pharr, S. and Robert Putnam (eds) (2000). *Disaffected Democracies: What's Troubling the Trilateral Countries?*, Princeton, NJ: Princeton University Press.

Plasser, Frizta, Christian Scheucher and Christian Seft (1999). 'Is There a European Style of Political Marketing? A Survey of Political Managers and Consultants,' Chapter 6, in B. Newman (ed.), *Handbook of Political Marketing*, Thousand Oaks, CA: Sage Publications, pp. 89–112.

Polsby, N. A. and Aaron Wildavsky with David A Hopkins (2008). *Presidential Elections: Strategies and Structures of American Politics*. Lanham, MD: Rowman & Littlefield.

Prete, M. I. (2007). 'M-Politics: Credibility and Effectiveness of Mobile Political Communications.' *Journal of Targeting, Measurement & Analysis for Marketing*, 16(1): 48–56.

Promise (2005). 'Reconnecting the Prime Minister.' Company paper, *Promise UK*. Accessed from www.promisecorp.com on 21 January 2008.

Punch, K. F. (1998). *Introduction to Social Research: Qualitative and Quantitative Approaches*. London: Sage Publications.

Rademacher, E. W. and Alfred J. Tuchfarber (1999). 'Preelection Polling and Political Campaigns,' in B. Newman (ed.), *Handbook of Political Marketing*, Thousand Oaks, CA: Sage Publications, pp. 197–221.

Reeves, P., Leslie de Chernatony and Marylyn Carrigan (2006). 'Building a Political Brand: Ideology or Voter-Driven Strategy.' *Brand Management*, 13(6): 418–428.

Rehfeld, A. (2009). 'Representation Rethought: On Trustees, Delegates, and Gyroscopes in the Study of Political Representation and Democracy.' *American Political Science Review*, 103(2): 214–230, May.

Robinson, C. E. (2006). 'Advertising and the Market Orientation of Political Parties Contesting the 1999 and 2002 New Zealand General Election Campaigns,' PhD thesis, Palmerston North: Massey University.

Robinson, C. E. (2009). 'Case Study 7.7: Market-Orientated Political Advertising in the 2005 New Zealand Election,' in J. Lees-Marshment (ed.), *Political Marketing: Principles and Applications*, Routledge.

Rori, L. (2008). 'Party Politics and Campaign Strategies: Policy Making and Organizational Changes of the Greek Socialist Party During the 2004 Electoral Campaign.' *Journal of Political Marketing*, 7(3): 295–322.

Rothmayr, C. and Sibylle Hardmeier (2002). 'Government and Polling: Use and Impact of Polls in the Policy-Making Process in Switzerland.' *International Journal of Public Opinion Research*, 14(2): 123–140.

Rottinghaus, B. (2008). '[US] Presidential Leadership on Foreign Policy, Opinion Polling, and the Possible Limits of Crafted Talk.' *Political Communication*, 25(2): 138–157, April–June 2008.

Rottinghaus, B. and Irina Alberro (2005). 'Rivaling the PRI: The Image Management of Vicente Fox and the Use of Public Opinion Polling in the 2000 Mexican Election.' *Latin American Politics and Society*, 47(2): 143–158.

Rowe, G. and L.-J. Frewer (2005). 'A Typology of Public Engagement Mechanisms.' *Science, Technology and Human Values*, 30(2): 251–290.
Rudd, C. (2005). 'Marketing the Message or the Messenger?,' in D. Lilleker and J. Lees-Marshment (eds), *Political Marketing in Comparative Perspective*, Manchester: Manchester University Press.
Rudd, C. and Geoffrey Miller (2009). 'Case Study 5.8: ACT New Zealand and Branding,' in J. Lees-Marshment (ed.), *Political Marketing: Principles and Applications*, Routledge.
Russell, A. T. and Ed Fieldhouse (2005). *Neither Left nor Right?: The Liberal Democrats and the Electorate*. Manchester: Manchester University Press.
Sackman, A. I. (1996). 'The Learning Curve Towards New Labour: Neil Kinnock's Corporate Party 1983–92.' *European Journal of Marketing*, 30(10/11): 147–158.
Sarantakos, S. (2005). *Social Research*. Basingstoke: Palgrave Macmillan.
Savigny, H. (2007). 'Focus Groups and Political Marketing: Science and Democracy as Axiomatic?.' *British Journal of Politics and International Relations*, 9: 122–137.
Savigny, H. (2008a). *The Problem of Political Marketing*. London: Continuum International Publishing Group Ltd.
Savigny, H. (2008b). 'The Construction of the Political Consumer (or Politics: What Not to Consume,' in D. Lilleker and R. Scullion (eds), *Voters or Consumers: Imagining the Contemporary Electorate*, Newcastle: Cambridge Scholars Publishing.
Scammell, M. (1995). *Designer Politics: How Elections Are Won*. London: St. Martin's Press.
Scammell, M. (2003). 'Citizen Consumers – Towards a New Marketing of Politics?,' in J. Corner and D. Pels (eds), *Media and the Restyling of Politics*. Accessed from http://depts.washington.edu/gcp/pdf/citizenconsumers.pdf on 3 May 2008.
Scammell, M. (2008). 'Brand Blair: Marketing politics in the Consumer Age,' Chapter in D. Lilleker and R. Scullion (eds), *Voters or Consumers: Imagining the Contemporary Electorate*, Newcastle: Cambridge Scholars Publishing, pp. 97–113.
Schneider, H. (2004). 'Branding in Politics – Manifestations, Relevance and Identity-Oriented Management.' *Journal of Political Marketing*, 3(3): 41–67.
Scullion, R. (2008). 'The Impact of the Market on the Character of Citizenship, and the Consequences of This for Political Engagement,' in D. Lilleker and R. Scullion (eds), *Voters or Consumers: Imagining the Contemporary Electorate*, Newcastle: Cambridge Scholars Publishing.
Seawright, D. (2005). ' "On a Low Road": The 2005 Conservative Campaign.' *Journal of Marketing Management*, 21(9/10): 943–957.
Seligman, P. (2006). 'Policies Fail Without Buy-In.' *Marketing*, 26 April.
Shand, D. and M. Arnberg (1996). *Responsive Government*. Paris: OECD.
Sherman, E., Leon Schiffman and Shawn T. Thelen (2008). 'Impact of Trust on Candidates, Branches of Government, and Media Within the Context of the 2004 U.S. Presidential Election.' *Journal of Political Marketing*, 7(2): 105–130.
Slocum, R. (2004). 'Consumer Citizens and the Cities for Climate Protection Campaign.' *Environment and Planning*, 36: 763–782.
Slote-Morris, Z. (2009). 'The Trust About Interviewing Elites.' *Politics*, 29(3): 209–217.

Smith, G. (2001). 'The 2001 General Election: Factors Influencing the Brand Image of Political Parties and Their Leaders.' *Journal of Marketing Management*, 17(9/10): 989–1006.
Smith, G. (2005). 'Positioning Political Parties: The 2005 UK General Election.' *Journal of Marketing Management*, 21(9/10): 1135–1149.
Smith, G. (2006). 'Competitive Analysis, Structure and Strategy in Politics: A Critical Approach.' *Journal of Public Affairs*, 6(1): 4–14.
Smith, G. (2009). 'Conceptualizing and Testing Brand Personality in British Politics.' *Journal of Political Marketing*, 8(3): 209–232.
Smith, G. and Alan French (2009). 'The Political Brand: A Consumer Perspective.' *Marketing Theory*, 9(2): 209–226.
Smith, G. and Andy Hirst (2001). 'Strategic Political Segmentation: A New Approach for a New Era of Political Marketing.' *European Journal of Marketing*, 35(9/10): 1058–1073.
Smith, K. E. (2006). 'Problematising Power Relations in Elite Interviews.' *Geoforum*, 37(4): 643–653.
Sparrow, N. and Turner, J. (2001). 'The Integrating of Market Research Techniques in Developing Strategies in a More Uncertain Political Climate.' *European Journal of Marketing*, 35(9/10): 984–1002.
Steen, J. (1999). 'Money Doesn't Grow on Trees: Fund-Raising in American Political Campaigns,' in B. Newman (ed.), *Handbook of Political Marketing*, Thousand Oaks, CA: Sage Publications.
Steger, W. (1999). 'The Permanent Campaign: Marketing from the Hill,' in B. Newman (ed.), *Handbook of Political Marketing*, Thousand Oaks, CA: Sage Publications.
Stirland, S. L. (2008). 'Inside Obama's Surging Net-Roots Campaign,' in *Wired GQ*. Accessed from http://www.wired.com/politics/law/news/2008/03/obama_tools on 1 April 2008.
Strömbäck, J. (2010). 'A Framework for Comparing Political Market Orientation,' in J. Lees-Marshment, C. Rudd and J. Strömbäck (eds), *Global Political Marketing*, Abingdon, Oxon: Routledge, pp. 16–33.
Teinturier, B. (2008). 'The Presidential Elections in France 2007– The Role of Opinion Polls,' in M. Carballo and U. Hjelmar (eds), *Public Opinion Polling in a Globalized World*, Berlin: Springer-Verlag.
Temple, M. (2010). 'Political Marketing, Party Behaviour and Political Science,' in J. Lees-Marshment, J. Strömbäck and C. Rudd (eds), *Global Political Marketing*, Abingdon, Oxon: Routledge, pp. 263–277.
Tetlock, P. (2005). *Expert Political Judgment: How Good Is It? How Can We Know?* Princeton, NJ: Princeton University Press.
Turner, J. (2009). 'Case Study 9.3: International Political Product Marketing,' in J. Lees-Marshment (ed.), *Political Marketing: Principles and Applications*, Routledge.
Ubertaccio, P. (2008). 'Network Marketing and American Political Parties,' in Dennis W. Johnson (ed.), *The Routledge Handbook of Political Management*, New York: Routledge, pp. 509–523.
Varoga, C. and Mike Rice (1999). 'Only the Facts: Professional Research and Message Development,' in B. Newman (ed.), *Handbook of Political Marketing*, Thousand Oaks, CA: Sage Publications, 243–258.

Vigoda, E. (2008). 'From Responsiveness to Collaboration,' Chapter 31, in N. C. Roberts (ed.), *The Age of Direct Citizen Participation*, ASPA classics, Armonk, NY: M.E. Sharpe, pp. 473–490.

Von Drehle, D. (2008). 'Person of the Year Barack Obama: Why History Can't Wait.' *Time Magazine*, 36–44, 29 December.

Walsh, K. (1994). 'Marketing and Public Sector Management.' *European Journal of Marketing*, 28(3): 63–71.

Washbourne, N. (2005). '(Comprehensive) Political Marketing, Expertise and the Conditions for Democracy.' Paper presented at the Political Studies Association Political Marketing Group Conference.

Weale, A. (2007). *Democracy*. Basingstoke: Palgrave Macmillan.

White, J. and Leslie-de Chernatony (2002). 'New Labour: A Study of the Creation, Development and Demise of a Political Brand.' *Journal of Political Marketing*, 1(2–3): 45–52.

Wintour, P. (2005). 'Postcode Data Could Decide Next Election.' *The Guardian*. Accessed from http://www.spinwatch.org/content/view/613/9/ on 8 May 2008.

Wring, D. (2002). 'Conceptualising Political Marketing: A Framework for Election-Campaign Analysis,' in N. J. O'Shaughnessy and S. Henneberg (eds), *The Idea of Political Marketing*, New York: Praeger, pp. 171–186.

Wring, D. (2005a). *The Politics of Marketing the Labour Party*. Basingstoke: Palgrave Macmillan.

Wring, D. (2005b). 'The Labour Campaign,' in P. Norris and C. Wlezien (eds), *Britain Votes 2005*, Oxford: Oxford University Press, 208–223.

Wring, D. (2007). 'Focus Group Follies? Qualitative Research and British Labour Party Strategy.' *Journal of Political Marketing*, 5(4): 71–97.

Practitioner Interview References

1. Ansell, John (2007), Advertiser for the Labour Party in the 1987, 1990 and 1993 general elections, and Advertiser for the National Party in the 2005 general election in New Zealand, interviewed by email.
2. Armstrong, John (2006), Journalist and political columnist for *The Herald* newspaper, Wellington, New Zealand, 1 December.
3. Barber, Michael (2007), Former Head of the UK Prime Minister's Delivery Unit, interviewed over the phone.
4. Beeson, Rich (2007), Political Director of the US Republican Party, interviewed at RNC headquarters, Washington DC, USA, October.
5. Billot, Victor (2006), President of the Alliance political party, interviewed in Dunedin, New Zealand, December.
6. Blumenthal, Sidney (2007), Former advisor to President Bill Clinton, Third Way advocate, and advisor to Hillary Clinton's presidential nomination campaign.
7. Borrowman, Duncan (2006), National Campaigns Officer for the Liberal Democrats, UK, interviewed on 10 April.
8. Boscawen, John (2009), Former ACT Fundraising Manager and Epsom Campaign Manager in 2005, Act Party Campaign Manager in 2008, and current ACT MP, interviewed over the phone, 16 March.
9. Brash, Don (2007), Former leader of the National Party in New Zealand, interviewed Mission Bay, New Zealand, 7 February.
10. Braun, Alex (2009), PSB (Penn, Schoen and Berland) Associates, New York, interviewed over the phone, January.
11. Brodie, Ian (2009), Former Chief of Staff in Prime Minister Stephen Harper's office from Harper's ascension to the position of prime minister until 1 July 2008, and current consultant at Hill and Knowlton, interviewed in Ottawa, Canada, 29 May.
12. Butler, Gareth (2006), Deputy Editor of *The Politics Show*, interviewed in UK, 18 April.
13. Bray, Garth (2008), TVNZ journalist and overseas correspondent in Australia, interviewed at ABC studios in Sydney, Australia, February.
14. Byrne, Dorothy (2006), Head of News and Current Affairs, Channel 4, interviewed at Channel 4, London, UK, 21 April.
15. Callingham, Judy (2009), Media Advisor to Helen Clark, former Prime Minister of New Zealand, interviewed in Herne Bay, Auckland, New Zealand, January.
16. Campbell, Alastair (2005), Former Chief Press Secretary to UK Prime Minister Tony Blair, interviewed at Millbank, London, UK, October.
17. Carson, Fraser (2006), New Zealand Labour Party Advertiser 1993–1999, Wellington, New Zealand, 29 November.

18. Carr, Bob (2008), Former Premier of NSW, Australia, interviewed in Sydney, Australia, February.
19. Carter, Matt (2007), Former UK Labour General Secretary, and Managing Director of London branch of Penn, Schoen and Berland Associates, interviewed at PSB, London, UK, 7 September.
20. Chalupa, Ali (2007), Former Kerry 2004 campaign staffer, and current staff at the DNC, interviewed in Washington DC, USA, October.
21. Clelland-Stokes, Nick (2009), Chief of Staff for Auckland Mayor John Banks, and former communications staff for South African Party, interviewed at Auckland Town Hall, 27 January .
22. Collins, Damian (2006), Managing Director M&C Saatchi UK, interviewed in London, UK, 18 April.
23. Davidson, Jo-Ann (2007), Deputy Chair of the RNC, interviewed at RNC headquarters in Washington DC, USA, October.
24. Di Lollo, Justin (2008), Former Political Advisor and current Political Consultant with Hawker Britton, interviewed in Sydney, Australia, February.
25. Duffy, John (2009), Advisor to Canadian Prime Minister Paul Martin, currently principal at Strategy Corp., interviewed in Toronto, Canada, 20 May.
26. Durdin, Martha (2009), Former staff in the Canadian Prime Minister Pierre Trudeau's office and current principal at Navigator Ltd, interviewed in Toronto, Canada, 19 May.
27. Duncan Smith, Iain (2006), Former leader of the UK Conservatives 2001–2003, interviewed at the House of Commons, London, UK, 18 April.
28. Edwards, Damien (2006), New Zealand First Advisor to Winston Peters, interviewed in Wellington, New Zealand, November.
29. Edwards, Brian (2009), Media Advisor to Helen Clark, former Prime Minister of New Zealand, interviewed in Herne Bay, Auckland, New Zealand, January.
30. Evans, David (2006), The Campaign Company, interviewed face to face in London, UK, followed up over the phone, April.
31. Evershed, Alexandra (2009), Ipsos-Reid, interviewed in Ottawa, Canada, 29 May.
32. Fenn, Peter (2007), Fenn Communications, interviewed in Washington DC, USA, October.
33. Fitzpatrick, Eammon (2008), Former Media Advisor, state level, current consultant at Hawker Brittain, interviewed in Sydney, Australia, February.
34. Gill, Mark (2007), Former Head of Political Research at Ipsos Mori, current Director of Woodnewton Associates, UK, interviewed in London, 5 September.
35. Gillan, Cheryl (2006), Shadow Secretary for Wales, UK Conservative Party, interviewed at Porticullis House, London, UK, 18 April.
36. Glover, David (2007), Gravitas Research, New Zealand, interviewed in Auckland, New Zealand, 10 August.
37. Gould, Bryan, (2007), Former UK Labour Party MP and Campaign Manager, then Waikato Vice Chancellor, interviewed at the Hilton Hotel, Auckland, New Zealand, 21 August.
38. Gould, Philip (2007), Labour strategist/pollster and advisor to the Blair New Labour opposition and government, interviewed at his residence, London, UK, 10 September.

39. Green, Damian, (2006), Conservative MP, interviewed at Portcullis House, London, UK, April.
40. Griffin, Richard (2006), Former Chief Press Secretary to Prime Minister Bolger in New Zealand, interviewed in Wellington, New Zealand, 29 November.
41. Griggs, Rob (2008), Former Political Advisor for Bob Carr and current Political Consultant with Hawker Britton, interviewed in Sydney, Australia, February.
42. Harris, Will (2006), Former Director of Marketing for the Conservative Party, interview at The Bank, London, UK, 19 April.
43. Harvey, Bob (2007), Former New Zealand Labour Party Adviser for election campaigns in 1969, 1972, 1975, 1984; Labour Party President 1998–2000 and Mayor of Waitakere since 1992, interviewed in Waitakere City, New Zealand, 13 August.
44. Hide, Rodney (2007), Leader of the Act Party, New Zealand, interviewed in Epsom, Auckland, New Zealand, 2 August.
45. Humphrey, James (2007), Former civil servant, with roles including Head of Corporate Communications and Strategic Communications at Downing Street; current Director at Woodnewton Associates and visiting professor at Government City University, UK, interviewed in London, UK, 5 September.
46. Hyder, Goldy (2009), M. Hill and Knowlton, interviewed in Ottawa, Canada, 28 May.
47. Inglish, Sue (2007), Head of Political Programmes, Analysis and Research, BBC News, interviewed at BBC White City, London, UK, 12 September.
48. Jones, Matt (2008), Former staff at UK Conservative Party headquarters during 2005 campaign, interviewed in Sydney, Australia, February.
49. Karia, Kamlesh (2006), Political Development Manager, UK Labour Party, interviewed at Labour headquarters, London, UK, 13 April.
50. Kartch, John (2007), Communications Director, Americans for Tax Reform, interviewed in Washington DC, USA, 22 October.
51. Keneally, Ben (2008), NSW Delivery Unit, Australia, interviewed by phone, 24 April.
52. Krohn, Cyrus (2007), Republican National Committee E-campaign Director, interviewed at RNC headquarters, Washington DC, USA, October.
53. Krohn, Cyrus (2009), Republican National Committee E-campaign Director, interviewed post-2008 presidential election over the phone, 3 February.
54. Langmaid, Roy (2008), Consultant from Promise, UK, advisor to UK Labour 2004–2005, interviewed over the phone, 9 April.
55. Lawrence, Neil (2008), Creative Strategist, member of the Rudd 07 campaign, Singleton Ogilvy Mather, interviewed in Sydney, Australia, February.
56. Lavigne, Brad (2009), National Director of the New Democratic Party of Canada and former advisor to the NDP leader, interviewed in Ottawa, Canada, 28 May.
57. Levin, Ben (2008), Former delivery staff in provincial governments in Canada, interviewed in Auckland, New Zealand, January.
58. Lloyd, David (2006), Former Head of Current Affairs and News at Channel 4, interviewed in London, UK, April.
59. Pleasants, Simon (2009), Communications Advisor in the office of the Prime Minister Helen Clark, Labour, interviewed over the phone, 16 January.

60. Mehta, Parag (2007), Director of Trainees for the Democrat National Committee/US Democrats Party, and former Dean 2004 presidential nomination bid staffer, interviewed at DNC headquarters, Washington DC, October.
61. Mehta, Parag (2009), The Office of the Public Liaison Presidential Transition Team, interviewed post-2008 presidential campaign and transition over the phone, 29 January.
62. McCully, Murray (2007), National Party MP and strategist in 2002, 2005 and 2008, New Zealand elections, interviewed in Browns Bay, Auckland, New Zealand, 13 August.
63. Macken, Sean (2008), Former Political and Policy Advisor, and current Political Consultant with Hawker Britton, interviewed in Sydney, Australia, February.
64. Mellman, Mark (2007), Kerry 2004 Campaign Advisor and Senatorial Advisor, interviewed in Washington DC, USA, October.
65. Middleton, Gavin (2006), ACT Party Staff, interviewed in Wellington, New Zealand.
66. Mills, Stephen (2009), UMR Pollster to New Zealand Labour Party from 1990s to present day, interviewed in Auckland, New Zealand, and has written comments subsequently.
67. Mortimore, Roger (2006), MORI polling company, UK (providing a general perspective reflecting on market intelligence industry), interviewed in London, UK, 11 April.
68. Muttart, Patrick (2009), Former Communications Consultant and the Deputy Chief of Staff in the Canadian Prime Minister's Unit and advisor to Prime Minister Stephen Harper, interviewed over the phone, 25 June.
69. Munro, Mike (2006), Former Chief Press Secretary for Prime Minister Helen Clark, Wellington, New Zealand, 28 November.
70. Nanos, Nik (2009), Pollster and CEO of the Nanos Research Corporation, a public and market research firm, interviewed in Ottawa, Canada, 28 May.
71. Nelson, Terry (2007), Bush/Cheney Campaign Political Director, 2004 election, and McCain presidential bid Campaign Manager, December 2006–mid 2007, interviewed in Washington DC, USA, October.
72. Nicolle, Brian (2007), Advisor to Rodney Hide and other former ACT Party leaders, interviewed in Epsom, New Zealand, December.
73. Noble, Leslie (2009), Strategic Advisor to the Progressive Conservatives and Campaign Manager for Ontario Premier Mike Harris in 1995 and 1999, and current Principal in Strategy Corp., interviewed in Toronto, Canada, 20 May.
74. Norquist, Grover (2007), President of Americans for Tax Reform and Republican activist, interviewed in Washington DC, USA, October 22.
75. Pattillo, Anne (2009), Pattillo Consulting, New Zealand, interviewed over the phone, 4 February.
76. Paxman, Jeremy (2007), BBC journalist and interviewer, interviewed at BBC White City, London, UK, 12 September.
77. Pringle, Michael (2006), National Administrator, Green Party, Wellington, New Zealand, 29 November.
78. Ranger, Paul (2006), Director of Campaigns, UK Liberal Democrats, interviewed at Liberal Democrat headquarters, Cowley Street, London, UK, 11 April.

79. Reid, Scott (2009), Senior Advisor and Director of Communications to Canadian Prime Minister Paul Martin and Director of Communications for the 2004 and 2006 Liberal Party election campaign, currently principal of Feschuk Reid, interviewed in Toronto, Canada, 19 May.
80. Rennard, Chris (2006), Chief Executive of the Liberal Democrats, interviewed in London, UK, April.
81. Ridder, Rick (2007), International Political Consultant, former advisor to Bill Clinton/Gore 1992 campaign, Howard Dean 2000 campaign, UK Liberal Democrats and Australian NSW Labor Party, interviewed over the phone, 23 October.
82. Riddell, Peter (2006), Journalist and columnist for *The Times* newspaper, interviewed at Portcullis House, London, UK, 11 April.
83. Robertson, Grant (2006), Former Senior Advisor to the Prime Minister Helen Clark, New Zealand, interviewed in Wellington, New Zealand, 28 November.
84. Robertson, Grant (2008), New Zealand Labour candidate and MP, interviewed over the phone.
85. Rogers, Chad (2009), Former Senior Advisor to Nova Scotia Premier John Hamm, providing strategic planning and communications advice to the premier and Cabinet from 1999 to 2003, currently a principle in Navigator Ltd, interviewed in Toronto, Canada, 19 May.
86. Rosenberg, Simon (2007), New Democrat Network, interviewed in Washington DC, USA October.
87. Roozendaal, Eric (2008), Minister for Roads and Minister for Commerce, NSW parliament, and former NSW Labor Party General Secretary/2003 Campaign Manager for Bob Carr, interviewed in Sydney, Australia, February.
88. Scard, Jo (2008), Former Labour Party UK staff member, UK journalist, Australian journalist and consultant, interviewed in Sydney, Australia, February.
89. Smith, Mike (2006), General Secretary of the Labour Party, interviewed in Wellington, New Zealand, 29 November.
90. Somerville, Will (2007), Senior Policy Analyst Migration Institute, Washington DC and former IPPR, UK, interviewed in Washington DC, USA, October.
91. Sparrow, Nick (2007), Pollster ICM UK/former pollster Conservative Party 1995–2001, and 2003–2004, interviewed at ICM Offices, London, UK, 5 September.
92. Stanzel, Scott (2007), Deputy Press Secretary, White House, interviewed at the White House West Wing, Washington DC, USA, 24 October.
93. Stockley, Neil (2007), PR Consultant and former NZ political staff/research for the New Zealand Labour Party, interviewed in London, UK, 11 September.
94. Taylor, Sara (2008), Strategist on the 2004 Bush–Cheney campaign and former Political Director in the White House, interviewed over the phone, 11(US)/12(NZ) March.
95. Tyson, Brian (2008), Political Advisor, Gavin Anderson and Company, Australia, interviewed in Sydney, Australia, February.
96. Ulm, Gene (2007), Political Consultant for Public Opinion Strategies, interviewed in Alexandria, Virginia, USA, 24 October.
97. Utting, John (2008), UMR pollster, Australia, interviewed in Bondi Beach, Sydney, Australia, February.

98. Wilson, Stuart (2006), ACT Party Staff, interviewed in Wellington, New Zealand.
99. Williams, Mike (2007), New Zealand Labour Party President 2000–2008, interviewed Te Atatu Peninsula, Auckland, 13 August.
100. Wright, John (2009), Senior VP Public Affairs with Ipsos-Reid Canada and co-author of *What Canadians Think*, interviewed in Toronto, Canada, 20 May.

Index

Advertising, 39, 55, 108, 128, 136–137, 141–142, 144, 149, 151, 153, 157, 161, 162–163, 216
Advisors, 33, 46, 55, 85, 93–98, 101, 161–163, 202, 216, 222–223
Ansell, John, 27, 39, 66, 137, 141, 142, 144, 161, 162, 202, 257
Authenticity (authentic), 73–75, 153–155, 216

Barber, Michael, 168, 169, 170, 178, 179, 187–188, 257
Blair, Tony, 15, 28, 50, 52, 58, 64–65, 67–69, 71, 87–88, 91–92, 94–95, 97, 116–117, 119, 122–123, 135, 140, 146, 168, 170, 172, 178, 179, 187, 189, 204, 216
Blumenthal, Sidney, 87, 136, 146, 160, 182, 184
Branding, 45, 55, 61, 62, 66–73, 77, 78, 96, 106, 121, 122, 154, 169, 201, 202, 204, 217, 221, 224
Brash, Don, 39, 57, 63, 64–65, 74, 88, 123, 131, 135, 137, 144, 257
Brodie, Ian, 15, 38, 63, 96, 98, 170, 177, 179
Bush, George W, 22, 37, 47, 49, 62, 68, 72, 91, 113, 120, 134, 140, 149, 169, 173, 175

Callingham, Judy, 27, 37, 89, 95, 96, 100, 154
Cameron, David, 57–58, 69, 117, 122, 136, 138
Campbell, Alastair, 19, 34, 83, 89, 94, 95, 96, 128, 160, 175, 180, 186, 188
Candidate analysis, 24–26, 218
Carr, Bob, 36, 39–41, 82–83, 87, 81, 95, 97, 101, 171, 175, 176, 185

Clark, Helen, 35, 86, 93, 95–97, 100, 133, 137, 145, 155, 172, 182, 183
Communicating a leader, 13, 132–135, 142–143, 153, 207
Communicating complex policy, 130–132
Communicating delivery, 182–186
Communicating re-positioning, 58, 62–63, 136–137, 220
Competition, 60–66, 143–145, 217, 219, 223
Consultants, 30–34, 54, 55, 96, 100, 122, 203
Consultation, 28–29, 183, 197–199, 208, 210, 211, 213, 224, 227, 228–230, 234–235, 237, 239

Delivery failures, 180–182
Delivery strategy, 174–175
Democratic political marketing, 193–211, 223, 224
Duncan Smith, Iain, 13, 51, 58, 85, 99, 121, 122, 136, 146, 159, 195

Edwards, Brian, 18–19, 35, 58, 65, 90, 96, 102, 155, 181, 188
E-marketing, 127, 129, 148–153, 208

GOTV (Get out the vote), 22, 138–139
Gould, Phillip, 19, 26, 33, 45, 50, 51, 52, 53, 56, 70, 87, 91, 92, 116, 117, 188, 193, 196, 198, 202, 204, 207, 212

Harper, Stephen, 15, 69, 74, 94, 96, 154, 170
Harris, Will, 52, 60, 94, 100, 117, 119, 137
Hide, Rodney, 36, 51, 64, 82, 87, 100, 101, 123
Howard, John, 17, 62, 75, 144

Ideology, 116–118, 204, 205
Inglish, Sue, 131, 132, 159, 160
Internal relationships, 57, 118–124, 155–158

Key, John, 36, 61, 88, 145

Langmaid, Roy, 13, 17, 66, 67–68, 71, 96, 100, 146
Lawrence, Neil, 51, 62, 64, 75, 101, 120, 136, 137, 142, 143, 144, 156, 161, 171
Leadership (or leading), 87–102, 134, 200, 216, 220

Market analysis methods, 16–20, 30, 216
McCully, Murray, 4, 52, 53, 56, 57, 66, 174, 195
Media, 83–84, 128–130, 131, 158–161, 175, 206, 208
Methodology, 3, 5, 7, 8
Mills, Stephen, 15, 19, 21, 34, 50, 56, 75, 79, 87, 89, 90, 100, 183, 188
Mortimore, Roger, 12, 13, 19, 22, 34, 56, 82, 93, 122, 204
Munro, Mike, 75, 86, 93, 95, 97, 100, 128, 133, 159–160, 195
Muttart, Patrick, 11, 12, 17, 54–55, 94, 172, 174, 177, 188

Nanos, Nik, 16, 30, 37, 74, 80–82, 198

Obama, Barack, 22, 25, 37, 48, 61, 70, 71–72, 106–107, 110, 111, 114–115, 149, 152–153, 157, 169, 173, 209
Opposition research *see under* Candidate analysis

Partnership democracy, 226–239
Party organisation, 104, 105–108, 119, 156
Paxman, Jeremy, 83, 127, 137, 159, 160

Positioning, 15, 27, 58, 60–66, 73, 78, 86, 116
Predictive market analysis, 26–27
Pre-election delivery, 171–174
Product, 45–50, 67, 136–138, 159, 219

Receiver-responsive communication, 145–148
Reid, Scott, 47, 74, 89, 129, 134, 140, 142, 143, 154, 161, 181, 185
Rennard, Chris, 37–38, 40, 49, 202
Rudd, Kevin, 40, 51–52, 57, 97, 101, 121, 137, 144, 156, 171, 175, 182, 197, 209

Segmentation, 20–24, 150, 193, 198–199, 218
Selling policy, 132–133
Smith, Mike, 105, 107, 111, 118, 155
Stanzel, Scott, 47, 129, 130, 132, 134, 149, 159, 206
Strategic communication, 56, 128–155, 186
Strategy, 4, 14, 15, 17, 41–42, 51–60, 79, 100–101, 106–107, 121–122, 135, 136, 149, 174–176, 213, 219–220

Targeting, 20–24, 107, 127, 129, 131, 142–143, 145, 150, 151, 160, 174, 180, 198, 201, 222
Taylor, Sara, 37, 91, 140

Unity, 68, 104, 221, 224
Utting, John, 14, 16, 27, 30, 40, 64, 75, 79, 87, 196, 201, 207

Vision, 56, 65, 116–118, 135, 156, 216
Volunteer(s), 18, 22, 49, 104, 105, 108–114, 138, 155, 218
Voter profiling, 20–24

Williams, Mike, 26